Advances
Membership
Categorisation
Analysis

SAGE was founded in 1965 by Sara Miller McCune to support the dissemination of usable knowledge by publishing innovative and high-quality research and teaching content. Today, we publish more than 750 journals, including those of more than 300 learned societies, more than 800 new books per year, and a growing range of library products including archives, data, case studies, reports, conference highlights, and video. SAGE remains majority-owned by our founder, and after Sara's lifetime will become owned by a charitable trust that secures our continued independence.

Los Angeles | London | Washington DC | New Delhi | Singapore

Advances in Membership Categorisation Analysis

Edited by

Richard Fitzgerald and William Housley

Los Angeles | London | New Delhi
Singapore | Washington DC

Los Angeles | London | New Delhi
Singapore | Washington DC

SAGE Publications Ltd
1 Oliver's Yard
55 City Road
London EC1Y 1SP

SAGE Publications Inc.
2455 Teller Road
Thousand Oaks, California 91320

SAGE Publications India Pvt Ltd
B 1/I 1 Mohan Cooperative Industrial Area
Mathura Road
New Delhi 110 044

SAGE Publications Asia-Pacific Pte Ltd
3 Church Street
#10-04 Samsung Hub
Singapore 049483

Editor: Jai Seaman
Assistant editor: Lily Mehrbod
Production editor: Victoria Nicholas
Copyeditor: Rosemary Campbell
Proofreader: Louise Harnby
Indexer: Martin Hargreaves
Marketing manager: Sally Ransom
Cover design: Jennifer Crisp
Typeset by: C&M Digitals (P) Ltd, Chennai, India
Printed by: Replika Press Pvt. Ltd, India

Library of Congress Control Number: 2014948352

British Library Cataloguing in Publication data

A catalogue record for this book is available from
the British Library

ISBN 978-1-4462-7072-1
ISBN 978-1-4462-7073-8 (pbk)

At SAGE we take sustainability seriously. Most of our products are printed in the UK using FSC papers and boards.
When we print overseas we ensure sustainable papers are used as measured by the Egmont grading system.
We undertake an annual audit to monitor our sustainability.

We dedicate this book to Stephen Hester; a great ethnomethodologist and inspirational teacher.

Contents

About the Authors

Frederick Attenborough is currently Lecturer in Communication and Media Studies at Loughborough University. He has written extensively in the area of feminist media studies, focusing on the media – as broadly conceived – from an ethnomethodological perspective. His publications include co-editing a special issue of the journal *Gender & Language* that focused on 'gender, language and the media' (2014, Vol. 8/2) as well as articles in *Discourse & Communication*, *Discourse & Society*, *Feminist Media Studies* and *Journal of Gender Studies* that have analysed what it is that we read when we read about sexism, rape, misogyny, and so on, in the media.

Richard Fitzgerald is Associate Professor of Communication at the University of Macau. Since completing his PhD at the University of Wales: Bangor UK he has held posts at Brunel and Cardiff Universities in the UK and the University of Queensland, Australia. He has written extensively in the area of Membership Categorisation Analysis, often with a focus on broadcast media. His publications have also included co-editing two special issues of the *Australian Journal of Communication*, focusing on Ethnomethodology and Conversation Analysis (2009, Vol. 36/3, with Carly Butler and Rod Gardner, 2013, Vol. 40/2, with Sean Rintel and Edward Reynolds) and co-editing *Media, Policy and Interaction* (Ashgate, 2009) with William Housley.

William Housley, PhD, DSc.Econ., is Professor of Sociology at Cardiff University, School of Social Sciences. He has written extensively in the areas of membership categorisation, team interaction, collaborative work and media communication. He has also contributed to the field of qualitative social inquiry and research methods. More recently his work has engaged with the emerging field(s) of digital social research, social media analytics, big data and disruptive technologies. This work is being realised through the COSMOS (Collaborative Online Social Media ObServatory) research programme. He is currently co-editor of *Qualitative Research* (published by SAGE), serves on the editorial board of *Big Data and Society* (published by SAGE) and is lead author (with Edwards, Williams and Burnap) of the forthcoming book *Digital Society: Theory, Method and Data* (SAGE, 2015).

Christian Licoppe, PhD, is Professor of Sociology, alumnus of the Ecole Polytechnique and acting head of the Social Science Department at Telecom ParisTech. Trained in history and sociology of science and technology, he is interested in conversation analysis and multimodal interaction analysis, and more generally ethnographic studies of multi-participant interaction in mobile and institutional settings. He has been extensively involved in the field of mobile studies, where he has studied the interactions of mobile users in location aware systems and the social consequences of the ways they refer to place and proximity. He is currently engaged in a large-scale video-ethnographic research project on courtroom interactions, in relation to the introduction of videoconference systems and the way they are part of a reshaping of such an institutional speech event.

Edward Reynolds is currently Lecturer in Conversation Analysis at the University of New Hampshire. His research focuses on the organisation of groups in conflict, in particular the ethnomethods of categorisation, comparison and conflict. His publications include co-editing a special issue of the *Australian Journal of Communication* (2013, 40/2, with Sean Rintel and Richard Fitzgerald) and research on the interactional organisation of deception in the *British Journal of Social Psychology* (with Johanna Rendle-Short, 2011) and the description of an undescribed practice of conflict-talk in *Pragmatics* (2011).

Sean Rintel is a postdoctoral researcher at Microsoft Research Cambridge (UK) in the Computer Mediated Living area and a Lecturer in Strategic Communication at The University of Queensland. He was awarded his PhD in 2010 from the University at Albany, State University of New York, chaired by Professor Emerita Anita Pomerantz. His research focuses on how the affordances of communication technologies interact with language, social action and culture. He has published on video-mediated communication, Internet Relay Chat, social media, online television websites, phatic technologies, memes and internet culture, and telerehabilitation. He edited the 2013 *Electronic Journal of Communication* Special Issue on 'Videoconferencing in Practice: 21st Century Challenges' (2013, Vol. 23/1&2). With Richard Fitzgerald and Edward Reynolds he co-edited the *Australian Journal of Communication* Special Issue of selected papers from the Australasian Institute of Ethnomethodology and Conversation Analysis Conference (2013, Vol. 40/2).

Robin Smith is Lecturer in Sociology at the Cardiff School of Social Sciences, Cardiff University, where he completed his PhD in 2010. His research interests coalesce in an ongoing programme of empirical work concerned with ways interaction and sense-making get done in public space, through mobility, and in other settings such as research team meetings. This work has been informed by Interactionist sociology, ethnomethodology and studies in Membership Categorisation Analysis. He has published a number of articles reporting on these matters, as well as contributing to the field of qualitative methodology more generally. He is a member of the editorial board of *The Sociological Review* and Review Editor for *Qualitative Research* (published by SAGE).

Elizabeth Stokoe is Professor of Social Interaction in the Department of Social Sciences at Loughborough University. Her research interests are in conversation analysis and membership categorisation, and she has published extensively on settings including university classroom education, police investigative interviews, dating and mediation. She edited a special issue of *Discourse Studies* on membership categorisation (2012).

Her work also includes *Discourse and Identity* (2006, with Bethan Benwell) and *Conversation and Gender* (2011, with Susan Speer). Much of her current work is focused on developing the 'Conversation Analytic Role-play Method', an approach to communication training for practitioners, as well as studying problems with traditional forms of role-play and simulated interaction.

Rod Watson is Professor of Sociology (Adj.) at Telecom ParisTech, Eurecom at Nice-Sophia-Antipolis, France. In his career, he has won three international prizes for both his theoretical and empirical work. His interests are in the creation of a greater synergy between ethnomethodology, conversation analysis and the analysis of membership categorisation activities than presently exists and to use these approaches to contribute to an anti-cognitivitic, anti-reificatory and methodologically non-ironic sociology (and linguistics). In addition to the publications already referred to in his chapter in this volume, two of his other publications exemplify his core analytic concerns: 'Ethnomethodology, Consciousness and Self' (*Journal of Consciousness Studies*, Special Issue, 'Models of the Self', 1998, Vol. 5/2, pp. 202–23) and 'Constitutive Practices and Garfinkel's Notion of Trust: Revisited' (*Journal of Classical Sociology*, Special Issue, 'John Rawls' "Two Concepts of Rules"', ed. Anne Warfield Rawls, 2009, Vol. 9/4 (November), pp. 475–99).

Acknowledgements

We wish to thank SAGE and particularly Jai Seaman and Lily Mehrbod for their support, encouragement and faith in this project.

1

Introduction to Membership Categorisation Analysis

William Housley and Richard Fitzgerald

Introduction

This book is about an ethnomethodological approach to the study of talk-in-interaction that is gaining wider popularity and interest from across the social sciences. Membership Categorisation Analysis (MCA) refers to the study of the range of practices that members of a given speech community deploy alongside complementary and aligned ethnomethods in the routine accomplishment of everyday social interaction. A core principle here is the anthropological notion of *membership* and its relationship to the categories of culture and society that form the stock in trade for the routine accomplishment and co-ordination of social life. Categories are central to social life and experience and an empirical understanding of their actual use in real-time at the situated and granular level can generate insights into a wide spectrum of social behaviours and problems. This book draws from the pioneering work of Harvey Sacks and his concern with membership categorisation (in addition to other aligned forms of conversational practice) and the wide range of rich and fecund studies that have followed. Many of these studies have explored the relationship between membership categorisation practices, language and identity in a variety of settings and through the study of a diverse set of activities. Of course membership categorisation practices are more than the study of identities and identity work-in-action but this is a convenient place to begin our journey. Identity matters have been and continue to be an important site for sociological and related inquiry; not least because they represent a field through which individual and collective life intersect.

Membership Categorisation Analysis and Identity

While the sociological and psychological interest in social identity has a long history, this interest has tended to conceptualise identity as either a role or as an analytic group, collecting people together and predicting how they will behave. Underpinning this notion of identity as a role (or further analytic type) has been the development of theories about the interrelationship between individual identity and group membership. In psychology, this has tended to stem and develop from the early work of Erikson (1993), who made the distinction between the individual 'self' and people's social roles as the primary frame for locating social identities. This focus on social identity is also developed through the social psychology of Tajfel and Turner (1986), who theorised group formation and individual perceptions of group behaviours under the heading of Social Identity Theory (SIT). While SIT was mainly concerned with group formation, this was followed by the development of Self-Categorisation Theory (Turner et al., 1987) and its interest in the dynamics of group membership. For SIT and Self-Categorisation Theory the focus remains fixed upon the way individuals integrate into groups and encounter other groups within perceived hierarchies. While these approaches are mainly concerned with theorising identity at social group level they have become shorthand for a general theorising about social selves (Haslam et al., 2010) or a general theory of social categorisation (Turner and Reynolds, 2010). This is especially relevant here as the tendency to treat Self-Categorisation Theory as a general theory of social categorisation is sometimes tethered to the goal of cognitive science in developing an explanatory mental schema for things in the world including people and social identities (Lakoff, 1987). However, while explicitly interested in social and cultural identity these approaches tend to remain couched at the theoretical level rather than examining how people actually make sense of their own social categories and the particular social environment in which they engage (Edwards, 1991, 1995a). This is in contrast to examining how identity is done, managed, achieved and negotiated in situ, whereby these approaches tend to pass over this lived experience in favour of a more abstract conceptualisation of social identity. Furthermore, the focus on the term 'identity' can remove from view the practical concern of describing the use of an array of social types and categories within a wider sense of social structure or culture as a routine aspect of naturally occurring ordinary activity. Thus, the sociological or indeed ethnomethodological use of this term requires some qualification and caution.

For sociology, the interest in 'identity' has been directed towards the question of how much the individual is affected by their society, and vice versa, and for psychology the interest is in how group and group identity operates; though, we would argue, each tends to generate an effective separation of the research phenomena from the actual phenomena of the day-to-day work of being and acting in a society – in vivo. As such, the theoretically driven approach to understanding social identity is largely removed from day-to-day lives and routine actions where social identities are both practical accomplishments and essential resources in achieving and co-ordinating everyday tasks and actions.

Within a sometimes polarised environment characterised by debates concerning macro vs micro explanation and other dichotomies (Knorr-Cetina and Cicourel, 1981) little attention was paid to examining how people understood social identity and how they used social identities in their everyday business. That is to say social identity is something people in society do, achieve, negotiate, attribute things to and act upon as part of their daily lives. It was this lived work of social identity of how people do things with identities as social categories that Harvey Sacks saw as offering the chance to develop a particular take on the sociological imagination; namely the study of society from the practical participatory view of members. Sacks then, rather than trying to delve into people's heads to gain an understanding of how people perceived and engaged each other in their society, or pursuing research that sought to categorise people into groups so as to predict behaviour, was interested in how people use and deploy ideas and notions of aggregated behaviours as they go about their routine business. This focus on the use of routine ordinary common-sense knowledge to competently navigate society was to be found in people's descriptions of their social world and conveyed through text, symbolic representation and interaction; where displays of practical theorising about the world and how it is organised and common-sense reasoning about how it works in particular instances are reflexively and accountably constituted through these and associated practices. Professional sociological categories were treated no differently in this regard, a stance that at the time was seen by some as a direct attack on the work of professional academic research. However, Sacks and Garfinkel (see Hill and Crittenden, 1968; Gellner, 1975) were simply pointing out that their work also relied upon common sense ('common' to the field of professional social science) practical theorising; an argument that generates less controversy today.

Thus, the study of 'identity' categories and social types is key to a general conceptualisation of social science and sociology and has provided a central theoretical, methodological and empirical anvil upon which many current research tools and concepts have been formed and forged. Harvey Sacks's concern with how everyday members of ordinary society, as competent members of a linguistic community, use categorisation in everyday life is novel but it also resonates with core sociological concerns and allied forms of inquiry. Sacks, of course, was completely cognisant of this disciplinary fact and this is a theme that will be explored during the course of this book in ways that demonstrate the conceptual and practical relevance of membership categorisation practices to contemporary social relations and contemporary topics of social inquiry.

It has been argued that Sacks's work on membership categorisation represented an operationalisation of Schütz's (1973) phenomenology (see Watson, this volume). The moral and practical 'typing' of persons, labelling and the like became a key concern for so-called micro studies of social life that ranged from education to everyday work settings (Atkinson and Housley, 2003). However, the significance of Sacks's concern with categorisation practices is that it represented a move to a much finer level of granularity that renders visible the relationship between morality, practical action and the social organisation of everyday social life through linguistic practice and the circulation, reception and use of texts. This is not to say that these are the only means through which social life and social relations are organised as an order of action; just that they remain a compelling feature of social organisation as a situated accomplishment by members. The importance of this focus on social categories and types (inclusive of what we might term identity) is expressed elo-quently in Sacks's classic 1979 paper 'Hotrodder: a revolutionary category': '... any person who is a case of a category is seen as a member of a category, and what's known about that category is known about them, and the fate of each is bound up in the fate of the other' (1979: 13).

This ontological orientation towards categories and categorisation as members' phe-nomenon:

> [D]irects attention to the locally used, invoked and organized 'presumed common-sense knowledge of social structures' which members are oriented to in the conduct of their everyday affairs ... This presumed common sense knowledge or culture is made available through a method by which the ordi-nary sense of talk and action is made problematic (for the purpose of analysis) and is conceptualised as the accomplishment of local instances of categorical ordering work. The aim of such analysis is to produce formal descriptions of the procedures which persons employ in particular singular occurrences of talk and action. (Hester and Eglin, 1997a: 3)

In this way, Sacks pointed to the routine common-sense theorising employed by mem-bers to explain, predict and describe others' behaviour as part of the routine work of everyday social action. It might be argued that Sacks was not so much interested in observing *that* people mention social categories in the course of their interaction or within textual forms but rather in the unique configuration of categories and their associated predicates and attributes through which social categories are deployed in any particular instance. That is to say, his interest was in just how they were brought to life in any particular instance, for the participants, just here, just now, and for just this purpose.

For Sacks, the ability of capturing this ordinary routine practical theorising and common-sense reasoning through tape recordings held out the possibility of examining society as a public achievement, a possibility that involved the examination of mem-bers' own understanding of society as they engaged with it. To Sacks this offered the possibility of developing a 'primitive' sociology based on empirical observations and recordings of people enacting (doing) society when going about their routine business. While he was not particularly interested in language to begin with, but rather in the stable reproduction of data, the affordances of the new tape-recording devices with the ability to record, play back and listen repeatedly allowed him to collect instances of locally achieved sense-making where people relied upon common-sense social knowl-edge and engaged in practical theorising. Thus, underpinning Sacks's developing interests was an orientation to an empirical 'proto-sociology' based on observing what people do as a way of engaging with the classic sociological question of how social order and organisation are possible.

It is from Sacks's early interest and examination of the practical work of members' 'sociological' theorising that Membership Categorisation Analysis (MCA) has developed, as a rigorous approach to the study of how social knowledge is organised and used during the course of everyday situations and events. The focus of MCA is on peoples' routine methods of social categorisation and local reasoning practices as a display and accomplishment of 'doing' society, or what has been described as 'culture-in-action' (Hester and Eglin, 1997b). Membership Categorisation Analysis is part of the broader research work of Ethnomethodology and allied disciplines, which includes Conversation Analysis (CA), and more recently Discursive Psychology. Ethnomethodology is a sociological approach founded by Harold Garfinkel (1964) that approaches the classic sociological question of 'how is social order achieved?' through studying what people actually do, how they conduct themselves and how they interact with others. In this sense, rather than *theorising* how society is organised, ethnomethodology focuses on how people routinely accomplish social life, where social facts are not treated as things but as accomplishments (Garfinkel, 2002).

The focus of ethnomethodology and of MCA is exemplified in the collection of studies brought together by Roy Turner entitled, unsurprisingly, *Ethnomethodology* (1974). While this work includes a section on the way institutional records are constructed and organised, and how theorising as a practical accomplishment might be scripted, the final section is on the methodological basis of interaction. It is in this section that Sacks and Schegloff produce two of the most influential and enduring discussions in their emerging observational discipline with its goal of dealing with 'the details of social action rigorously, empirically and formally' (Turner, 1974: 195). Although both published previously (Sacks, 1972b; Schegloff and Sacks, 1973), the two chapters in Turner's collection, 'On the analysability of stories by children' (Sacks, 1974) and 'Opening up closings' (Schegloff and Sacks, 1974), point to the emerging research trajectories in what has become known as Conversation Analysis and Membership Categorisation Analysis. The foci of the two papers followed different trajectories, with CA developing rapidly and finding an audience in the linguistic area of pragmatics, rather than sociology. However, while this move towards linguistics certainly did not cover all CA-inspired work (see for example Pomerantz and Mandelbaum, 2005) the linguistic appeal of CA also corresponded, until recently (Heritage, 2013; Watson, this volume), with a lessening of the ties to an explicit sociological agenda; these debates remain current.

While the rapid rise of CA tended to overshadow Sacks's concern with categories and categorisation, under the heading of MCA his work has continued to be developed into a principled analytic approach used across a range of disciplines where the focus is on how people display a working social knowledge about social categories, and their actions both in and about a setting. Of course, although developing a strong focus on social interaction, MCA is not confined to spoken interaction. From the early lecture on a child's story (which we discuss in detail below) to the lecture on the 'Navy Pilot' (Sacks, 1995, Vol. 1, Lecture 14, 205–22) various materials have provided a rich source of members category work which have included newspaper headlines (Hester and Eglin, 1992; Lee, 1984) and wider newspaper coverage (Eglin and Hester, 2003), and continues with contemporary texts drawn from social media (Stokoe and Attenborough, this volume).

In the following sections we turn to focus on some of the main aspects of Sacks's category work before tracing these aspects towards contemporary themes in MCA research. However, before doing so it is useful to note that MCA is not so much a fully worked out methodology but rather a collection of observed practices employed *by members*. Thus MCA has not tended to establish a fully worked out set of methodological tools to be applied to data, but rather to develop a concern with the empirical examination of just what people seem to be orienting to in order to achieve whatever it is they are doing. That is to say MCA is interested in observing, uncovering and detailing the methods, techniques and orientations employed by members as they go about their routine tasks. Thus MCA is not so much a method of analysis but rather a collection of observations and an analytic mentality towards observing the ways and methods people orient, invoke and negotiate social category based knowledge when engaged in social action. In this way, and as we work through Sacks's basic observations in the following sections, it is worth bearing in mind that the concepts and analytic 'tools' outlined are those drawn from observing people *doing category work* (Licoppe, this volume). In this sense, the initial observations about how social categories work in the story below provide an introduction to the phenomena of categorial work, which allows us to begin to open up and examine in ever increasing detail, subtlety and analytic sophistication just how shared social knowledge (a baseline definition of culture) is profoundly flexible and adaptable to task and purpose. We begin, then, with Sacks's well-known discussion of the kinship story before moving to some of the recent areas that have been developed from Sacks's original work.

Harvey Sacks and Membership Categorisation Analysis

For Sacks the classic sociological question of 'how is social order possible?' is not answered by asking people what they do but by examining what people actually do, i.e., how *they* engage with and make sense of the world in doing or going about their everyday routine activities. As mentioned previously, with the advent of the portable tape recorder, Sacks was able to collect recordings and snippets of everyday interactions and he became increasingly interested in the way people used social categories for describing people in the world and how these social categories were used to account for, explain, justify and make sense of people's actions. As Licoppe (this volume) demonstrates, this routine category work can have consequences for the participants if not performed adequately. For Sacks, then, the classic question of 'social order' could be found in the way such categorisation work embeds and trades on assumed taken-for-granted knowledge about the social world and, in particular, how the actions of social categories are made to operate within as well as organise interaction in particular instances.

The classic illustration of how taken-for-granted knowledge of social categories and routine assumptions about how they operate in particular instances is found in Sacks's detailed exposition of the first two sentences of a 2-year-old child's story, 'The baby cried. The mommy picked it up' (Sacks, 1974). The enduring analytic power of these two sentences is found in the gestalt shift Sacks achieves through his careful unpacking of the 'simple' story to reveal how complex layers of social knowledge and social action are inbuilt and trade on 'common sense' knowledge of who was involved, what happened and why. This simple yet profound observation, which we discuss below, revealed the scope and potential for examining members' social reasoning practices through a focus on members' use and methods of social categorisation and the work this is put to in doing some form of social activity.

Membership Categorisation Analysis – the Basics: 'The Baby Cried. The Mommy Picked It Up'

As indicated above, Sacks's interest in social categories was developed over a number of years and appears throughout his lectures and publications, where it finds its clearest exposition in his discussion of a child's story – 'The baby cried. The mommy picked it up' (Sacks, 1972a, b, 1974, 1995). In 'On the analysability of stories by children' (1974) he embarks upon the analysis of this story by assuming an un-problematic but nonetheless remarkable understanding of the events by his readers/listeners.

> The sentences we are considering are after all rather minor, and yet all of you, or many of you, hear just what I said you heard, and many of us are quite unacquainted with each other. I am then dealing with something real and something finely powerful. (Sacks, 1974: 218)

What Sacks proposes, then, is that this story is heard and understood by many who hear it as meaning what was intended by the author of the story. That is to say, it is perfectly recognisable to unacquainted members without recourse to whom the particular people involved are, and who it is told to. Sacks (1974: 218) then poses a question as to whether it is possible to arrive at a methodological apparatus for explicating this mundane, yet detailed 'known in common understanding' in order to

> ... give some sense ... of the fine power of culture. It does not, so to speak, merely fill the brains in roughly the same way, it fills them so that they are alike in fine detail ...

> What one ought to seek to build is an apparatus which will provide for how it is that any activities, which members do in such a way as to be recognisable as such to members, are done, and done recognisably.

The premise, then, is that the child's story is mundanely recognisable, and that, as such, the goal is to try to account for this recognisability through the building of an apparatus that can deal with these abstract references to persons and actions. To this end, and in the subsequent analysis, Sacks introduces a number of concepts or tools including 'membership categorisation devices', 'membership categories', 'category bound activities', the 'rules of economy and consistency', and the 'viewers and hearers maxims' to tease out an analysis of how this common understanding is arrived at.

Membership categorisation 'devices' are, for all practical purposes, the lynch-pin for the analysis. The 'device' is the 'organisational relevance' providing for, collecting together and organising social categories and their relevant actions, *in any particular instance*. Categories are described as references to persons such as 'fireman', 'brother', 'prime minister', 'teacher', etc., or in this instance 'baby' and 'mommy'. Categories, then, may be used by members in such a way as to form co-membership with other categories in an organisational and situational relevant 'device'. This means that references to such categories as 'butcher, baker, candlestick maker' can be seen to be connected in terms of occupations, or rather the device of 'occupations', which provides an organisational relevance for *these* categories for *this* topic here and now. That is to say, the use of any *particular* categories, 'baby' and 'mommy' are heard to go *together* within the organisational device, 'family' in this instance, and further that *these* categories in *this* device also involve working knowledge of background expectancies such as their expectable actions and their legitimate attributions in relation to each other. This points, then, to the way that categories are selected, used and configured by members with an orientation to the topic at hand, that their use in any particular situation is purposeful or practical for that topic, rather than simply abstract references.

Furthermore, Sacks (1972a) suggests that the categories 'baby' and 'mommy' comprise a further class of categories which go together in a strong associated pairing, or 'standardised relational pair', such as 'doctor/patient', 'mother/baby', 'girlfriend/boyfriend', etc. This class of categories are common pairings, whereby mention of one *suggests* the other. However, although quite recognisable as 'going together', the category 'doctor' may not necessarily be found with 'patient', for example, the pairing of doctor/nurse may be heard to have an equal level of practical association. Some category pairs or 'standardised relational pairs' such as 'husband and wife' suggest stronger ties, where one category references the other to such an extent that mention of one of the categories may include reference to the other. In this sense, certain categories stand in relation to each other as a signature of the normative parameters of culture and social relations that are routinely configured, interpreted and reproduced by members.

The associated category-bound actions (or predicates) of social categories comprise a kind of stock of knowledge-in-action or *culture-in-action* (Hester, 1994; Hester and Eglin, 1997a), which involves common-sense knowledge about the world and how social categories are expected or assumed to act in general and in particular situations. That is to say, while there are any number of ways categories, devices and their associated actions can be configured prior to their use, it is only through their use in any particular situation that they become operative for the participants. From this basic categorisation 'apparatus' Sacks then offers some further observations, which he refers to as 'rules of application', that provide some further insights as to how social categorisation practices are realised.

Sacks describes two 'rules of application', the 'economy rule' and the 'consistency rule' (1995: 221), that work to inform and organise participants' interpretation and understanding of categories in use. The economy rule states that when a member refers to a single category from any device then this is an adequate reference to a person for all practical purposes here and now and without further need of elaboration (e.g., 'mommy, baby' need not be described beyond these categorisations). The 'consistency rule' is derived from the observation that if a member of a given population has been categorised within a particular device then other members of that population can be categorised in terms of the same collection (e.g., mommy and baby are in the device 'family'). Sacks then derives a corollary known as the 'hearer's maxim' (1974), which posits that if two or more categories are used to categorise two or more members of some population and those categories can be heard as categories from the same collection, then: hear them that way (e.g., mommy and baby are heard as belonging to the *same* family). These rules of application and corollary therefore work as practical registers that reinforce the observed or described actions of persons which draw upon common- sense understandings for their practical sense making through the *occasioned* use of membership categorisation devices.

Sacks, then, shows how a common-sense understanding of the story can be made analytically interesting. By proposing that the use of 'baby' and 'mommy' can be heard as belonging to the same 'device' of 'family', this provides for a hearing that identifies the 'baby' as a young child, and the 'mommy' as the mother of *that* child. They are related through the 'obvious' device of co-members of the *same* family. Further, the actions contained in the story are sequential in that the mommy picks the baby up after, *and because*, it is crying. Thus, through common and recognisable 'category attributes' related to the categories 'mommy' and 'baby', whereby babies cry and their mothers pick them up to comfort them when they are crying, the actions carried out in the story can be heard as recognisable, common, *expected* actions and attributes of the categories displayed. Furthermore, that this recognisable and mundane action can be heard to be done is itself *unremarkable*, i.e., we do not need to look any further to understand what the story means as all that is needed is contained in the two sentences.

It is with this apparatus, then, that Sacks provides an empirically grounded analytic set of observations that seeks to produce principled empirical observations of naturally occurring social categorisation.

However, before going on to examine recent developments of Sacks's work it is worth pausing to examine some of the criticisms that have been raised about his analytic discussions. While his *Lectures* (Sacks, 1992, 1995) offer a vast array of insightful observations they are transcripts of his lectures and so they do not contain a systematic method or a coherent set of procedures. Rather his observations (edited by Jefferson and with introductions to each volume by Schegloff) offer a unique and valuable insight into Sacks's own working through various ideas and observations, including impromptu responses to questions from the student audience. While this provides an excellent insight into the process and development of Sacks's analytic interests, a tendency has also been identified (Edwards, 1995a; Hester and Eglin, 1997b; Schegloff, 1995;

Watson, this volume) in some of his analysis and discussion towards giving a more solid, fixed or reified property to some categories and their organisation in social action. As Watson (this volume) points out, this is not that surprising given the intellectual trends at the time, and this deserves some critique – but within a framework of his overall work. While this has been raised by various analysts (and is discussed in depth by Watson, this volume), this tendency was first tackled head-on by Hester and Eglin in their introduction to the book *Culture in Action* (1997a), who tease out a set of principles and concepts and critique the possible analytic separation of the observed phenomena (i.e. categorisation practices) from the actual lived tasks the phenomena are embedded within.

In other words, at some points Sacks seems to be advocating an analysis which could produce decontextualised accounts of category work. This, as Schegloff (1995) in his Introduction to Volume 1 of Sacks's *Lectures* argues, has the potential for the analysis to be *promiscuous*, where the analyst relies upon *their* understanding rather than those displayed by the participants (see also Fitzgerald, 2012; Fitzgerald and Rintel, 2013; Housley and Fitzgerald, 2002a; Stokoe, 2012a; Watson, this volume). Thus, rather than reiterate the locally occasioned character of sense-making, some of Sacks's own concepts serve to undermine his insistence on an empirical focus upon locally occasioned work. Although acknowledging that Sacks's own words contribute to the perceptions of static forms of knowledge and analytic decontextualisation, subsequent work in MCA clearly demonstrates the contextualised underpinning of in situ occasionality, evident in the overall thrust of his analysis, and evident in the contributions to this volume.

While Sacks's story provides an excellent way of introducing the principles of MCA, we now move from the static text of the child's story to interactional conversational work where further levels of complexity are observable; as any category work is irredeemably part of a flow of interaction and therefore necessitates a concern with the mutually elaborative work of both categorial and sequential aspects of 'talk-in-interaction'. For MCA, this means treating category work as flowing through the interaction as sequential and topical relevancies emerge and recede through various tasks. It is important then that in any analysis of members' category work this is conceived as part of a multidimensional flow of interaction in which sequences and categories are multi-linear, flowing through time, changing and adapting according to the immediate and distal relevancies if, as, and when they become salient to the participants' orientations.

Membership Categorisation Within Multi-layered Interaction

While Sacks's story provides a detailed example of the culture-in-action embedded within the two sentences, and demonstrates an elegant way of analytically unpacking the organisation of category work, he was also interested in members' category work within interaction and as interactional work. For Sacks (1995) it was equally of interest not just how categories were organised but also how they were invoked, used and negotiated within the flow of interaction. For MCA, this means conceiving of members' category work within an inextricably entwined multi-layered sequence that permeates multiple layers of participant orientation and interactional tasks.

Treating category work as part of the flow of any interaction highlights that interaction and the tasks at hand do not routinely reside at just a single layer of category orientation, such as the explicit use of social categories, but within multiple layers of category work oriented to by participants. From this position it becomes important to understand MCA as a way exploring members' category work within a multi-layered sequential flow of interaction that continually changes as the interaction moves from speaker to speaker and action to action. For Sacks and later Watson (1994) this involved examining the sequential turns of interaction through a categorial lens, as 'turn generated', or more recently 'turn formed' (Watson, this volume), categories. Treating turn sequence as but one layer of category work conceives of interaction as multi-layered and as a site where further layers of category work and category-based orientations become analytically observable in a rich mutually implicative interactional texture. In the next part of our introductory discussion this layered interactional work is explored through an example of MCA analysis drawn from a radio phone-in (Fitzgerald and Housley, 2002; Housley and Fitzgerald, 2002a). We begin at the level of sequentially formed categories, highlighting the way sequential turns can be seen to have categorial organisation, before building further layers of membership category orientations. For the second level we examine how a caller's opinion about a topic is eventually tied to a membership category, which then serves to account for that opinion. At the third level of analysis we highlight how the context of the interaction, a radio phone-in, is oriented to by the participants through a categorisation device for the interaction – a kind of 'who we are and what we are doing' device (Butler and Fitzgerald, 2010) – that the participants orient to at various points in the programme.

Multi-layered Organisation of Category Work

For Sacks, sequential actions could be treated and analysed in a similar way to membership categories, in that they can be seen to involve and make relevant various attributes for these actions. For example, to ask a question requires the asker to construct an utterance that can be recognised as a question, and relatedly the obligation of the answerer is to produce a recognisable answer to *this* question in the next turn slot. The attributes tied to a sequential action then are 'turn generated' (or, following Watson, this volume, 'turn produced' or 'turn-formed',) as they relate only to the interactional action and the job that action is doing. At this level the idea of 'turn-formed' does not stipulate in advance of the occurrence who should fill the slot, indeed as a 'turn-formed category' slot this is adequately categorised through the action, i.e., 'caller/called' or 'questioner/answerer'. The occupation of these categories is a sequential matter, as who occupies the turn-formed category 'questioner' is fulfilled by the person who performs the action.

Sequential turn-formed categories are occupied only for the duration of their occurrence, and upon satisfactory completion the sequential category membership is ended.

The questioner does not remain the questioner; rather, the questioner may then become the answerer or something else, including a new turn-formed category 'questioner', in the next sequence. In other words, they are turn-formed categories occupied for the duration of the sequential action that can, in turn, touch off new turn-formed categories, as seen in this example taken from a UK radio phone-in programme.

EXTRACT 1: TURN-FORMED CATEGORIES

```
01N: Frances Smith from from Birmingham what do you think
02F: urrr..I.feel that the age of consent should stay at
03   twenty one()I believe that society is going to send a
04   message to young people..that..um..gay sex is OK
```

In this opening sequence of a radio phone-in the interactional work of N involves moving F from 'off-air' to 'on-air' and into a sequential position to speak about the topic. N achieves this through producing the full name and location of F during which time N occupies the sequential category 'introducer', which is then followed by N producing a question/invitation to speak. In this way, the speaker, N, occupies the turn-formed category of introducer before mid-sentence shifting categories to question/inviter. F then begins to speak and in so doing occupies the sequential category 'answerer' by fulfilling the turn-formed requirements of the response to N's question. In this example, the turn-formed categories of introducer/introduced and questioner/answerer are made operative and fulfilled only for the duration of the turns.

Through the deployment and occupation of turn-formed categories and the completion of such categories, these categories are seen to 'continually flow' through the interaction being occupied, used, completed, re-used, modified etc., as the interaction unfolds. This highlights the continually changing occupation of such categories, whereby, as speaker change occurs, the predicates associated with the turn-formed categories change with them. The term 'turn-formed categories' is also useful as it highlights the *social* obligation involved in occupying such categories where the non-fulfilment of the category action can be drawn attention to or sanctioned by, for example, asking someone to speak up, to repeat the question, to ask if what they said was a question or to describe their action as a statement rather than a question. In other words, they are an important feature of accountable action.

Membership Categorisation in Interactional Sequence

In a similar way to turn-formed categories, members' explicit use of category references and descriptions are embedded in a multi-layered sequential environment. For example, returning to the previous extract of the phone-in opening, F invokes various membership categories along with associated predicates as the work of the call progresses. Following N's introduction F begins to give her opinion on the topic, the proposed of lowering the age of homosexual consent from 21 to 18 years of age. Her opinion at this point is not explicitly tied to any membership category. However, as the call progresses, and in response to N's question, F does claim membership of a category.

EXTRACT 2: CATEGORY FLOW

```
01N: Frances Smith from from Birmingham what do you think
02F: urrr..I.feel that the age of consent should stay at
03    twenty one()I believe that society is going to send a
04    message to young people..that..um..gay sex is OK
05    and..uh..I just don't agree..I think it's unnatural..I
06    think with the fear of Aids..it's very frightening..
07    that..our young men can go out and and..and..and..will
08    not be so much worrying whether the girls can become
09    pregnant as to whether our (.)sons are going to catch
10    Aids
11N: can I disassociate..try and disassociate the two issues
12    here and lets talk about them separately. One is the
13    public health ()one [and one] is the one of excluding
14F:                       [ yes   ]
15N: that..of of ethics and whether..ur..[um((inaudible))    ]
16F:                                      [I' m..well..I' m a]
17    Christian and I do believe it is against the Christian
18    ethics I believe St Paul spoke quite strongly against
19    homosexuality
```

At line 2, F begins to offer her opinion on the topic of lowering the age of male homosexual sexual consent. The point she makes is that she holds a concern for the well-being of young people who may get involved in this type of activity *because* society is giving the wrong message. In the course of this opinion she offers various categories in relation to the topic. She suggests that '*our young men*' and '*our sons*' are vulnerable to catching AIDS; that societal concern will shift from unwanted pregnancy to fear of infection. While not explicitly claiming membership of any category, F's reference to 'our young men', 'our young sons' and 'the girls' works to collect these categories together in a device 'family' with F possibly speaking as a 'concerned parent'. For the audience, the opinion and concern could reasonably be predicated to the category parent. As the call continues, however, any initial and tentative predicated category assumption is replaced with an explicit category relationship tied to her opinion.

When N attempts to narrow the debate, F claims membership of the category 'Christian', '16F: I'm...I'm a Christian and I do believe [it] is against Christian ethics...'. The category membership claimed by F is now explicitly tied as a reason for her opinion. That is to say her opinion is now made a predicate of her membership of the category Christian such that her opinion about the topic is now tied (Reynolds and Fitzgerald, this volume) and made accountable to her 'new' category membership. Furthermore, her claim to membership of the category Christian serves to retrospectively account for her foregoing contribution in relation to that category in that it can now be seen as an explicit category-based opinion. Her past and future contribution can now be seen in the light of this newly available category and associated predicates of the category.

This example highlights, and as Stokoe and Attenborough (this volume) discuss in more depth, the on-going in situ nature of members' category work whereby category and predicates do not remain static but are continually developed, clarified, made accountable and even retrospectively modified. Having examined an instance of category work at the level of sequence and topic we now turn to a further layer of category-based orientation.

Omnirelevant Categories and Devices

As demonstrated in the previous example, members' category work flows through the interaction being developed and transformed over the course of interaction as new categories are used and are made topically relevant in both description and incumbency. However, while new categories may be made relevant and further category work undertaken at any time these do not necessarily make the previous categories redundant, or mean that they cease to operate, for they may now form part of the background relevancies to the participants. That is to say, while the development of categories within the interaction may continue apace, previous categories may remain or be re-invoked within the interaction. Moreover, some categories and devices may be potentially relevant for the whole or at any time during the interactional event, such that they are 'omnirelevant' categories. As Sacks (1995: Vol. 1, 594–5) observes in relation to a group therapy session:

> What I want to be able to say is that 'therapist'/'patient' is 'omni-relevant' for the 'group therapy session'. I don't want to say that it's the only collection of category used or usable in this session; that would clearly be absurd. And I don't want to say it's the only collection that's omni-relevant; there may be many that are omni-relevant. It is one omni-relevant collection.

Here Sacks observes that although categories may be deployed and negotiated in the course of the interaction, as topics develop and shift there may remain omnirelevant categories that are, or may be, oriented to as relevant throughout the interaction. In terms of the radio phone-in extract above, the categories of 'host' and 'caller' are omnirelevant as these organise the programme and remain relevant throughout the show even though the category of 'caller', F in the example above, is occupied by a series of 'callers'; that is, omnirelevance indicates that categories and devices operate at a local contextual level of 'who-we-are-and-what-we-are-doing'. Thus, to describe these categories as omnirelevant is to say that they can permeate the interaction at different levels, for example operating at an organisational level and at an immediate level and invoked as relevant at particular points in the interaction. It is then at the immediate level, when they are invoked and oriented to by the participants, that they become observable/accountable as operating at the organisational level. This means that just because the example above can be described as a radio phone-in, it does not mean that this context or the constituent identities/categories are always immediately relevant or oriented to for any particular task undertaken by the participants. For MCA, this has to be shown as being oriented to by the participants (Fitzgerald and Rintel, 2013; Fitzgerald et al., 2009; Hester and Hester, 2012; Rintel, this volume). For example, while within the particular radio programme discussed above it is possible to describe the institutional roles of the participants as 'host' and 'caller', we avoided these labels in the data and discussion as these categories need to be seen to be oriented to and relevant for the participants. The analytic focus then is on how the participants occupy and make observable and relevant the categories 'host' and 'caller', i.e., how the participants 'operationalise' their category membership through performing certain category specific actions such as introducing the programme/topic, introducing the callers, inviting callers to speak, discussing issues raised with the callers, and managing caller transition. That is to say, in performing these actions N is both doing 'hosting' and also making relevant another programme-relevant category 'caller'. These are programme-relevant categories as they relate to the programme 'radio phone-in' rather than to the actual business of topical debate where topical relevant categories are used. In this way, MCA approaches members' category work in interaction as embedded within a multi-layered and multi-sequential environment while embracing the complexity of interaction and the orientations of, and to, those present.

As discussed above, while MCA offers various analytic tools it does not stipulate a formula or process to follow when undertaking analysis. Rather the relevant analytic tools are assembled by the analyst in relation to the particular data being examined, as *occasioned* by the data. Central to MCA then are a modest collection of routine categorisation features that Sacks observed in his analysis of the child's story which have subsequently proved to be resilient over time and provided a rich resource through which to develop a remarkable insight into the complexity of members' reasoning practices in a range of settings. Thus, while there was some early criticism of the approach, for example whether Sacks intended to continue to focus on members' category work (Schegloff, 2007a; see also Stokoe, 2012a; Watson, 1994), subsequent

MCA research undertaken has nonetheless developed a strong and flexible methodological framework which continues to produce a robust cumulative body of research.

So, to reiterate, the achievement of MCA has been in developing an empirical understanding of members' interactional category work within a complex multi-layered
social environment and which in turn has provided a basis for the study of more complex categorial organisation including category-based moral ordering (Jayyusi, 1984;
Watson, 1978), the display of social norms (Housley and Fitzgerald, 2009a), and traditional social science topics such as racism (Whitehead, 2009), gender (Stokoe, 2003)
and childhood (Butler, 2008). An additional and important dimension of Membership
Categorisation Analysis also relates to practical categorisation work around non-
personal collections, categories and modes of predication within particular activities
(see Hester and Eglin, 1997b; Housley and Fitzgerald, 2002a; Housley and Smith, this
volume). The 'sociality' of artefacts, objects and things finds resonance in the symbolic
interaction of Mead where mind, self and society are extended into a wider cosmic
frame of being and becoming that is inclusive of interaction between subjects and
objects within a broad continuum of sociality that is inclusive of but more than just
individuals, groups and institutions. More recent developments have cited actor-
network theory (Latour, 1999; Law, 1994) as a lens through which the ordering of
actors, objects (and other material formations) and networks can be re-specified. The
debate and connections between actor-network theory and ethnomethodology lie
beyond the scope of this book but deserve further scrutiny in terms of common roots
but also important differences. Approaches to the study of members' non-personal
category use have adopted an empirical approach. As we have noted elsewhere:

> MCA had also, in some respects, developed from the initial Sacksian concerns
> with personalized membership categorization devices into an interest in the
> use of non-personalized membership categorization devices in members' talk.
> For example, McHoul and Watson (1984) examine how common-sense
> knowledge of the children's own locality is used as a resource in the explana-
> tion of formal geographical knowledge ... Further work which has extended
> the analytic role of MCA into the domain of non-personalized categories, as
> opposed to Sacks's early emphasis on the descriptive categories of person,
> includes work carried out by Coulter (1983). He seeks to locate categories of
> social structure within both institutional and organizational conversational
> contexts as well as everyday non-institutional contexts. (Housley and
> Fitzgerald, 2002a: 63)

Further advances in the field of membership categorisation have involved an engagement with related and aligned aspects of interaction. Of course, while the study of
membership categorisation practices has dealt with talk and texts from the beginning,
other orders of action and their relationship with different modes of interaction are
also reflected upon within the *Lectures* (Sacks, 1995). Perhaps the most important of
these less frequented avenues has been the development of the 'viewer's maxim' to an

understanding of how membership categorisation might operate in terms of mundane visual order (see Hester and Francis, 2003) and in relation to other orders of ordinary interaction where membership categorisation practices (amongst others) are salient and recognisably relevant resources for the routine situated accomplishment of social organisation and conduct. The arrival of new forms of communication technology and the emergence of social media often constitute 'places' where the multi-modal characteristics of the interaction order are reassembled within specific communication formats oriented to affordances of connectivity across time and space. An understanding of how categorisation practices move between 'audio' and 'video' cues is increasingly a practical problem for networked members utilising new forms of communication technology (Licoppe, this volume; Rintel, this volume).

The study of membership categorisation practice, as an aspect of everyday order, is beginning to develop apace with the flowering of a coherent set of studies bound together through common problems, analytic descriptions, core studies and common sites of interest. Whilst the analytic flexibility of MCA, as a branch of ethnomethodological enquiry, provides an opportunity to explore new domains it also remains firmly a part of a broader programme of research and inquiry that is deeply implicated in key sociological issues and debates.

Chapters in this Collection

The chapters in this collection bring together some of the foremost authors in Membership Categorisation Analysis. Each of the chapters examines a particular set of concepts within MCA and develops these in relation to contemporary directions in the field of Ethnomethodology and Conversation Analysis. In this sense each of the chapters advance the analytic sophistication of particular concepts within the overall development of MCA as an approach. As will be discussed in more detail as we introduce each chapter, this includes examining category predicates, entwined categorial and sequential flow, the contextual layering of omnirelevance, the relationship between categorial identity and interactional sequence, and the consequences of not being 'ordinary'. As a methodologically oriented collection the chapters also provide a wide range of data examples that contribute to both substantive and emergent topical areas as well as discussions around data collection and use. For example, Stokoe and Attenborough utilise data examples from personal instant messaging, rolling TV and online print media, Rintel uses data taken from couples in long-distance relationship using video chat facilities, Edwards and Fitzgerald use videos posted on the social media sharing site YouTube while Licoppe uses video linked judicial hearings. By utilising an increasingly wider range of data sources the chapters highlight how MCA contributes to a range of analytic interests as well as contributing to the discussion of what counts as 'data' for discourse and language research.

So far in this chapter we have covered the basic concepts within Membership Categorisation Analysis through Sacks's work and traced subsequent directions that are currently being developed. Following on from this introduction to MCA, each of the chapters develops some of the main concepts discussed above. The collection kicks off with a discussion by Watson, who focuses on the fundamental concepts underpinning MCA and the main conceptual shift necessary in undertaking MCA research. Watson argues that MCA is not a set of tools to be applied but relies on an analytic attitude to observing and documenting the categorial work, methods and techniques utilised in any particular event. That is, to get to the heart of successful MCA research entails an important conceptual shift in analytic mentality from selecting and applying methodological tools to explain what members do, to putting members at the centre of the analysis and allowing members' category work and the methods used in any particular situation to emerge. In doing this Watson also addresses some of Sacks's writings that have sometimes seemed equivocal on this point and which have potentially obfuscated the development of MCA. As Watson and others (Edwards, 1995a; Hester and Eglin, 1997a) have shown, within some of Sacks's writings and lectures there is a tendency at times to lean towards treating some membership categories and associated features as somehow pre-existing or as fixed in time and space prior to any particular instance of their use. For example, the categories of 'male' and 'female' within the device 'sex' are described as 'natural' categories as opposed to categories which are 'occasioned' in situ. While echoing previous critiques of this, Watson provides an in-depth level of critical detail to this element in Sacks's work and from this argues strongly for the praxeological *principle* clearly underlying his work.

From this position, Watson then moves on to raise the issue of context and how the focus on single elements of action or categorisation ignores the way any action and categorial work is part of a complex interrelationship of contextual relevancies. Here Watson introduces the term 'gestalt contexture' to make the complexity of context conceptually visible and analytically approachable through the way interactional and categorial elements are seen to exist and be visible through each other. In this way membership categories and their use, relevance and invocation shift through time while their immediate and essentially reflexive retrospective and prospective here-and-now relevancies are preserved.

During the course of Chapter 3 Stokoe and Attenborough address and develop a major theme in recent MCA research focusing on the relationship between category work as part of sequential practices. The aim of the chapter is to present and exemplify a practical and sequential approach to MCA. In their discussion they demonstrate that not only are these mutually entwined, but entwined within an essential reflexivity where each relies upon the other. To this end the chapter focuses on the particular set of reflexive practices described as 'prospective and retrospective' (Watson, 2009a), where initial categorisations are subsequently reassessed within an on-going and dialogic (Leudar et al., 2004; Nekvapil and Leudar, 2002) inter-textual media. After initial discussion of the practice the authors then examine this practice as part of a particular media practice during a breaking and rolling news story.

Drawing on a range of spoken and written discourse data, Stokoe and Attenborough show how practices of description and categorisation get used in and as part of sequential practices to do particular kinds of inferential work. The authors consider these description-categorisation practices as sequentially paired actions (Watson, 2009a, this volume) where the first is *prospective*, the second *retrospective*. From this, they consider how the practice is used within rolling news coverage of a breaking news story where a news channel replaces routine news coverage to dedicate coverage to a single breaking story. Examples such as the attack on the World Trade Center (Jaworski et al., 2005) have become noted as a particular form of news coverage, described by Liebes (1998) as 'disaster marathons' where journalists working in the absence of any certainty, lacking immediate information but with the need to fill air-time, provide descriptions of actions (bombings, mass-shootings, etc.) and categories which 'fit' with the present actions but which then have to be modified and changed as more information becomes available. What becomes clear through their analysis is that the on-going reassessing of the initial and later categorisations, involving pro-spective and retrospective categorisation, constitutes a key mechanism for the practical negotiation of news work during such events where actions and biographical details of potential suspects get prospectively and/or retrospectively categorised – using category-implicative features – in various different ways before a breaking news story solidifies into a report of 'what actually happened'. The chapter considers the implications of these findings for MCA research as well as debates about analysis, inference and context in discourse and interaction analysis.

Chapter 4, by Christian Licoppe, addresses the essential principle underpinning the analytic attitude of MCA by exploring how members' own membership category analysis is an expected part of being socially competent. In this Licoppe returns to one of Sacks's initial observations that people *work* to be 'ordinary' (Sacks, 1995) by focus-ing on the routine everyday work of *being* socially competent, demonstrable through in-situ and accountable Membership Categorisation Analysis work. The data for the chapter is taken from a judicial hearing, conducted over video link, where being able to be seen to perform category analysis 'correctly' can and does have serious conse-quences when not deemed adequately performed. Here the perceived inability to perform routine Membership Categorisation Analysis is not only treated as a lack of social competence, in this case it results in continued incarceration.

The chapter then turns to the very basis of Sacks's observations of categories and their understanding as taken for granted social knowledge and *their* culture in action. In so doing the discussion forcefully provides an important bearing on the overall view of MCA research by refocusing on one of the profound observations made by Sacks and bringing this conceptual point to the fore. That category analysis is first and fore-most a routine members' practice and it is the task of MCA research to observe and reveal the ways in which categories are oriented to *by members*.

In Chapter 5 Reynolds and Fitzgerald focus on the relationship between a member-ship category and associated features, or predicates, of that category. The authors highlight how MCA has successfully been able to highlight and demonstrate how and in what ways various activities, rights and obligations are routinely related to member-ship categories and membership devices. While this reflexive relationship between category and predicated feature, initially restricted to 'category bound activities' (Sacks, 1974) and subsequently developed by Watson (1983) as 'category bound predicates', has proven immensely useful it has also tended to serve as a catch-all term for *all* relationships between category features. In Reynolds and Fitzgerald's discussion they argue that it is possible to examine the subtle *differences* in the ways category features (rights, knowledge, activities, etc.) are deployed. Through their analysis the authors explore this relationship by examining further levels of refinement to further understand the relationship between membership categories and locally invoked associated features.

Using a collection of data where participants are engaged in public arguments (Reynolds, 2011, 2013) the authors trace out three distinct differences in the types of relationship between categories and category features. The first relationship adopts Sacks's (1995) term *'category tied'* and refers to the link between a category and category features which are made explicit by participants; the second *'category bound'* relationship identifies where category-based features are *treated by members* as *naturally* related to a category, in a taken for granted, but nevertheless explicit way; and thirdly, *'category-predicate'*, where category features are implied by the operation of a membership device or category. The authors identify and explore the different *forms* of relationship between category features and categories/devices to show how these further levels of observations are analytically useful.

In Chapter 6, Rintel examines the concept of omnirelevance as a central feature of 'technologised interaction' (Hutchby, 2001a). As Rintel observes, the concept of 'omnirelevance' has recently re-emerged within Membership Categorisation Analysis as attention is given to participants' multiple orientations to various levels of context within interaction or 'reflexive oscillation' between interaction and context (Fitzgerald and Rintel, 2013) organised through membership devices. Omnirelevant devices then tie the particular interactional moment to the contextual pattern of the activity by drawing attention to 'who-we-are-and-what–we-are-doing'. Rintel utilises this concept in examining couples engaged in remote video interaction, or 'technologised interaction', interaction in which the material and social affordances of technology are 'laminated and compounded' (Hutchby, 2001b: 448–9) such that technology is a frame but not a determiner of social action. The combination is illustrated through examples in which couples cope with distortions in video calling through orienting to omnirelevant laminations of relationship and technology categories. From this Rintel observes that the notion of omnirelevance can provide a principled and nuanced understanding of an omnirelevant technological device the couples orient to as a background organising device. In this chapter omnirelevance provides a principled and grounded approach to exploring the practices through which interaction is technologised and the wider sociological interest in the interdependence of technology and society. In so doing the chapter makes important inroads into further understanding the lived experience of technologised interaction while also developing the concept of omnirelevance and the subtle dynamics through which interactional and task context are oriented to and managed in situ.

In the concluding chapter Housley and Smith explore the situated use of membership categorisation practices within research team interaction. The chapter explores real-time examples from a research team setting where social scientific matters are being routinely attended to, and builds on methodographic studies of related phenomena (Mair et al., 2013). The chapter examines how interview data is coded and explores the interactional processes and centrality of membership categorisation to negotiation and deliberation around the topics of consistency, validity and reliability (amongst others) as they relate to data and practical interpretation. Furthermore, the chapter explores the process of coding data within a research context where computer assisted qualitative data software (CAQDAS) is being used. Housley and Smith note the visibility and centrality of membership categorisation work to coding practices and methodological reasoning within social scientific research teamwork where, in this particular case, large amounts of interview data are being processed by a number of different team members. This provides for an analysis of and insight into the interactional accomplishment of data coding by research team members where matters of framing, alignment, repair and recognisability feature as matters of membership categorisation work and associated reasoning practices.

In summary, this book delivers a suite of chapters that explore interrelated advances in studies of membership categorisation. The chapters make connections with established literature, open new avenues for research and provide further grounds for a cumulative paradigm of research that complements an ethnomethodology that is critically and practically engaged with a *sociological* programme where social facts are treated as uniquely and adequately human accomplishments. We believe that this collection is timely and we hope that it provides inspiration to both early career and more established scholars who have an interest in language, interaction, culture and society. The study of membership categorisation practices is a field that is a rich resource for empirical inquiry, where the stability of social categories and the practical requirement to realise social organisation for all practical purposes is underscored by rapid social and cultural transformation. In this sense, membership categorisation, as a matrix of ethnomethods, is inexorably and inevitably tied to the mundane reproduction of human society.

2

De-Reifying Categories

Rod Watson

Introduction

This will be very much a sort of loose 'state of the art' retrospective chapter; one that builds upon and extends some of my earlier considerations of 'Membership Categorisation Analysis'. That is, it is intended as a quite straightforward methodological overview of the origins, development and prospects of the analyses of membership categorisations. I shall attempt not to conflate observations from various phases in (say) Sacks's works on this topic and shall focus on some of the origins of reification in the analysis of membership categorisations, reification in this case often being a first step on the way to analytic cognitivism.

I shall look at how Harvey Sacks began to expunge reification from Membership Categorisation Analysis, but – especially at the outset – did not fully do so. Finally, I shall suggest how we might methodologically carry forward the anti-reification aspects of Sacks's project whilst eliminating those aspects that facilitate reification. I hope to do this without taking any of the extreme or eliminative positions that have characterised the debate over membership categories. Further, I shall offer some illustrations and further indications of what I feel may be the way ahead. Later in the chapter, I shall take up some issues concerning loose/flexible contextual organisations and the like, and through all this I shall offer some suggestions for a *rapprochement* between sequential and categorial analysis in the study of conversational organisation.

'Reification' in sociology involves a version of what philosophers such as Alfred North Whitehead have termed the 'fallacy of misplaced concreteness'. It involves the analyst's attribution of a false substantiality to some social phenomenon, mistakenly conceiving of that phenomenon as a thing, or as thing-like, having the properties of concrete things, where sometimes these properties are even held to be quantifiable and measurable.

Of course, much of classical sociology recommends and employs techniques of reification as a resource (often tacit or unacknowledged) and this is something that is both studied and opposed by conversation analysis and ethnomethodology, and particularly Wittgenstein-based ethnomethodology. Dorothy E. Smith, in an influential paper, has, as we shall see below, examined the method of reification in sociology, rightly in my opinion dubbing it the 'ideological practice' of conventional forms of the discipline (Smith, 1974). Similarly, Jean Widmer (2010: 69–72) and Douglas Maynard with Thomas P. Wilson (1980) have examined reification from an ethnomethodological point of view. However, few if any have extensively considered issues of reification *within* the family of ethnomethodological and conversation analysis approaches.

Sacks's earliest work often tended towards treating membership categories in a way that was, to a significant extent, reified. He talked about membership categories as having 'incumbents' rather in the way that the pioneering role theorist Ralph Linton had conceived, in reified ways, of normatively defined 'statuses' in the social structure as being ascribed to and 'occupied' by 'incumbents'. Persons occupying a given status also enacted the 'roles', i.e., the behavioural aspects, that were 'attached' to that particular status. As Sacks often presents it, membership categories seem to be presented as 'things' that were 'produced and deployed' by a 'machinery' or 'apparatus'. Whilst, of course, even at this time Sacks also wrote praxeologically about membership categories, his conceptual vocabulary often suggests a 'structural-ist' residue, which, I shall argue, derives largely from the often awkwardly conjoined Chomskyan and componential-analytic origins in his work. Certainly the Chomskyan element is at odds with the praxeological thrust of Sacks's work, given that the latter is resolutely anti-Cartesian.

Sacks's approach to conventional collections of membership categories also had its quasi-'structuralist', reified aspects in the case of his initial data (Sacks, 1972a). The relevance of a given collection was, for Sacks, an assembled object, occasioned by and through suicidal persons' telephoned conversations with suicide prevention counsellors concerning their reported search for help related to their personal troubles.

As is clear from his first published paper 'Sociological description' (1963: 4) Sacks drew a great deal from Harold Garfinkel's and Alfred Schütz's works. Sacks's study of membership categories can, in part, be seen in terms of his (*inter alia*) imparting a radical linguistic turn to Schütz's (1962, 1964, 1966) concern with person-typifications, typifications of persons and actions. In so doing, he wrought a radical departure from Schützian or typification-based studies such as David Sudnow's 'Normal Crimes' (1965). The latter contains no reference to co-selection rules, duplicative organisation or other properties in terms of which Sacks construed ordinary membership categories and their application. Sacks's first article included a 'representative metaphor', the 'commentator machine', and set out, highly formally and schematically, various relations between what lay members say and their 'other' actions. It was Sacks's first foray into the formal, mechanistic imagery that was to pervade his work and was also to influence his (and others') sequential as well as categorial analysis.

There is a point of view that Sacks intended terms such as 'apparatus' or 'machinery' as a 'mere' metaphor or simile, apt in that it brought into view the 'how' aspects, the culturally methodic aspects, of knowledge-in-action. I do not consider that he intended an apt simile; instead, I hold that he saw both Chomsky's transformational grammar and componential analysis – despite some big differences between them – as precedents for a production model for conversation. At that time (the 1960s), both componential analysis and (especially) transformational grammar were 'in the air', as it were, that is they were quite pervasive ways of analysing 'language'. It was all too easy to be influenced by these approaches, and I consider that, in large part, Sacks's mechanistic imagery derives from them. However, despite some infelicitous turns of phrase I do not consider that Sacks's use of reifying imagery ever led to a systematic, thoroughgoing cognitivism – not even in his earliest work.

However, Sacks did derive and adapt many of his analytic procedures from a form of cognitive anthropology variously called 'ethnosemantics', 'ethnoscience' or 'componential analysis'. Quite as much of the mechanistic way in which he presents the operation of these procedures comes from this origin as his reading of Chomsky's transformational grammar. His conception in 1963 of the commentator machine evokes the transformational grammar model, but soon afterwards he introduces a quite distinct approach, componential analysis. In his PhD thesis (1966) Sacks claims he wants a 'generative grammar' of social activities such as reporting, describing and – significantly – conversing. Part of this last-named concern was to devise a 'grammar' of how co-conversationalists use categories in classifying each other: he referred to the 'special principles' that persons use to refer to each other. At that point, his interest was to study 'natural groupings' of categories – groupings that members of the society feel 'go together'. This concern derives, arguably, from componential analysts' similar objectives – objectives that, in a sense, were quasi-structuralist in that they implied 'structures' such as semantic grids.

Indeed, Sacks cites a classic 1965 issue of *The American Anthropologist* dedicated to studies in componential analysis, in which this conception of 'natural groupings' of terms is a central concern. Despite its partial origins in descriptive linguistics, some aspects of componential analysis also bear some resonances with what is in principle a very different approach, the transformational grammar model. Transformational grammar, too, involves reference to subtending or underlying elements. Indeed, this perceived affinity helped lead Aaron V. Cicourel, whose early work rendered some major ethnomethodological themes, into combining the two into his notion of 'generative semantics' (Cicourel, 1974: 74–98). Sacks, though, increasingly gained much more *specific* resource material from componential analysis, so I shall concentrate on that influence.

Componential Analysis and Membership Categorisation

So what is 'componential analysis'? Basically, it is a form of cognitive anthropology, one that is distinctive in that takes the 'linguistic turn' in quite a radical way. In so doing, it establishes a peculiar form of reification that, in so far as it was carried over into Sacks's work, had a 'knock-on' effect for early conversation analysis. The influence of componential analysis on early ethnomethodology and its cognates is often unrecognised but is attested to both by Garfinkel himself (in Hill and Crittenden, 1968) and by Edward Rose (idem.). Indeed, Garfinkel has himself avowed that he derived the term 'ethnomethodology' from componential-analytic terminology such as 'ethnobotany', 'ethnophysiology', etc. (Garfinkel, in Hill and Crittenden, 1968: 5–11).

Whilst it is not possible here to do componential analysis the justice it deserves, we can say that it applied the principles and approaches of descriptive linguistics to one of the most generic concerns of anthropology, that of classification. In so doing, it also (and importantly for ethnomethodology and conversational analysis) re-focused anthropology on the primacy of ordinary members' own knowledge and use of categories rather than those attributed to or imposed by analysts. In Kenneth Pike's term (1964: 55), componential analysts tend towards the 'emic' rather than 'etic' level. This concern with 'folk knowledge' had some significant affinity with ethnomethodology's Schützian concerns with lay society-members' common-sense knowledge and reasoning.

Given that componential analysis, an anthropological approach, had, as I have said, adopted many of its conceptions and methods from descriptive linguistics, it also took on what are for ethnomethodologists and conversation analysts some of the positives and negatives of that type of linguistics. The positives were many and highly significant. They included a focus upon how ordinary language (or just 'talk') figured within the on-going flow of ordinary activities, and this included a correlative focus upon ordinary speakers' cultural competence and background knowledge, although *how* this background knowledge was conceptualised by componential analysts in terms of semantic structures is highly dubious from the mature ethnomethodological and conversation analytic standpoints.

The contrast with very many conventional sociologists' and anthropologists' analytically unhelpful – not to mention invidious – conceptions of society rendering members as cultural and judgemental dopes (and, for sociologists, as essentially society-members without language) was quite striking and highly suggestive for ethnomethodologists and conversation analysts. In its competence model of membership, componential analysis was thus a significant resource for both ethnomethodologists and conversation analysts.

The negatives – again from an ethnomethodological and conversation analytic point of view – were, however, potentially quite debilitating. They included what we might call a residual (at the very least) cognitivism and a concern for the establishing by the analysts of segments, cases, classes and contrasts that – whilst it focused upon how native speaker themselves construed these – still involved a significant interpolation by the analyst (despite him/herself), in constructing the frames, genres and semantic structures of domains that were purported to stand as background knowledge informing members on actual occasions and instances of speaking. On top of all these concerns were the highly proactive research techniques sometimes employed by componential analysts to 'flush out' the information they required. Componential analysts' elicitation techniques tended to fly in the face of their entirely laudable claims that the analyst should not impose, or accord primacy to, her/his conceptions and procedures over those of ordinary members, as very many conventional sociologists and anthropologists did and still do.

Componential analytic anthropologists employed interventionist elicitation procedures (plus, inevitably, the researcher's unexplicated background knowledge) to establish various conjunctive and contrastive sets of terms which derived from terminological groupings of equivalences and segregates. These were analytically assembled so as to form various terminological and semantic grids – again, 'ethnomedicine' and the like. These grids comprised the components of what (according to the analyst) a member of that culture needed to know in order to act in specific instances and situations in a manner that is recognisable as unproblematically competent to fellow members of that same culture. There was, therefore, some consideration of action in componential analysis, though the place of action was not so central as the place that Sacks accorded it.

The culture is, then, presented by the componential analyst as a set of stabilised, relatively freestanding semantic grids. This is why componential analysis was sometimes called 'ethnographic semantics' since its analysis started from studying the purported 'folk taxonomies' that categorised those members' shared world of persons, states, actions and objects. Again, the place of action in the analysis in Sacks's work increasingly differed from that in componential analysis, given the latter's focus on these folk taxonomies.

These purported taxonomies included rules of usage such as those for the combinatorial use of culturally standardised classes, and so on (all this was stipulated by the analyst). The 'typicalised' (Sacks) actions of persons in the culture were often analysed by a kind of mapping exercise where the analyst 'referred the action back' to the semantic grid that was held by that analyst to inform it. In componential analysis, the semantic grids themselves are frequently conceived as static, rigid and in principle standing apart from the specific actions for which they served as resources – actions such as particular attributions of 'mental states' or particular identifications of plants or animals.

Such semantic structures are assumed by componential analysts to be cognitive ones, too: they structure cognition. Cognition is, thus, conceived in terms of culturally based 'systems' (Frake, 1962), but, of course, this did not guarantee an anti-cognitivist position as Wittgensteinians might define it: nor, to be fair, did componential analysts particularly seek this.

As one might readily recognise, these semantic grids as analytically formulated by componential analysis were conceived as reified, thing-like entities having thing-like properties such as externality, resistance and constraint. The formulation of these grids showed the methodic pattern described by Dorothy E. Smith (Smith, 1974: 45–6) in her exposition of the reifying ideological practice of sociology, namely: (i) extracting a set of terms or expressions from the actual circumstances of their production; (ii) having effectuated such a decontextualisation, rearranging the terms to demonstrate an order among them; and then (iii) re-attributing them in their rearranged form to the action(s) from which they were originally detached.

We can see, I think, some links with some membership categorisation studies in all this. There is one tendency in membership categorisation which is still highly 'structuralist' in the taxonomic, formalistic, logic-chopping sense – one that is at least a minor theme, perhaps originating in Sacks's work on 'pn adequacy' and the like (Sacks, 1972a). That is why some formalistic linguists and discourse analysts like it, but it is a tendency from which I feel we should disaffiliate; it is, indeed, one from which Sacks himself progressively disaffiliated. Even from the beginning, he eschewed elicitation techniques for the analysis of naturally occurring actions, and also moved towards treating those actions as generically *expressing* categories and categorial relations rather than treating them as derivations from a relatively free-standing semantic grid. He made a definitive move toward treating categorisation as an array of practices, constitutive practices.

Still, Sacks initially adapted much from componential analysis: arguably, he even adapted the term 'conversational analysis' from it, where he intended not so much a theoretical rubric as a datum, an empirical topic for study. That topic is members' own *in situ* common-sense analysis of the 'emic' categories they used – plus, of course, the utterance sequences they employed in the course of so doing. In this way, he adapted and extended from componential analysis this conception of members as being cultur-ally competent rather than the cultural or judgemental dopes that conventional sociology regularly and damagingly assumed they were; this assumption still persists more than it should. Sacks shared with Garfinkel a notion of the culturally methodic or 'systematic' nature of actions, and this too came, in another sense, from componen-tial analysis. Finally, it could be argued that Sacks took a concern for *situations* from componential analysis – for instance, Frake's famous analysis (1964) of occasions of drinking among the Subanun: some examples of componential analysis focalised more than just semantic grids.

Whilst restricting the categorisation issue to terms for persons, Sacks nonetheless still adapted the rules of use of categories from componential analysis (the consistency rule, the economy rule, the category relevance rule, etc.). He conceives of these as a machin-ery or apparatus. Furthermore, in his earliest work on categorisation, (Sacks, 1966; and Sacks in Hill and Crittenden, 1968), he tends to analyse actions by referring them back to complex, assembled structures of 'standardised relational pairs' of membership categories, for example collections 'Rp' and 'K'.

Sacks also adapted his criterion of adequacy from componential analysis. In the Purdue Symposium on Ethnomethodology (Hill and Crittenden, 1968: 42), he says that he expects of the cultural apparatus that he formulates that it should be able to 'give (him) his data back'. This expectation shows an elective affinity with componen-tial analysts' conviction that their formulation of the 'analytic machinery' going into the production of a given action, for example drinking, should be able to 'reproduce that action'. In addition to componential-analytic moorings, we can see, in this 'reproducability' criterion, a strong elective affinity with formalism and transforma-tional grammar. This is not to deny, of course, that transformational grammar and componential analysis are significantly different analytic rubrics but they are signifi-cantly analogous in that they involve referring specific utterances to an underlying 'grid' (though the purported location of that differs).

Sacks's Praxeological Approach

As I have observed above, despite these formal and 'structuralist' (in the linguist's sense) moorings, right from the beginning Sacks began to 'praxeologise' and contextualise membership categories (including the issue of co-selection of categories in given contexts). He treated categorisation – and all description – as itself an *activity* through which, very often, other activities could be effectuated (what Roy Turner in another context, called 'double duty'). In this respect, categories were treated in a similar way to utterances. Just as utterances were transformed by lay speakers into activities and professional analysts alike, so categories too were conceived as activities. Not only was categorising itself an activity but, through that, the question could be asked: what is this categorisation doing? In past papers I have argued that some of these 'doings' include such things as the allocation of blame, guilt and responsibility (see, *inter alia*, Watson, 1978, 1997b).

Sacks (1972a) also treated the structures of standardised relational pairs not as freestanding but as *occasioned* by (in this case) the activity of searching for help by people reporting troubles. He gradually shifted away from mapping actions onto *categorial* grids. Crucially, he eschewed elicitation techniques – techniques criticised by Anthony Wootton in his coruscating critique of componential analysis (Wootton 1975: 28–42, 109–10n) – to look at actual, naturally occurring actions as recorded on audio- (and later video-) tapes, which minimised intervention. Sacks moved increasingly towards a treatment of membership categorisations as *in situ*, *in vivo* phenomena, and towards treating categorisation as, through and through, an array of sense-making *practices*.

In turn, this initiated a move (never quite completed) towards eventually treating those actions as generic, as *in themselves*, expressing categorisations and categorial relations, instead of these actions being referred back to a notionally separate semantic grid. Instead, we can now look at, say, the diagnosis of disease as self-contained within its naturally occurring setting and organisation. Sacks makes the crucial move from *categories* to *categorisation practices*, and this is what, ultimately, triggers off the de-reification project. This is not only the case in relation to categorisation, but also to the situations of which such categorisation practices are a part. The situation, too, was seen as produced through persons' actions rather than being, say, a structural 'emplacement' of these actions. Categorisation practices were, then, part of an *in vivo* weave or contexture of social actions rather than being actions in a (relatively freestanding) 'context'.

This move is crucial because it shifts categorisation analysis away from being a kind of EM/CA placeholder for role theory in conventional sociologies. Ralph Linton's 'structuralist' distinction between 'status' (a position) and 'role' (the performance of status-relevant activities) was pervasively influential in sociology, even profoundly influencing analysts of face-to-face interaction such as the early Goffman. It is all too easy to treat membership categories as though they were status roles or 'slots' occupied by 'incumbents' who acted according to the category and who gained their identities from these 'slots'. Sacks's early vocabulary for membership category analysis does render a hostage to fortune in this conception in some respects, as does his early conception of utterances as 'slot' and 'filler'. However, two aspects of his work operate against this tendency: (i) treating categorisation as (linguistic) activities; and (ii) demonstrating how these activities show an immense flexibility and range – far more than could be derived simply from a rigid categorial 'grid' *à la* componential analysis. Sacks's categorial analysis was part of a broader 'linguistic turn' in which he was a pioneer in sociology.

I think that subsequent researchers into membership categorisation have often failed to exploit the huge range and variety of categorisation, and related practices, that Sacks outlines in his *Lectures on Conversation* (1992) and elsewhere – things like turning a one-person problem into a two-person problem (Sacks in Hill and Crittenden, 1968), the MIR device, ex-relationals, and so on. Very few, if any, of us have addressed the immense scope of Sacks's analysis of categories-in-action or of the wide and flexible range of activities done through categorisation (viz. Sacks, 1992: Vol. 1, *passim*). Nor, perhaps, have many of us been sufficiently sensitive to the reflexivities of categorisation practices, for example that a given context does not simply imbue a categorisation with its specific, 'situated', sense but also that category reciprocally contributes to the con-stitution of the occasion or context as 'what it (i.e. that occasion or context) actually *is*' for participants. I shall also argue below for a consideration of the reflexive, back-and-forth determination of category and sequence.

Without a proper and quite exhaustive appreciation and knowledge of the range of uses, predications and contextualisation procedures of which categorisation activities are a part, we are left with a skeletal structure of categories more or less structurally conceived plus just one or two rules of application regarding reference, co-selection, predication and the like, with a pared-down or even absent characterisation of context, occasionality and contingency, let alone of improvisation. In turn, this will lead, per-haps has led, to a situation in which we risk presenting society members as 'categorisation dopes', homunculi who are incapable of doing anything with member-ship categories beyond quite rigid, simple, duplicatory and reductive acts. Given this narrowness of vision, no wonder categorial analysis gets seen as a 'milk float' com-pared with the 'juggernaut' of sequential analysis. Membership categorisation is only a limited vehicle if that is all one makes of it.

Amongst my attempts to occlude any tendency towards this in work in which I am involved are the comments on glossing practices, turn-formed categorisations, and other sequentially organised activities described in this chapter and, *inter alia*, catego-risations and spatial references, categorisations and practical onomastics and categorial characterisations of markets (McNally and Watson, 2013). Many others, notably Peter Eglin and the late Stephen Hester, are involved in their own re-workings of categorisa-tion analysis, which, I feel, have an analogous outcome.[1] Thus, although the presentation of the categorisation 'apparatus' has, in some cases, appeared as more rigid than Sacks (eventually) did, antidotes are at hand.

What these various antidotes have in common is, again, the broadening of our examination of the range and flexibility of activities done through categorisation. Of course, members seldom, if ever, do categorisation 'for its own sake'. Even Einstein's bombardment of membership categories was offered to make a point, with wit and a fine sense of contingency, all of which categorisation analysts would do well to try to emulate: He said:

> If my theory of relativity is proven correct, Germany will claim me as a German and France will declare I am a citizen of the world. Should my theory prove untrue, France will say that I am a German and Germany will declare that I am a Jew. (Address at the Sorbonne, Paris, December 1929; from *The New York Times*, 16/12/1930)

We can see here that co-selections of conjunctive and disjunctive membership categories can be 'assembled objects' as Garfinkel put it, relative to given theme or point, for example affiliation versus disaffiliation, and relative to a given contextual condition (Einstein's success or failure). They are not invariant 'structural' relations.

Sacks thus did a great deal to de-reify categorisation analysis so that it resembled far less a rigid, static, grid-like structural entity and was more like a hugely wide ranging contextually sensitive complex of practices – practices whose incarnation was not always talk-in-interaction but in sites such as written texts and the like (viz. Lee (1984) and Watson (2009a), where categorial practices were seen to be adjusted to the specific sites of public space). Much of this transformation comes from Sacks's switch of the analysis to an even more exhaustively 'emic' status than that facilitated by componential analysis's formalistic out-of-context reifications of semantic structures.

Sacks treated membership categorisation analysis as a primordial phenomenon, an analysis done by lay members rather than, in the first place, by analysts. He treated such laic categorisation analysis as a *topic* to be analysed rather than as an analytic framework or *resource* for doing analysis – and members' ordinary practical activities are far greater in range and flexibility than are the practices of analysts (see also my comments on conversation analysis as a datum or topic, above). We need more studies, too, that afford us a broader view of the produced *sites* of membership categorisation (Watson, 2009a), so that, for instance, site-specific usage may be examined. We cannot assume the 'automatic' transposability or extensibility of conversational categorial practices to other sites, for example online chatrooms (viz. Verdier, 2010).

In the light of all this, then, the question remains: how can we employ Sacks's pointers to take his categorisation project further, to de-reify and de-cognitivise it more exhaustively? Of course, the key move is to more fully extend the praxeological approach to this form of analysis, and part of this is to treat practices, including categorisation practices, as both *contextualised* and *contextualising*. Such practices contribute to the very character of the context in which they are situated. One additional benefit of this might be to help reintegrate conversation analysis with that most praxeological of approaches, ethnomethodology – especially in its Wittgensteinian mode, where, arguably, practices are most clearly and precisely focalised.

Membership Categories and Action Sequences

Now, if we are, as ethnomethodologists or conversation analysts or both, interested in the organisation of talk-in-interaction, I think these sequences are highly instructive. Emanuel A. Schegloff, in some arguments (Schegloff, 2007a, 2007b), has insisted that membership categories only be admitted to the panoply of conversation analysis if they be analysable so as to fit in completely with the properties of conversational sequences (and so with sequential analysis). I concur, to a significant extent, and hope to illustrate that concurrence below.

We may also concur, to a significant extent, with Schegloff's (2007a) strictures on categorisation and person-reference in relation to sequential analysis.[2] However, we do not need to concur with any suggestions that purely sequential relevancies be accorded *a priori* the status of what Frederick Crews (1987) has termed a 'master transcoding device', to be given some kind of 'monopoly' over conversational phenomena.

We should not accept that sequential organisation be seen as the driver of conversational organisation, however important it be, nor should we as analysts seek to drive sequential relevancies, as master transcoding devices, through any given body of data. Indeed, I think the examples I have given indicate that membership categorisation practices have potentials and properties of their own – such as category boundedness – that themselves help to shape conversational organisation, both at the levels of utterance production and sequence production. The question then becomes one of figuring out how sequential and categorial phenomena operate in unison in the fashioning of conversational organisation, without aprioristically according predominance to either. If there be any such precedence in any specific instance, then that is an empirical and occasioned matter, not one that can be decided by the analyst in advance. As a follow-on, I feel that this approach will also assist us in effectuating a *rapprochement* of Conversation Analysis with Ethnomethodology, particularly in respect of the latter's focus on situated practical reasoning in action. In turn, this will help us guard against linguists' attempts to reintroduce formal analytic methods into both Conversation Analysis and Ethnomethodology. After all, it took us many years to expunge formal analytic methods of the sociological kind from those approaches.

We might, then, hope for a situation where we see categorisation practice as (also) a *sequential* object, and sequences where categorisation practice not only demonstrably makes an appearance, but also exerts an influence in shaping the discourse. Indeed the seeds of such a concern were sown several decades ago (Watson, 1977; Drew, 1978). I myself examined conversations in which racial and religious discriminations are made and authorised and where these activities could not be adequately analysed without references both to sequential and categorial features (Watson, 1978). I see what the French linguistic anthropologist Maud Verdier (2010: 636) means when she designates such concerns as comprising a new 'field' of enquiry, though this does not mean we should reify that field (see below). I certainly do not think this new field can be a simple collation of the previously separate domains of sequential and categorial analysis.

We need to start again, treating category and sequence as each having what Aron Gurwitsch termed 'functional significance' in the complex of situated conversational organisation. Amongst other things, such an approach will help avoid one type of what has come to be called a misbegotten 'culturalist' approach to membership categories – that is (*inter alia*), the analysis of categories as constituents of the cultural content that is made available in conversational sequences. Whilst it is a truism that the exhibition of cultural knowledge may indeed be part of the work that membership categorisations do, a far more profound point is that categorisation activities operate at a methodic or procedural level in the actual production of the conversation as an organised phenomenon. Treating membership categorisation in terms of lay members' glossing practices, and treating both as (also) sequential objects, is just one way of respecifying categories in sequential terms and sequences in categorial terms. I have, in previous papers, pointed to Sacks's final consideration of categorisation practices, in what I now term 'turn-produced, turn-distributed categories', where examples of these are categorisations being 'identities-for-the-conversation' (see below), and indeed one of my earliest preoccupations in ethnomethodological conversational analysis has been to show how, in any specific instance, categorial and sequential considerations may coalesce (Watson, 1978).

A Praxiological Solution

In his later work on telephone interlocutors as 'caller' and 'called', Sacks says that these identities, generated by who calls whom '... are terms that apply to people in a way that has them as *categories* and not merely the person that they are, someone with a name' (Sacks, 1992: Vol. 2, 360–6). Particularly at the beginning and endings of conversations, these categorisations organise the distribution of oriented-to sequential rights and obligations and Sacks (1992: Vol. 2, 163ff.) observes that people can hardly ever 'get out from under' these. These turn-produced categories, then, methodically shape such features of conversational organisation as the distribution of particular utterance types amongst interlocutors at particular points in their discourse, and thus organise the conversational constraints that pertain, both there and then and in the conversation's development.

For instance, it is the interlocutor categorised as 'caller', not the 'called', who has the category-bound right and obligation to initiate a call closing. If the *called* party wishes to close the call, they have to do so through orientating towards that category-bound prerogative, inducing the caller to initiate a *closing*. Consequently, the called party may introduce a 'close offering' such as saying to the caller, 'this must be costing you a lot of money'. (Indeed, Manny Schegloff himself once said this to me to get me off the phone: he doesn't just study this stuff.) I think that this approach marks Sacks's ultimately divesting himself of the reification of membership categories and espousing a thoroughgoing praxeological approach to the analysis of these categories – that is, an approach that is praxeological without residue.

Under what I now call 'turn-produced categorisation', I have applied Sacks's conception to the embodied and visual availability of categorial identities in some of the serial organisations of urban public space. I do not think we need to endorse Schegloff's latterday assumption that the analyst should restrict their consideration to talk-in-interaction, particularly as Schegloff himself has not, in effect, always done so (Schegloff, 1972). After all, as people such as Lena Jayyusi have also extensively shown, the phenomenon of the interlocutors' specific categorisation being visually available to co-conversationalists can itself inform their talk. This is, of course, a central feature of categorisation as an embodied practice, where we might begin to examine categorisations as arrays of methodically produced visual indications and visibility arrangements. Indeed, to disattend this matter and treat categorisation practices purely as phenomena for talk-in-interaction is itself a decontextualisation technique that itself risks reification.

Another example: queues or waiting lines are familiar serial orders in public space where turn order is typically organised on a 'first come, first served' rule of service. Visible membership categories operate in every aspect of this turn order. Even the turns themselves can usefully be seen in terms of categorisation practice – 'first in line'/'head of queue', second in line'/'next up', 'last in line'/'tail of queue', etc. Such categories are, by and large, distributed via order of arrival at a queue one wishes to join. To treat these as one kind of turn-formed membership *category* helps us to focalise these turns as 'loci for the imputation of rights and obligations' (as Sacks, in Sudnow (1972) says of membership categorisations). For instance, the person(s) at the head of the queue has (have) obligations to monitor the service point for precisely when s/he/they should move forward – no noticeable gap in the queue, no overlap. In a sense, the concept of turn-formed categories is the 'other side of the coin' to category-formed turns, where, as the anthropologist Ethel Albert has reported (discussed in Sacks 1992, Vol. 1, 624–32), among the Burundi on ceremonial occasions, princes speak first, then commoners, then servants, etc.

Whilst Sacks only mentions generally and in passing that this is an issue of categories (Sacks, 1992: Vol. 1, 630) we may indeed treat this phenomenon as an example of 'category-formed turns' (my term, not Sacks's). Such turns, in Burundi, resolved the issue of what Sacks calls the order of speakers or of speaking. When a prince speaks in his proper turn, he is heard as speaking under the auspices of the category 'prince' and no other. Categories can, then, be loci for hearing rules, just as, Sacks also presciently notes (Sacks, 1992: Vol. 1, 630), when someone in our society is categorised as a 'celebrity' everything he or she says or does is heard as speaking in the capacity of a celebrity and no other category.

The very *constitution* of a turn in a queue can itself be a matter of categorisation practice. For instance, if there are four persons standing near each other, are they four turns in the queue or just one? If, for instance, they are on this occasion visually available as a duplicatively organised unit of categories such as a 'family' (canonically, parent or parents plus children) they might be taken as comprising a single turn in the queue, not, say, four separate turns. We might see here that categorisations are not simply part of the 'context' of the queue but are also, at the level of laic method, part of its very production. A final categorisation practice in the queue I shall mention here is that some persons visibly categorised as, for instance, 'disabled' or maybe 'elderly', might have rights to proceed straight to the head of the queue. In some parts of France, those categorised as 'firefighters', 'soldiers' or as 'pregnant women' can go straight to the head of the queue. We might term these 'distal' categories. Each kind of category, considered as a *practice*, along with its predications can be seen as helping to shape the very composition of the queue. Of course, the queue is a sequenced object, too, and thus sequencing conventions also shape the queue's composition, often – as I hope to have indicated – in a way that is inextricable from the methodic categorial and embodied practices involved.

In all, I suggest that it is not possible to ethnomethodologically understand the turn taking systems we call 'queues', in either lay or professional terms, without reference to categorisation practices. The practices of 'categorisation' and 'sequencing' are not only inseparable but reciprocally – constituting and reciprocally – shaping. This reciprocity is, indeed, one among many of the 'essential reflexivities' of conversational organisation. To ignore it is to submerge a basic constitutive feature of the queue, and again to relegate categorisation practice to the level of unexplicated resource. Should this happen, the analysis of queues will rest on an unexamined common-sense foundation, vulnerable to Zimmerman and Pollner's (1970) 'topic and resource' criticism (see below).

The payoff of this approach is also clear in other kinds of respects. For instance, a parenthetical fragment of Lorenza Mondada's thought-provoking 2003 paper 'Working with videos …' (Mondada, 2003: 58–9), on the videos of surgeons' actions can be reanalysed with reference to categorisation practice in ways that more fully explicate it. The surgeon is conducting laparoscopic surgery on the patient, accompanied by his assistants in a way that involves adjacently paired actions. The surgeon says 'coag' in the first pair-part and one assistant coagulates or cauterises the blood flow from some incision.

The adjacency pairing is crucial, for it is the only cultural method of making some action happen *next*, as an immediate next action. However, this adjacency pairing is also categorially 'processed'. The term 'coag' is a first pair-part of an adjacency-pair of actions but it is also in address terms, a category-bound one: it is bound to the category 'assistant (surgeon)' and to none of the other categories, thereby *selecting out* the assistant and none of the others to perform the second pair-part action, the actual effectuation of the coagulation. (One might consider that another first pair-part designation of another action could, as a category-bound predicate, select out the 'theatre nurse' or 'theatre porter' to perform another second pair-part).

We might say that this is a 'mere' case of recipient design, but as usual the term 'mere' reduces or trivialises a complex and consequential activity. We should also add the rider that categorisation practices may well not resolve all activity – allocation issues, for example; where there is more than one assistant surgeon in the operation (which is the case here) then there is still an intra-categorial division of labour to be determined: but the activity is still bound to the category 'assistant-surgeon' – no other *category* of person is allocated the task of cauterising the bleeding, nor does any other person bid or volunteer for it. This is surely an outcome of the categorial organisation of this participation framework, an organisation which is, unfortunately, not explicated. The analysis thus relies upon a tacit, unexamined resource. Not explicating the work done by these categories runs the risk of rendering the study of common sense status 'naturally theoretic' rather than of thoroughgoing analytic status.

Of course, we cannot, as analysts, explicate every feature of a setting, but to overlook a major feature that informs a setting (such as categorial organisation) is to risk severely compromising the analysis. The classic paper by Zimmerman and Pollner (1970) on 'topic and resource' is centrally relevant to this matter. As ethnomethodologists, we must cease to use the categorial organisation of this or that participation framework as a tacit resource in analysing the framework, but instead turn it into a topic worthy of explication and analysis on its own behalf. Then we can treat categorial analysis as genuinely part of ethnomethodology by conceiving of it as constitutive practice. Moreover, seeing membership categorisation strictly in terms of 'person-description' (Schegloff, 2007a), whilst deserving serious consideration, again often stipulates too narrow a rubric for the analysis of these categorisations. As I hope this brief excursion into the analysis of participation frameworks has indicated, categorisations serve a range of activities that extend beyond that of mere person-description or person-reference.

Consequently, an *explicit* introduction of categorial analysis would add a great deal to our current understanding of participation frameworks and 'recipient design' in worksite studies. This is an aspect which, it seems to me, is surely underdeveloped, even submerged, in sequential analysis considered as a separate rubric of analysis, one that might benefit from membership categorisation concerns where – and only where – the data strongly warrant them. This basic example of the categorial 'processing' of an adjacency pair also helps us to explicate the division of labour as common-sense, *intersubjective* accomplishment rather than the pseudo-objectified one of Durkheimian metaphysics. This is something Anderson, Sharrock and Hughes noted long ago (Anderson et al., 1991: 240–1), though again – regrettably, in my view – without explicit reference to categorial analysis.

The working of the intersubjective division of labour also operates to define who does *not*, must not, perform a particular task and thus helps define inclusion and exclusion as well as the activity-type and footing-type participation in given task-performances. These are all parts of a gestalt contexture within which these performances occur. Categorisations-in-action, such as occupational titles and vernacular designations of parties to a worksite-based task comprise one practical instrument in the performance of specific tasks. They are part of what that pioneer of ethnomethodological worksite studies, the late Egon Bittner (1974), referred to as the 'terms' and 'determinations' of formal-organisational work as these are defined by persons deemed competent and entitled to do so. The pattern of categories in a particular worksite is part and parcel of these terms and determinations and, indeed, has a major influence in constituting the footing or 'participation framework' in which parties to a worksite arrange their reciprocal alignments and activities. In this respect, to treat (as Schegloff (2007a) does) membership categorisation as merely 'person-description' or 'person-reference' is to stipulate *a priori* too narrow a range of activity for them. As I hope I have indicated here, categorisations serve a far greater range of functions than just person-description. There is substantial foundation in Sacks's earlier work for this, especially in his *Lectures on Conversation* (1992), where from a relatively early point he indicates the great range of activities transacted through categorisation.

However, and puzzlingly, ethnomethodological studies of worksite context and practices have seldom, if ever, treated membership categorisations as an integral part of the allocation and performance of tasks in work contexts or of, say, differential participation status of parties to a given task. This is especially puzzling because it is in some ethnomethodological studies of work that one finds the strongest conception of context, that of *gestalt contexture*. Puzzling, too, is that this conception makes not a single appearance in what is perhaps *the* major collection of articles on interaction and context, the canonical Duranti and Goodwin reader *Rethinking Context* (1992), which perhaps shows that the praxeological respecification of 'context' and the eradication of all 'structural' residues still has some a long way to go. The contributors to Button's equally canonical *Ethnomethodology and the Human Sciences* (1991b) seldom if ever mention it in any significant way either; it is not even in the index. This is a pity, because this concept of Aron Gurwitsch's has been around in ethnomethodology, if only *sotto voce*, since its inception, and has become, perhaps, the *locus classicus* of the concepts 'reflexivity' and particularly, 'indexicality' for later ethnomethodology. The concept gained greater prominence in Garfinkel's later work (Garfinkel 2002), but, as I observed, originally derives from the work of Gurwitsch, with whom Garfinkel was in contact when he (Garfinkel) was at Harvard University.

A 'gestalt contexture' is a particular phenomenological conception of context where the elements in a given contextual pattern are said to 'exist through each other'. The functional significance or specificity of sense of these elements is, in any particular instance, dependant on that of the others. If an element is torn from a locally given pattern then the significance of both particular and pattern are modified. The gestalt contexture has, then, an 'instanced', locally specific, patterned coherence in which each element is reflexively related to the other and in which the elements and the pattern are, in a back-and-forth way, constitutive of each other (Garfinkel, 2002: 158 ff.; Wieder, 1974: 186–90). I refer to such contextures as 'kaleidoscopic' in their singularity.

Membership categorisations or categorisation practices, when they occur, are without exception endogenous features of such contextures. They are not to be seen in terms of an 'externalist' position (see below), that is, as somehow being distinctive in 'standing outside' the specific instance. Nor, yet again, are they mere 'labels' or simple identifications of persons but are integral to such contextures and must be analysed 'from within' as part of the gestalt coherence of the contexture as a 'whole' (i.e. as a patterned configuration). Again as an integrand, the category is reflexively embedded in the contexture, including its serial organisation; it has functional significance (to use Gurwitsch's term) in that it elaborates the contexture and is elaborated by it.

Such contextures and their elaborations are highly specific and thus must be analysed case by case: consequently, what Wittgenstein calls the 'the attitude of disdain toward the particular case' has to be overcome in sociology as well as philosophy. Here, social order is located in the particular, not in formal abstraction or generalisation. In this respect, for instance, the co-selection of categories acquires a particular here-and-now *local* sense and significance rather than being the straightforward product of a relatively decontextualised 'apparatus'. (I have addressed this issue as it applies to conversation analysis: see Watson (2008)). Categorial analysis is, in this central respect, very different from the 'baseball cap' conception for sociological analysis, where, purportedly, one size fits all.

It has already been mentioned that such categorisations are overwhelmingly found, in particular, in intersubjectively – given divisions of labour in the oriented-to specification and allocation of tasks and in the reciprocally oriented-to rights and responsibilities of the various parties within the particular worksite contexture. Moreover, membership categories can work as participants' glosses – endogenously produced glosses – of arrays of particulars within the context. One of the classic ethnomethodological instances is to be found in the study by Wieder (1974: 169–70), where an interactant categorised as a 'staff member' asks an interlocutor categorised as a 'resident' of a parole institution to inform on his fellow residents. The resident's retort, 'You know I won't snitch', is suffused with categorial relevance, that is, it is a person visibly categorisable as 'staff member' who is being addressed in a relevant institutional setting. This, of course, renders *what* is said, too, as a move in a gestalt contexture. We hear the utterance that way, and hearing it that way elaborates the sense of the (staff member-resident) setting just as the setting elaborates the sense of the utterance. This is, again, a classic instance of reflexivity, where an item is identified as a pattern element, is elaborated by that pattern and, in turn, elaborates that selfsame pattern. Thus, 'snitching' is identified in terms of the category-pair 'resident' (or 'inmate') and staff 'member' and, in turn, highlights the contrastive relations (in this case) between the relevant categories. In so doing, it realises the 'staff member'-'resident' category pair for (as Garfinkel terms it) 'another first time'.

Similarly, the concept 'gestalt contexture' can assist in Conversation Analysis's sequential analysis. The late Jean Widmer (2010) pointed out that Schegloff's paper 'Confirming allusions' contains vulnerabilities linked to the fact that membership categorisations are not examined (Widmer 2010). Widmer examines a particular sequence to show that what is done and done in sequence, what is accepted and refused, is predicated on the categories 'salesperson' and 'customer'. In certain cases (and, of course, certain cases only), categorial analysis helps to fill in what is elided by sequential analysis *simpliciter*.

All this is not to plead for an ultra-fragmented or relativising conception of membership categorisation but for a 'family resemblance' model where, as situated descriptive, referential or identification practices (though not the only kind of any of these; there are more canonically utterance-sequenced ones too, of course), categorisations show a criss-crossing network of similarities, overlaps and differences from case to case, from one 'another first time' to the next, without ever being coterminous.

In fact, in a brilliant but perhaps too little cited paper, John Heritage (1978) gives us an approach to descriptions and family resemblances that is both conceptually sophisticated and empirically researchable. Adding to Heritage's model, we might once more say that membership categorisations are glosses that permit members to linguistically produce common-sense, practical equivalence classes ('train driver', 'Anglican', 'head of queue') where persons are similarly classed in the face of 'detail' differences; for example an Anglican may be classified as such whether they are also categorisable as 'low church' or 'high church', 'vicar', 'verger', 'sidesman/woman', 'choir member' or 'congregation member', etc. The point is that the lay members' equivalence class (or membership category, considered as a gloss) 'Anglican' gathers and glosses all these differences. Membership categories as glosses and as part of 'broader' glosses remains a fertile but underdeveloped aspect of Membership Categorisation Analysis, upon which I have been working.

I also hold that an analysis of the serial organisation of categorisation practices might, on occasion, help us to understand something that, for instance, ethnomethodological worksite studies have to be concerned with – the *durée* or participants' intersubjectively experienced temporal organisation of work settings. Categorisation practices are part of the production and distribution of the task-related practical identities deployed in the performance through time of the activities involved in specific work settings. The study of queues at service points seems to me to begin to illustrate this, but, of course, there are a huge number and variety of other categorially given modes of temporal organisation too – not least, as I have claimed, the temporal organisation of natural conversation. In these modes, categorisations and serial orders of activities each contribute their own reciprocal or functional significance to the overall gestalt coherence of the phenomenon. That is to say, categorisations and action sequences each have their own organisational significance within a 'larger' temporally ordered phenomenon, such as a situated conversation; each helps shape that phenomenon.

To give another example of the work of categories in the *durée* of action, this time from non-work activities, an analysis I have been conducting with some co-researchers (Conein et al., 2013), which focalises the co-ordinated actions of pedestrians entering a department store, indicated that the timing of holding the door open for others, subsequent to one's own passage through, is category-sensitive. For instance, persons passing through the door will hold the door open longer for a subsequent pedestrian categorisable as an 'elderly person'. Again, this includes categories as part of the intersubjective experience and deployment of time or timing in action. We might say that this is one of many features of categorisations that present them as 'wild phenomena', that is as 'found' phenomena 'in the field' whose detailed uses could not have been aprioristically modelled in any detail through the invocation of a theory that is based on 'external standards'.

'Methodological' Considerations and Categorial Analysis

The above suggestions will, I hope, serve to occlude at source any tendency towards a reification of conceptions of the concept 'membership category' and to similarly occlude any of the present tendencies towards a residual reification. Alongside and, I believe, partly as a result of, such reification, there has emerged a new(ish) reified analytic domain running parallel with ethnomethodology and conversation analysis, namely 'Membership Categorisation Analysis' or 'MCA' as a real risk attendant upon Verdier's definition of categorial-sequential analysis not merely in one-dimensional terms (i.e., the terms in which I present it here) but as a 'new field'.

This 'new field' or domain is often presented as autonomous, relatively separated from, say, purely sequential or other modes of analysis and is sometimes even conceived as being, to a certain degree, in competition with these other modes. As Hegelians and some Marxians have long told us, along with reification comes alienation, and the development of MCA has frequently meant an increasing separation from, and even opposition to, the other analytic modes that operate under the *aegis* of ethnomethodology and conversation analysis.

This process of reification and alienation of 'MCA' has had several negative consequences. The often oppositional position of 'MCA' has resulted in a polemicising of argument on both, or all, 'sides' of the debate. Such polemics have generated more heat than light: they have left little room for more measured, dimensional or nuanced argument and, consequently, shown less subtlety and sophistication in the claims that proponents of one mode (not just 'MCA') have levelled against the others. As a result, there has been less room for the kind of detail that might go into 'bridge-building', mid-points, integrated positions and the like, and it is such an integrated position that is sought in the present discussion. The de-reification of conceptions of membership categories may well be a necessary, though not a sufficient, factor in the de-reification of the analytic domain termed 'MCA' considered as a relatively freestanding, boundary maintaining sub-field – even a sub-discipline – within ethnomethodological and conversation analytic studies.

We cannot even take the term 'within ethnomethodological and conversation analytic studies' for granted concerning this emergent reified conception of 'MCA'. Indeed, the dissolution of this conception would also get rid of the detachable, 'bolt-on' quality that it is beginning to acquire and which is, arguably, already a done deal in conversation analysis – to its detriment, I think. There is already a perceptible tendency for, say, linguistics and discourse analysts (to say nothing of practitioners in fields such as media or cultural studies) to detach a reified 'MCA', as a purportedly 'self-contained' single entity, from the base disciplines that inform the most profound uses of categorial analysis, namely ethnomethodology and conversation analysis considered sociologically.[3] Having been lifted out of its natural footings in these disciplines, 'MCA' as a denatured, leeched-out conception of categorial analysis is then transplanted into a frame of reference whose presuppositional base is inimical to that giving this mode of analysis its distinctive *raison d'être* and its analytic depth. Quite apart from the errors of logical category that such transplantations all too often engender, the actual process of transplantation comprises one of the purest cases of alienation one is likely to find in academic activities (admittedly, a hotly contested title).

We still find instances of such alienation in some approaches to (categorial) identities. What I have referred to as the 'bolt-on' quality of MCA in relation to approaches bearing various levels of affinity and disaffinity to EM/CA sociologically conceived is paralleled – and in some ways facilitated – by the retention of an obsolete 'externalist' view of membership categorisation vis-à-vis any given conversation sequence. Indeed, this view is a component of the reification of categories, of their analytic presentation as 'freestanding' so far as the particular instance is concerned, or partly so – 'half-digested' into the conversation so to speak. As such, the adoption of such an externalist position is seriously mistaken.

To take a relatively recent and, perhaps, surprising instance, John Heritage (2012), citing Liz Stokoe on membership categorisation, nods towards the possibility that aspects of social identity that are 'outside' the talk can be admitted to the concerns of CA sequentially conceived through the analysis of what they contribute to the colloquy in terms of meaning and action. Admittedly, this is a passing remark in the closing paragraph of his article, and he puts the term 'outside' in quotation marks, thereby perhaps, wisely, indicating a less than full commitment to the externalist position concerning categorisations: nonetheless, the term 'outside' is left to do its reifying work, and perhaps expresses an understanding of membership categorisation still located in Sacks's earliest work.

However, the analysis of membership categorisation has moved on quite fundamentally since then, as the work of John Lee, Stephen Hester, Peter Eglin and other, even more recent analysts (and the current volume) attests, and any remarks on the place of membership categorisations in talk-in-interaction, and derivatively, of the place of MCA relative to CA (and EM) would be wise to take these developments into account. Again, the moves of some MCA advocates to make their mode of analysis into a 'separate domain' has surely helped to facilitate the preservation of the externalist position: a classic case of the old Lancastrian adage, 'Be careful what you wish for – you might just get it.'

Wittgenstein, in his later philosophy, argued that the abolition of the 'internal'–'external' distinction would dissolve a whole range of self-imposed problems and mistakes that fed into what we now call cognitivism. I agree that this is an abolition to be supported along with those others that support conventional sociologies – 'action'–'structure', 'subjective'–'objective', 'individual'–'society', etc. The 'internal'–'external' opposition certainly does its own sad work in sustaining the 'externalist' view of membership categorisations.

To take the strongest case, what use would it be to treat turn-produced, turn-distributed categorisations such as 'caller'–'called', 'head of queue'–'tail of queue', etc. as 'external' to the interactional systems that they describe and organise? These categorisations are engendered by the turn-organisation of instances of these specific formations themselves. Each is intrinsic to the specific instance of the formation concerned. The 'internal'–'external' distinction does very little, if anything at all, here, to analyse the situation concerned. Membership categorisations are – here but also in other cases – no more 'external' than, say, the phrasal, clausal or sentential components of the construction of a particular turn at talk: there seems little reason to single out membership categorisations as 'external' items.

Even if we take an earlier formulation of membership categorisation – say, Sacks (1972b) – the inadequacies of an externalist position are already evident. Of course, members of any society trade on the standard common-sense knowledge of their society, on 'what anyone knows', and so on, as the late Ted Cuff (1993: 54) says. However, using data of an invited story in which a version of a marriage breakdown is expressed, Cuff shows that even when using Sacks's early work on categorisation, any notion that categorisations are 'imported' into the specific instance does not afford us an analytically adequate formulation of that instance. As Cuff puts it (1993: 52):

> We are proposing, then, that unqualified, general categories of husband and wife are inadequate for repairing the sense of what is being reported (in this account – Ed.). Rather, hearers might require some more specific identity such as 'bad' or 'dissolute' husband for them to find who it is who is engaging in a range of activities like gambling, lying, refusing to work and support his wife and children in this marriage. The qualified identity 'bad husband' might then serve to collect together these various activities, which can be heard as a collection of the sort of things done not simply by husbands but by 'bad' husbands.

In this sense, identity-selections are 'packaged' into specifically sensible combinations and 'fine-tuned' towards the 'topic', 'theme' or 'subject matter' of a sequential order such as a story. That is, even if one does not endorse the abolition of the 'internal'–'external' distinction upon which the externalist view depends, we need to look at the localisation of categorial identity-selections, co-selections, qualifications and modifications, as localisation procedures are what EM is all about. However, whilst I applaud Heritage's comment about the admissibility of categorisation data to CA, I feel we should increasingly question what it is that is 'external' about any element of discourse, not least membership categorisations. In this regard, it is encouraging that noted analysts such as Jay Meehan (2006: 195–8) analyse membership categorisations as part and parcel of the sequential analysis of interaction in a particular setting, that of citizens' calls for service from the police.

Along with the dissolution of conceptions such as 'externality' that serve to reify membership categorisations, we can also hope to nip in the bud any related conception of a 'research method' for analysing these categorisations. Certainly this is the case if by the term 'research method' is intended a single, unitary, 'across-the-board', codified-in-advance research technique that is intended to be utilised in the same fashion as the 'cook-book rules' for the sample surveys of much formal-analytic quantitative sociology or the qualitative data software packages so frequently employed by those whose conception of 'qualitative analysis' is, at bottom, similarly formal-analytic.

Any use of a reified single 'MCA' domain as a pretext for attempting to develop any such associated, invariant, research method should be precluded by a praxeological, contextually sensitive project of respecification of categorial analysis. Such a project is, indeed, now required more generally in the light of methodological conservatives' critiques of ethnomethodology *per se*. These attempts at a *rapprochement* between ethnomethodological studies and the formal-analytic approaches that are characteristic of conventional sociologies include both (a) critiques of current ethnomethodology for not having *a* unified research method and (b) recommendations, whether in the interest of *rapprochement* or, even more ruinously, concerning the incorporation of ethnomethodological studies into formal analysis.

One of the latest methodologically conservative critiques or counsellings of this kind comes from the applied linguist Alan Firth (2009), who, astonishingly, rebukes the currently unreconstructed ethnomethodology for research methods that are '... eclectic, some may say haphazard and arbitrary, relying on a seemingly capricious assortment of ethnographic field work, audio-and video-recordings, experimentations ...' (and the list continues) (2009: 77). Of course, such comments are familiar incantations, far from new: see, for instance, the oral contributions by positivistically inclined sociologists such as David Rose, Robert McGinnis and others, broadly transcribed in 1968 in the *Proceedings of the Purdue Symposium on Ethnomethodology* (eds., Hill and Crittenden). Firth's recommendations virtually replicate these original ones, namely that ethnomethodologists enter into a debate with, and take into account, conventional sociologists (although it was never the case that even the most methodologically radical of ethnomethodologists had ever ceased to do either of these things).[4]

So, then, can we speak of ethnomethodology as possessing a 'methodology', on to which, if analyses of membership categories be allowed to remain within the ambit of ethnomethodology, categorial analysis might be heir? Well yes, so long as we can muster the minimal savvy required not to mischaracterise it is a 'research method', a technique, or even 'strategy' (as Silverman and Gubrium, 1994, for instance, also misconceive it), in the first place. If we do, we may avoid the rookie error into which Firth and others would lead us. Instead, we might see ethnomethodology as, for good and clear reasons, exhibiting an evolving 'analytic mentality' that partakes of (*inter alia*) a range and varying mix of non-ironic, anti-cognitivist, praxeological, context-sensitive, naturalistic dispositions. It is these dispositions that I have attempted to deploy here in my critique of the reification of the conception of membership categorisations, bearing also in mind the crucial distinction and relation between members' and analysts' relevancies. We might then begin to speak of categorial analyses (in the plural) as not being unitary and interchangeable but as varied, minutely fitted to purpose and as connected by 'family resemblances' under the *aegis* of an analytic mentality. It is such dimensions of EM's analytic mentality that Firth so signally misunderstands.

The notion of the 'analytic mentality' has its origins in a description devised by the sequential/conversational analyst, the late Jim Schenkein. Schenkein writes of an analytic mentality as consisting, among other things, of a set of dispositions, orientations, habitudes and commitments that one brings to a phenomenon which is topicalised for analysis (his were naturally situated conversation and also texts). His characterisation is appropriate to ethnomethodological/categorial analyses in its essential 'vagueness', its open-endedness or open-texturedness and in its abstention from the stipulation or codification of a purportedly rigidly reproducible research technique. What seems at a superficial glance to be 'vagueness' in an approach, can be a resource, a flexibility, not a drawback. Indeed, in this discussion of analytic mentality I have not even touched upon the issue of idealisation and reconstructed logic in the formal-analytic characterisation of research methods or techniques and the respects in which these idealisations risk the importing of an analyst-stipulated 'external standard' to what should be the study of specific social contexts as examined 'from within'.

The reason for any apparent 'vagueness' – read, then, 'open-endedness', 'flexibility', 'adaptability', 'potential for improvisation', 'suitability for purpose', 'fine-tuning to the object of study', and the like – lies in the commitment to the inspection of any given single social setting in its distinctively identifying detail and in terms of the specific 'methods' (to use a gloss) through which participants produce a given setting as a sensible phenomenon – sensible, that is, to themselves, in the first place. Ethnomethodologists', including (let us hope) categorial analysts', analytic mentality must be minutely attuned to the distinctiveness of these methods and their fittingness for the settings they produce. This is where Garfinkel's methodological precept of the 'unique adequacy requirement' for the analytic characterisation of a setting comes in. The analyst must ideally possess or acquire as a practitioner the cultural competences employed by the participants themselves in the production and constitution of any given setting – even when those competences are part of some body of expert knowledge, some 'finite province of meaning' (it helps that these provinces are, as Schütz explains, ultimately rooted in mundane reason). Beyond this, whatever means, whatever instrument of observation or reasoning the analyst can deploy in order to grasp the constitution of the local setting, in the most sensitively attuned way, can legitimately be brought to the analytic process. The terms, the coherence of the analyst's approach are set by the fine organisation of the object of study as apperceived by participants themselves, not by the organisation of an analyst-driven idealisation of a set of components composing a mechanical 'one-size-fits-all' research method. It is members' *in situ* use of methods, not those of the analyst, that counts.

As for the multifarious analyses of membership categories as 'wild phenomena' or as 'practices in the wild', the upshot of the above 'methodological' (in the general sense) considerations is, again, that just as there can be no *unitary* research domain of 'MCA', nor, therefore, can there be a single, unitary research method which can be attributed to such a domain or driven through just any body of data. Instead, the approach to be taken is far more demanding. As I have indicated above – and there is a reason for this 'methodological' section of this paper to be placed after, not before, the examples – we should consider membership categorisations, including co-selections in their distinctive phenomenal detail, and in terms of the setting-specific 'methods' through which members produce that setting, as a sensible phenomenon (note that the term 'methods', too, is a gloss). The approach of ethnomethodologists, including categorial analysts, must be sufficiently flexible as to be minutely adjusted to these methods.

In a strong sense, then, the methodic practices of 'the-analysis-in-this case' must be finely attuned to the methodic practices of the participants. Whatever analytic 'take' that can be used to capture and topicalise participants' locally specific production of a given, distinctive setting may legitimately be used. Given the vast and rich variations of social settings in everyday life in society, it is not surprising and certainly not 'haphazard' that ethnomethodological analysts' 'methods' themselves are highly variable. This variability is not a defect, not 'capricious' (*pace* Firth, 2009: 77) but the outcome of what is perhaps the most highly principled and exhaustive naturalistic approach there is. What Garfinkel terms 'wild phenomena' – of which membership categorisations are an example – cannot be theoretically modelled in advance for ethnomethodology, in any adequate way. Nor, by the same token, can there be a standard research method that is adequate to their analytic apprehension as *particular* cases, in all their richness, in all their fullness, in all their 'kaleidoscopic' singularities. Again *pace* Firth, it is the imposition of a single research method on this subtle diversity that is 'arbitrary' and 'capricious'.

For the analysis of membership categorisations, the upshot of the above 'methodological' considerations is that combinatorial forms of categorisations, where (and if) they occur, are occasioned by and integral to the gestalt contexture in which they occur, not merely to a set of 'rules of application'. We may, too, expect that what Gurwitsch terms their 'functional significance' will vary according to context, and that properties such as duplicative organisation will be contextually occasioned, and contextually determined, too. Perhaps this phenomenal variation will be great, perhaps minor, but we may roughly expect the practices we call 'categorisation' to be, on the whole, connected, at least and at best, by family resemblances, or by overlaps of varying types and degrees. Any analytic approach by ethnomethodology to these phenomenal variations will perforce itself be varied, tied into the distinctively identifying features of any given setting.

Practices are 'self-embedding': they produce the self-same dynamic contexts in which they become on-goingly attuned and situated. As examples of constitutive practice, categorial practices are, once more, particularly perspicuous examples of this kind of reflexivity. Membership categorisations are often particularly evident as constituting the very contexts (e.g. in glossed terms such as 'doctor'–'patient' consultation') in which they themselves are embedded. There is, simply, no formal analytic research method that can grasp this back-and-forth reflexive determination of category and context. Consequently, there is no point in incorporationists' attempts to subsume ethnomethodological, including categorial, analysis into (some idealised conception of) a formal-analytic sociology with its associated, purportedly unitary, research methods, let alone into a discipline such as linguistics that has yet to shake off the ghost of cognitivism (let alone formalism). Such approaches are designed to model a 'reproducible' social/communicative order in the abstract, the former to consider order in its concrete, essentially local, phenomenal detail. This line of approach suggests that the true place of categorial analysis is in what has been (perhaps somewhat erroneously) termed 'ethnomethodological ethnography'. It is certainly true that in Harvey Sacks's work,

(Sacks, 1992: Vol. 1), his profound observations on membership categories expressed, amongst other things, a fine ethnographic sensibility (viz. Watson, 2009a). This is a sensibility that commentators on Sacks have often – and perhaps sometimes wilfully – overlooked. However, I want to suggest that – though to a degree yet to be empirically determined – categorial and sequential analysis can each be respecified so as to bring about a mutual *rapprochement* under the *auspices* of canonical conversation analysis, too: categorial analysis is not simply the 'minor ethnographic side' of Sacks's work or his heritage. Taking this on board permits of a radical respecification of ethnography, too, and particularly of an ethnography of communication of a type that Hymes and his associates, who were still far too much in thrall to linguistics, can hardly, at that point, have envisaged (though an important qualification of this point is that they were, to their great credit, among the very few that were professionally open-minded enough to sponsor some early conversation analysis).

However, the above characterisation of the 'analytic mentality' that is deployed in categorial analysis has not simply been done in order to note the radical incompatibility of such ethnomethodological studies and the formal-analytic studies of orthodox sociologies; it also carries implications for categorial analyses themselves. In my view, the appropriate 'analytic mentality' for the study of categorisation phenomena is that of single instance or, at least, instance-by-instance analysis, with perhaps the possibility of a 'family resemblance' conception in view.

Elsewhere (Watson, 2008b) I have argued against the 'research technique' of making collections in the sequential analysis of conversational objects. In that paper, I argued that utterances and utterance sequences were non-extractable features of the gestalt contexture of the conversation and that it was this contexture that give that utterance or sequence its here-and-now, distinctively situated sense. To extract the utterance or sequence from that sensible context and force it into a relation with other, similarly decontextualised utterances to attempt to form an equivalence class gives far too much away to formal-analytic sociology. Instead, I argued for the analysis of single instances of utterances and sequences in their distinctive, specific contextual embeddings, in their phenomenal 'just this-ness'. I consider that the analysis of categorisation practices is amenable, *a fortiori*, to this self-same argument. The making of collections in order to find what the early Sacks called a 'reproducible' model seems to me misconceived, for the reasons I hope to have outlined here.

A useful derivative of the approach I here recommend is that analysts will find it more difficult to drive a wedge between 'Sacks the sequential analyst' and 'the ethnographic Sacks'. Whilst there is of course a significant difference between these tendencies in his work, and particularly in his *Lectures in Conversation* (1992), it is not a hard and fast, for-all-purposes distinction. Membership categorisation analysis often brings out the elective affinities in these two tendencies.

Consequently, I feel we should treat the analysis of membership categorisations with some modesty, even caution. It is quite possible that the analyses of membership categories will turn out to be a minor or occasional, though still not negligible, theme in ethnomethodology and (especially) conversation analysis: certainly, there are, for instance, other forms of person-description that are partially or wholly independent of membership categorisation. Whilst we might not accept all the constraints imposed by Schegloff on the analysis of membership categories, methodological constraints there must be, and rigorous ones too – just not all the specific constraints that Schegloff requires. MCA, or some forms of it, is already too vulnerable to 'knock-down' criticisms, and if we cannot improve things we should not make them worse.

One positive outcome of all this, which I have explicitly sought since my earliest papers on categorisation in the 1970s (viz. Watson, 1977, 1978), might be to end the sense that sequential and categorial analysis are two warring camps, or that only one of these can contribute to 'true conversation analysis'.

Conclusion

To conclude: I feel that starting *de novo* on the study of the integration of categorisation practices with sequential ones would benefit canonical ethnomethodology quite as much as conversation analysis. From the inception of ethnomethodology, and especially from 1970 on, Garfinkel has insisted on the centrality to sense-making of members' mastery of the natural language. I think that with a few exceptions such as Garfinkel and Sacks's 'On formal structures of practical actions' (1970) paper and some largely pious comments by Garfinkel on local occupational 'lingoes', this precept of ethnomethodology remains relatively underworked. Whilst there is no single solution to this problem, a focus on categorisation practices in natural language would help redress the balance in specific contexts, so long as that focus is exhaustively praxeological, for example treated as an integrand of the practices comprising 'talk-in-interaction' or of other naturally situated serial-interactional organisations. Moreover, we should never forget that categorisation practices are part and parcel of constitutive practice: that is, they form part of our ensemble of cultural knowledge-based sense-making activities, routinely deployed in ordinary life.

What, then, might we anticipate for the future of Membership Categorisation Analysis? Certainly, we should resist any 'backsliding' tendency towards its becoming a placeholder for role theory or still less a simplistic theory of 'identity'. We should also resist any move towards subjecting Membership Categorisation Analysis purely and exclusively to the methodological constraints of canonical conversation analysis (thought these are by no means irrelevant). This is especially the case if this form of analysis continues to import and incorporate formal methodological constraints and analytic characterisations derived from linguistics. Rather, we should seek to move membership categorisation analysis towards a more classically ethnomethodological analytic mentality, for it may well be here that this form of analysis finds its 'natural home'.

We also stand in need of more analyses of membership categorisation practices in other cultures. Fortunately, there already are some, for example Leudar and Nekvapil (2000) and Dupret (2011a, b). These studies, particularly by the latter author, treat membership categorisations in highly particular institutional contexts. For instance, Depret has produced some perspicuous analyses of the use of membership categorisations in Arabic media contexts (Dupret, 2011b) and in judicial activities in Arabic contexts (Dupret, 2011a). Such analyses, which avoid reification through strictly dealing with categorisations in context, can enrich and expand our battery of anti-reifactory, analyses of categorisations. Dupret says:

> ... categorization, far from proceeding from formal semantics, are sensitive to the context of their formulation, which is necessarily situation in time and space'. In view of this, we are moving toward a conception of categorization not only as constitutive practice but as *endogenous* (intra-setting) constitutive practice. (2011b: 325)

This, I think, is a most perspicuous formulation. What I think might happen on the basis of some current trends, and, like Sacks, what I hope will happen, is that we shall have a kind of 'grammar' for membership categorisation practices – but not a grammar of the kind that Sacks wished for, one that was based on a misbegotten analogy with transformational grammar, and, indirectly, componential analysis. Instead we might anticipate something akin to a 'logical grammar' (Wittgenstein) or 'logical geography' (Ryle) of particular membership categories considered as practices in a given contexture. This is a big 'maybe' and, as I have said, would involve, above all, the abandonment of the attitude of disdain for the particular instance and a suspicion of 'data collections' that collate specifically situated, distinct uses of membership categorisations (Watson, 2009a). What efforts would such an abandonment involve?

Firstly, it should be said that in focusing on single instances, *all* the analytical turns I have described above must be taken together; after all they elaborate, and are elaborated by, each other. The contextual, praxeological, etc. analyses of turns must be analysed as an ensemble.

How, further, to analyse categorisation practices? Well, to adapt a quotation from Goffman to our purposes, we may, in each instance, follow each categorisation for whatever is does and wherever it seems to lead and press it to reveal the rest of its family. In so doing, we may come to abandon the search for or reliance on overarching characterisations of 'membership categorisation as a whole' in favour of instance-by-instance analysis with – perhaps, and only perhaps – a family resemblance model as a cautiously pursued 'grammatical' derivative. Such derivatives do not, however, accrue 'automatically': they have to be earned. Certainly, we should begin with such modesty. I am wont to quote Goffman, here (1961: xiv). He puts it in a way that should make us cautious about aspiring to a single, monolithic approach such as 'Membership Categorisation Analysis':

> Better, perhaps, different coats to clothe the children well than a single splendid tent in which they all shiver.

Notes

1 Sadly, on the rare occasions when sequential analysts in CA (e.g. Schegloff, 2007b) have discussed catego-risation activities, they have accorded insufficient attention to these later developments. Thus Schegloff's discussion (2007b) of categorisation, for example, is less a 'tutorial', more a history class. In glossing over the more recent attempts at development, these sequential analysts have tended to conflate very different contemporary 'takes' on how to develop categorial analysis, lumping them all together as though there were a 'party line'. There is not.

2 However, Schegloff seems relatively unaware of the range of more recent discussions about, and updating of, categorial analysis, let alone the distinctions between the arguments proposed by different analyses. His critiques, then, tend to apply more to the earlier forms of categorial analysis.

3 By 'considered sociologically', I mean to refer to a range of issues concerning the praxeology of lay and professional sociological description in their local contexts as set out by Garfinkel and by Sacks by way of a radical alternative to the established forms of sociological analysis (which they dub 'formal analy-sis'). See, for example, Garfinkel's early articles (e.g. Garfinkel, 1959), Sacks' first article (1963) and in particular his early lectures (Sacks, 1992: Vol. 1). For comments, equally radical, on these issues, see Garfinkel's and Sacks's contributions in Hill and Crittenden (1968) where Sacks's contributions include some little-known formulations of membership categories in relation to issues of sociological description. See also Garfinkel and Sacks (1970) for a conceptual re-working of these initial concerns.

4 For instance, one of Harold Garfinkel's more recent works (2002) is sub-titled *Working Out Durkheim's Aphorism* – hardly an ignoring or dismissal of classical sociology (tellingly, Firth does not list this study in his bibliography). Right from his earliest critiques of Parsons through to his considerations of eth-nomethodological and conventional sociological approaches as two incommensurate, asymmetrical but nonetheless 'paired' technologies of social research (which Firth does cite but whose full implications he manifestly fails to take into account), Garfinkel has never ceased to debate with conventional, formal-analytic sociologies. However, he has never been so unwise as to make the undermining concessions that Firth seems to envisage: that is another matter entirely.

3

Prospective and Retrospective Categorisation

Category Proffers and Inferences in Social Interaction and Rolling News Media

Elizabeth Stokoe and Frederick Attenborough

Introduction: Sequences, Categories, Categories, Sequences ...

A key context for any collection of works on Membership Categorisation Analysis (MCA), including the current chapter, is the relationship that MCA has with another ethnomethodologically orientated method for analysing interactional and textual practice, conversation analysis (CA). To set the scene, then, we begin with a short history that outlines the way that relationship has traditionally been articulated. Most readers will know that CA and MCA both emerged out of Sacks's (1992) ground-breaking *Lectures in Conversation*. However, many commentators have observed, over the years, that they developed 'largely in isolation from one another', and tended to focus on related, yet consequentially different aspects of discursive, rhetorical and performative practice (e.g. Plunkett, 2009: 24). CA has typically foregrounded 'the normative structuring and logics of particular courses of social action and their organisation into systems through which participants manage turn-taking, repair, and other systemic dimensions of language' (Heritage, 2005: 104), while MCA looked instead to 'members' methodical practices for describing the world, and displaying their understanding of the world and of the common-sense routine workings of society' (Fitzgerald et al., 2009: 47).

These different analytic foci have often been translated in different sorts of empirical studies. While CA works principally across large conversational data corpora to identify, cumulatively, robust structural patterns in turn-taking, repair, sequence organisation and action formation, MCA more routinely produces localised case studies of distinct interactional and textual settings of the turn-generated 'identities-for-interaction', moralities, cultures, and the many other categorial matters that can be found therein. In this way, slowly, over time, an artificial 'division of labour' developed such that 'sequence' and 'categorisation' fell into different (and hierarchically organised; see Stokoe, 2012a) methodological terrains. Conversation analysts have often criticised MCA for failing to engage with sequential matters (e.g., Schegloff, 2007a), membership categorisation analysts, in turn, have suggested that conversation analysts set 'categorization relevances at zero' (Watson, 1997a: 50). It is perhaps unsurprising, then, that in this context, studies in which *both* categorial *and* sequential aspects of talk and text are subject to analysis have been 'hardly done' (Hansen, 2005: 67, emphasis added) – at least until recently.

Part of the problem in bringing the two approaches together, according to Stokoe (2009, 2010b), has been a generally held assumption that categorial phenomena are 'disorderly'.

> We cannot simply go into the field and observe how, when, where, and with whom people talk with others about [identity] groups ... Finding data ... would amount to a search for the proverbial needle in the haystack. (Van Dijk, 1987: 18, 119)

> Because we cannot know in advance when a person will explicitly invoke a ... category, there is no way to plan data collection of them ... collections ... in all likelihood, would not be instances of the same interactional phenomena. (Pomerantz and Mandelbaum, 2005: 154)

And so conversation analysts, in particular, have argued that 'establishing the mechanisms by which a specific identity is made relevant and consequential in any particular episode of interaction has remained ... elusive' (Raymond and Heritage, 2006: 677).

However, in recent years there has been something of a rapprochement between the two 'camps', with many conversation analysts attending to categorial matters such as race and ethnicity (e.g. Whitehead, 2013; Wilkinson, 2011) or gender (see Speer and Stokoe, 2011). Indeed, in a recent paper focusing on the core CA topic of 'action formation', Heritage (2013) argues that phenomena such as 'identity' are at 'the heart of action formation' and should be 'reflexively incorporated into the analysis of what contributions to interaction are accomplishing in terms of meaning and action' (p. 573).

In this chapter, we continue to make the case for the systematic analysis of membership categories and related phenomena, and show that the apparent 'disorderliness' of 'category relevances' is a methodological artefact, and not an empirical reality. Taking up Sacks's (often idiosyncratic) observations about membership categories, we show how to track categorial concerns in the same way that CA pursues sequential practices. We draw on large conversational and textual data corpora in order to identify, cumulatively, robust sequential patterns in interaction (e.g., turn-taking, repair, sequence, organisation, action formation), aligning with more recent MCA studies that also work within a framework of cumulative research and with larger datasets. Both Van Dijk and Pomerantz and Mandelbaum assume that the category has to come first. But here, our suggestion is that sequential matters come first. As we (Stokoe, 2012a, 2012b) have shown elsewhere, by focusing on a large corpus of institutional materials, which have distinct overarching sequential organisations – e.g., openings, tellings of complaints, confessions, and so on – we can show how matters of identity crop up, and are dealt with repeatedly, and often in remarkably similar ways, across similar action-oriented environments.

We aim, therefore, to present, and exemplify, a practical and sequential approach to Membership Categorisation Analysis (MCA). Drawing on a wide range of spoken and written discourse data, from everyday conversation between friends as well as from institutional settings, we analyse a series of examples, each involving practices of description and categorisation, and show how those practices get used in and as part of sequential practices to do particular kinds of inferential work. When one party describes another's actions (e.g. 'he never calls me up'), that description may then be treated, by the same party or a recipient, as category-relevant (cf. Stokoe, 2012a; see also Deppermann, 2011; Hauser, 2011). In turn, either party may then *proffer a category* in response (e.g. 'that's men for you'). Within these practices, the first part may be considered *prospective*; the second, *retrospective* (cf. Watson, 2009a). As such, categorial work may be considered an essentially sequential phenomenon. Having established this point and its relevance across different contexts, we consider its application across a collection of 'breaking' news stories in which journalists, working in the absence of any legal or socially sanctioned certainty, have to try to tie descriptions of criminal actions (bombings, mass-shootings, etc.) to the 'right' kind of category. What becomes clear is that prospective and retrospective categorisation constitutes a key mechanism for the practical negotiation of this search for 'right-ness': the actions and biographical details of all potential suspects get prospectively and/or retrospectively categorised – using category-implicative features – in various different ways before a breaking news story solidifies into a report of 'what actually happened'. Overall, the chapter considers the implications of these findings for methodological debates in MCA and, more generally, for debates about analysis, inference and context in discourse and interaction analysis.

Prospective, Retrospective, Proffers and Inferences

In this section, we show how speakers invoke, produce, propose and sustain common-sense knowledge about members of categories, and show the regularity with which one can identify a distinct categorial practice comprising *description* and *categorisation*. The analysis will show how these components are produced by speakers, within or across a sequence of turns, in particular action-oriented environments. Alongside this, we show how people use categories in ways that show that the notion that categories carry inferences, and do implicative work, is a members' resource. By '*inference*-rich', Sacks (1992) meant that categories store 'a great deal of the knowledge that members

of a society have about the society' (pp. 40–1). A particular 'woman' may also be correctly categorised as a 'mother', 'lady', 'wife' or 'daughter', but each category carries a
different set of category-bound activities, predicates, or rights and obligations that are
expectable for an incumbent of that category to perform or possess. Categories and
their *inferential* upshots can be *implied*, but not overtly stated, by mentioning some
category-incumbent features. For instance, Sacks discusses how a suicidal man uses
descriptions such as 'I was a hair stylist at one time, I did some fashions now and then,
things like that' to imply for himself possible incumbency of a homosexual identity
(this was in 1960s California). He claims that 'there are ways of introducing a piece of
information and testing out whether it will be acceptable, which don't involve saying
it' (p. 47). As Edwards (2009, personal communication) argues, it is not the job of
analysts to be more specific about categorisation practices, or, more generally, about
designedly ambiguous descriptions and actions, than members themselves are. The fact
that we cannot be definitive about relevant categories and inferences is what gives
language practices their *defeasibility*: that Sacks's suicidal man was 'homosexual'
remains *provisional* and, crucially, *deniable* (Benwell and Stokoe, 2006).

Extract 1 comes from an online 'chat' between two friends, Callum and Isla, on
Facebook's instant messaging application.

EXTRACT 1: JM FACEBOOK CHAT

```
 1 Callum:  you can teach me ☺
 2                  (2.0)
 3 Isla:    I charge by the hour ☺
 4                  (35.0)
 5 Callum:  you sound liek a prostitute there haha
 6          but i wont take it like that
 7                  (69.0)
 8 Isla:    haha while that wasn't exactly the intention
 9          it was the connotations lol - joke with
10          my friend here - she just said the same
11          thing to another guy - agian in a different
12          context but with that sort of banter lol
```

Callum and Isla have been talking about sports coaching. A gloss on the mundane
(and accountably ironic) work of naming and labelling that takes place here might
be something like 'what is this relationship that we are proposing to enter into?' As
part of the action-oriented, sequential context in which the participants work towards

answering this question, a category is invoked that orients to, and makes relevant as a topical issue, each participant's 'gender'. An analytic gloss on this activity might involve the labelling of a 'discourse' or 'repertoire' of gender, gender stereotyping, or, at a push, sexism. MCA, however, shows not just *that* this kind of thing happens, but also *how* it is accomplished by retrospective and prospective categorial description, attribution and modification.

Consider, for instance, Callum's initial 'you can teach me' (line 1). It formulates, and summarises, the conversation that precedes it. To 'teach', in and of itself, involves a material action, rather than a category. But it invites Isla to see, and to identify, a particular kind of category that might be linked to that kind of action. To suggest that Isla can 'teach' him is for Callum to propose, and to open up for discussion, Isla's incumbency of the category 'teacher'. Indeed, because categories will often sit together in paired relationships, each with duties and obligations in relation to the other, 'you can teach me' also proposes the relational pairing 'coach and/or teacher–student' as 'the one' that each party to the interaction is collaboratively engaged in developing. As we can see then, whilst members can 'work forwards' from a category to the kinds of activity that incumbents of that category might do, they can also invite others to 'work backwards' from an activity (or predicted activity) to a certain kind of category, and category incumbent (see Watson, 2009a).

It is, in fact, on the basis of Isla's response, 'I charge by the hour' (line 3), that we can pursue this line of analysis: it is what she, herself, proposes as the type of relational pairing that Callum has suggested. Her response orients to Callum's initial action and, in doing so, offers up the kind of action that incumbents of the category 'teacher' might carry out: a 'teacher' not only 'teaches', but might also be reasonably expected to 'charge' for those services. They are, then, apparently on the same page here about the 'teacher–student' pairing: one party's description of [something] is treated as category relevant by another who proffers a category in response. A gloss on this activity might be something like: 'I hear your description as possibly referring to an incumbent of [category X]; do you agree?'

And yet, as we can see from line 5 onwards, if categories are inference-rich, then they are also indexical: links between categories, actions and predicates do not 'go together' in any decontextualised way; rather, their 'going together' 'is achieved and is to be found in the local specifics of categorization as an activity' (Hester and Eglin, 1997b: 46). Here, then, if a categorial-pairing is about to become accepted by both parties, then we, as analysts, might expect, given the topic under discussion – sports training and coaching – something like 'coach', 'trainer' or 'teacher' to become apparent (e.g., 'you'd make a great coach!'). But Callum takes the category work thus far down a different path, treating Isla's 'I charge by the hour' as an activity relevant to incumbency in a rather different categorial pairing, being 'liek [*sic*] a prostitute'. In this way, the pupil becomes a customer, learning not about sport but about sex; the teacher becomes a prostitute, giving advice not about cardiovascular, but sexual, stamina. Note also how this turn is carefully designed:

consistent with the stance taken in earlier turns in the sequence, Callum ends the first part of his turn with a written laughter particle ('haha'), he says that Isla '*sounds like* a prostitute', so downgrading the definitive nature of the categorisation, as well as noting that she only *sounds like* a prostitute *there*, in a temporally specific way. In these ways, he displays awareness that even implicit attributions of the category pairing 'prostitute–customer' are potentially risky, although, as we can see, Callum's management of risky categorisation-work is somewhat undermined in the continuation of his turn at line 6: 'but i wont [*sic*] take it like that'. This reifies the category-activity connection that Callum has constructed, whilst he simultaneously proposes ignoring such a connection. Isla begins her response by reciprocating Callum's stance towards this category work ('haha') and, as we can see by her inclusion of other 'laughter' indicators ('lol'), her response invites its recipient to treat the whole thing as ironic or humorous; as something that comprises their 'banter' (line 12). However, she both resists and goes along with the categorisation 'prostitute' in several ways: as something that her initial turn ('I charge by the hour') was not making relevant ('that wasn't exactly the intention'); as something that may be prospectively referred to ('it was the connotations lol'), and via the reporting of a concurrent Facebook chat with another friend who was involved in a similar prospective–retrospective categorisation activity ('she said the same thing to another guy … with that sort of banter lol').

In terms of the methodological underpinnings of MCA, what we can see here are two things: first, the inference-rich nature of categories; and second, the back-and-forth sequential nature of categorisation as it takes place whilst both parties work towards (though never fully or completely arrive at) an answer to the question of what kind of relationship they have. On the one hand, then, we see that categories allow both parties to stay on the same page in this 'on-going' collaborative work of naming and labelling their relationship. On the other, we see that every bit of that categorial work is effectively a 'first-through attempt'; it may be accepted, but it may be modified again, afresh, each time: a relational pairing is proposed, developed, or rejected, through the sequential organisation of interaction.[1] Our methodological point is that categories are not, in fact, like 'needles in haystacks'. Or rather, if they are, then the haystack has a certain structural order: across different contexts, look to sequential moments of naming and labelling, and you will find moments of categorial work in which the same kinds of category practices crop up.

Let us do that here, focusing on an extract in which the same activity of describing and categorising is taking place. Extract 2 comes from an initial meeting between a community mediator (M) and four clients who, together, are describing a complaint about one of their neighbours and are 'Party 1' to a dispute about which we find people engaged in naming and labelling some hitherto un-named action. C1, C2 and C3 allege that their neighbour, a single mother with several children, goes out at night leaving her children unattended. Here, the clients are talking together about the problematic character of their neighbour as someone who does not talk to them or other neighbours.

EXTRACT 2: ES: DM-C02 NEIGHBOUR DISPUTE MEDIATION

```
 1  C1:  D'y- ↑I don't think she ca:res actually she's not spoken to any
 2       of all of us has she in [all the time she['s be]en here[.
 3  C2:                          [No:,              [No, ]        [never
 4       spoke.
 5            (0.8)
 6  C3:  Never spoke.
 7            (.)
 8  C3:  She jus' dresses up,
 9            (1.4)
10  C3:  [(What's it,)]
11  C1:  [Like a tart.]
12            (0.4)
13  C2:  °Ye:[h.°
14  C3:      [Heh hah heh.
15            (0.2)
16  C3:  Yeh.
```

Extract 2 completes a long discussion between the clients about their neighbour (Stokoe, 2013). Our interest is in what happens at line 8 ('She jus' dresses up,') in which C3's turn will, in C1's response, be treated as a prospective categorisation. Prior to line 8, of course, C1, C2 and C3 are already collaboratively characterising their neighbour as someone who 'doesn't care', and does not speak to them (lines 1–6). C3's continuation of his own earlier turn is unclear and, anyway, in overlap with C1's category proffer: that their neighbour as someone who dresses 'like a tart'. Unlike in Extract 1, participants' subsequent turns ratify, more or less unambiguously, C1's categorisation, with agreements from C2 and C3 and affiliative laughter. The overall action of Extract 2 is different, of course, to Extract 1, as the clients work as one party to complain about an absent third party. In Extract 1, Callum's categorisation is relevant directly to his recipient; he and Isla are not collaboratively categorising *someone else*. However, in the same way that we saw in Extract 1, one speaker's turn may be treated as a *prospective categorisation* of someone (or something), and then, retrospectively, categorised via a *category proffer*. C1's category 'tart' characterises how their neighbour dresses, in ways that fit with, and perhaps formulate as a conclusion, much of what C1, C2 and C3 have been saying about her. Rather than being a person like they imply themselves to be (civil, interested in their children's welfare, neighbourly), her interests lie in some kind of wanton and irresponsible self-indulgence (Stokoe and Edwards, 2015). The way she dresses, and the category that it invokes, are tied to the same range of behaviours in which she goes out at nights, goes on holiday, leaving her children at home, and fails to discipline them properly.

In Extract 3, from a conversation between friends, Sophie is complaining to Emma that she is not seeing enough of her new boyfriend. We join her as she reports that, after their last encounter, he did not make arrangements for a next date.

EXTRACT 3: VH-1 FRIENDS' CHAT

```
1    S:  Once I left 'is though 'e was like 'e didn't say anything t'-
2    E:  Oh::::
3                 (0.2)
4    E:  That's ↑me:n.= that's what James was like: (.) on Sunday::
```

Sophie does not complete her turn, but we will see from Emma's responses that she has understood its trajectory as an item of evidence for both her complaint and her upset. Emma demonstrates her understanding of, and empathy with, Sophie's situation, in her response at line 2 ('Oh::::'). She then provides an upshot of Sophie's account, generalising the described activities of the boyfriend to those typical of 'men in general', 'That's ↑me:n.', with marked emphasis on the categorial term. The category is used to encompass a host of unspecified meanings of what 'men' are like. Emma then moves from the *general* category 'men' to describe an *instance* in her own boyfriend ('that's what James was like …'), which both evidences the generalisation and affiliates with her friend's complaint. Extract 3 demonstrates again our recurrent practice through which one speaker's descriptions are turned into a membership category by another; how speakers move between description and categorisation, and how recipients may proffer categories as a way of proposing intersubjectivity; as a way of showing that 'my mind is with you' (Sacks, 1992: 295).

Finally, Extract 4 comes from a telephone call to a mediation centre (M) in which a council worker (C) is calling on behalf of a woman whose house backs onto cricket club grounds. The woman has complained to the council that balls from the club are damaging her roof, and make it unsafe to sit in her garden. C wants the mediation centre to mediate between the woman and the club.

EXTRACT 4: DC-16 NEIGHBOUR DISPUTE MEDIATION

```
1 C:  […] she can't go in 'er ga:rden an' it's dam- she's
2     paid for: (.) tiles bein' fixed on 'er roof:. without
3     even contactin' them,=she's says- she knows they're re-
4     (0.2) they kno:w they're responsible    [hh      ] but she
5 M:                                          [.pt Yeh.]
```

```
 6  C:   doesn't want to confront them: she's [eighty three ]
 7  M:                                        [.hhh ↑↑No: I]'d be uh
 8  M:  ↑ye:[ah.     ]=it's not *i-* uh y'know: *i-* b- *i-*
 9  C:      [(Um)]
10          (0.5)
11  M:  Obviously age: (.)  c- *i- i-* (.)  could [be an i:ssue]
12  C:                                            [Ye:ah:       ]
13  M:  with'er but- .hh [↑y'know]  it's ↑not something that-=
14  C:                   [(Yeah) ]
15  M:  =(0.3) a lo:t of people: um: do: easily.
```

C is narrating the woman's circumstances and complaints: not being able to use her garden – a mundane entitlement for someone who owns one – and paying for damage caused by the club. At lines 3–4, C reports that the club knows that they are responsible for the damage. Note the repair from 'she knows they're re-' to 'they kno:w they're responsible' (lines 3–4), replacing the pronoun 'she' with 'they'. The repair fixes any notion that it is only the woman's version of events that the cricket club caused damage: the club itself accepts responsibility. M acknowledges this (line 5), and C proffers a category-relevant account for why her client has not 'confronted' the club herself: 'she's eighty three' (line 6). Although this description does not explicitly categorise her as, say, 'old', 'eighty three' infers a host of possible category resonances relevant to why this person does not want to complain directly to the cricket club (e.g., 'too old', 'frail', 'intimidated', etc.). M's response, 'Obviously age: (.) c- *i- i-* (.) could [be an i:ssue]' (line 11) shows that she has understood the category proffer, and turns this *description* into an explicit *categorisation*. However, M suggests that although age might be the category in play for C, in fact 'a lo:t of people:' (line 15) do not find confrontation easy. Thus M displays her understanding of the categorial basis of C's complaint, but does not fully align with it, replacing 'age' with 'people in general'.

Extracts 1–4 comprise a sample data corpus that provides evidence to contradict a common assumption about the 'non-capturability' of identity topics for research. Particular social actions like description and categorisation systematically bring into play particular self- and other categorisations of the persons involved. We have also seen how Sacks's notions about the inference-rich nature of categories, introduced earlier, are built into the very categorial practices themselves. It is not just that categories are, in theory and before empirical observation, 'inference rich', but that we can see that, and how, people treat categories *as* carrying inferential resources, in the design of their turns in which categorial formulations appear (Stokoe, 2012b). In other words, the inference-rich nature of categories is observable from the endogenous orientations of participants. This is revealed in the way that description gets treated as category-relevant, how parties *proffer categories,* and how participants *prospectively* and *retrospectively* move through the contingencies of description and action.

Categories as Resources in 'Breaking News'

We turn now to show how the type of analysis illustrated above may be particularly relevant to the mediated phenomena of 'breaking' and 'rolling' news, which, while the subject of some academic attention (e.g. Nacos, 2003), has received surprisingly little attention from the spectrum of discourse analysis. There are two relevant studies here. Firstly, there is Liebes's (1998) work on the way television coverage of news events can produce 'disaster marathons'. These are characterised by the lack of a readily available 'script', a high degree of repetition, and a concentration on what in other times would be passed over or provide only a sound bite. Such events focus on blame allocation as a device for maintaining narrative progressivity, as well as the transformation of horrific images into iconic representations detached from their original context. Secondly, drawing in part from Liebes's work, Jaworski, Fitzgerald and Constantinou (2005) examined live media coverage of 9/11, identifying characteristic features such as 'strategic silences' that 'not only act to cover for lack of new news, or give emphasis or gravitas' but also create 'an emotional space in which collective shock, grieving or wonder are managed through news presented as phatic communion' (p. 121). Other features, such as handling an absence of factual information are relevant to our case study, below. We will examine the way descriptions of events and persons, in the evolution of 'what happened', deploy the machinery of categorisation to imply and infer causes, victims and perpetrators, event types, responsibility, and so on, in ways that are designedly provisional and defeasible but that also slowly consolidate around the 'facts of the matter'. Our case study is the bombing of government buildings in Oslo and subsequent mass shootings of teenagers at a Labour Party youth camp on the island of Utøya, Norway. These events comprised the '2011 Norway attacks'; the perpetrator was quickly identified as Anders Behring Breivik. However, initial rolling news and published reports linked the 'attack' to Islamic terrorists.

As in other forms of interaction, categories and their inferential possibilities are an omnirelevant resource for breaking news. But yet there are some important differences. News has conventions and regulations about what can and cannot be claimed. For example, 'objectivity' involves distance, and distance involves talking through external sources and witnesses (e.g. Clayman and Heritage, 2002). As something 'unfolds', categories get locked, unlocked and re-locked into place. In the pre-digital age, much of the news came pre-packaged: such was the news cycle, involving a once daily newspaper and television news bulletins at pre-arranged times throughout the day. For the most part, the relevant categories of events, persons and so on, were defined prior to their publication in a newspaper article or as content for the newsreader's autocue. Increasingly, though, the media is becoming more like interaction, in which categorial practices are worked out live, and sequentially. This is principally because the news cycle now moves faster than the bureaucratic/source cycle: the once-daily newspaper has been complemented by websites with constantly updating textual, visual and audio material; the pre-arranged news bulletin has been complemented by 24-hour rolling news stations. The *daily* rhetorical achievement of the news is now a *ten-minute cyclical* achievement. Categorial reasoning is not just sequentially organised but publicly observable: when something happens, and before anyone knows what it is that has happened, breaking news involves the locking-in of certain names and labels that may have to be constantly tweaked and revised. These 'first-time through' categorisations are where we find what are, at some point, going to be 'quiet centres of power and persuasion' (Baker, 2000): this is reality-in-the-making.

In our data, we will show how categorisation is a resource for making predictions about who may be guilty of a crime, what type of crime was committed, and in confirming suspects as suspects or as innocent parties. Whilst under suspicion, suspects may be described *prospectively* with the aid of category-implicative features that hint at guilt; yet if they are subsequently found to be innocent, they have their biographies re-worked, in articles that *retrospectively* delete and override those initial features. Alternatively, when the suspect of a crime is yet unknown, the features of the crime may be listed as relevant to a type of criminal (e.g., terrorist, psychopath) or named suspect. Similarly, in cases where people who have, for years or decades, been passing as an ordinary citizen or admired celebrity but are subsequently – sensationally – identified as a criminal, then the biographical re-workings run in the opposite direction (e.g. the recent case of South African paralympian Oscar Pistorius; the case of British radio and television presenter Jimmy Saville). In constructing media coverage, journalists deploy their members' knowledge of membership categorisation.

Membership categorisation analysts have often looked to legal and criminal contexts as a source of data in their work, from Watson's (e.g. 1978) study of police–suspect interviews in the case of sexual assault (see also Wowk, 1984) to Lee's (1984) analysis of newspaper headlines in the case of rape. Other work is also relevant, including Clifton's (2009) analysis of the Waco siege and the FBI's recordings with David Koresh, focusing on how Koresh positioned himself as the 'victim' of the FBI-as-perpetrators, thus subverting the normative victim–perpetrator 'standardised relational pair' with Koresh as perpetrator. Also particularly relevant is Eglin and Hester's (1999, 2003) comprehensive analysis of media coverage of the Montreal Massacre and the gunman's categorisation of his victims as a 'bunch of feminists'. Eglin and Hester show how, of the many ways of categorising these victims, the selection of 'feminists' politicised his crime, thus providing a basis for a political and rational, rather than, say, psychopathic, 'evil' or 'mad', categorisation for his actions.

Our data comprise numerous newspaper articles about the case described, gathered from the archive Lexis Nexis, as well as from rolling online news that we screen-captured contemporaneously. The data were collected as part of a larger project on categorisation and media reports of serious crime, focusing on stories that made headline news for several days, nationally as well as internationally.

'Norway': From 'Muslim' to 'Nutter'

We start with the case of the bombings and mass shootings in Norway, for which Anders Behring Breivik was arrested and convicted. In 'known' cases of crime, where the facts of the matter have been established, the categories of 'victim' and 'offender', within the membership categorisation device 'parties to a crime', are easy to track and understand (Lee, 1984): an 'offender' perpetrated the offence, and a 'victim' was the passive recipient of the offence and its ill effects (Watson, 1978). In this way, the blame shifts towards the offender and away from the victim. But this is not, yet, what could happen in the Norway case. In the absence of any institutional certainty, initial descriptions started the process of allocating, and distributing, relevant category incumbencies. There were 'victims', to be sure. But what else was there? Were the initial explosions an unintended accident, or deliberate, and caused by an offender? Through its categorial work, breaking news, rolling 24 news, became the first, inchoate form of detective work. Let us begin with an extract from BBC rolling news online, in which two presenters (P1 and P2) in the BBC studio in London are discussing what has happened with a correspondent (C) on location in Oslo.

EXTRACT 5: BBC ROLLING NEWS (22/07/11)

```
 1. C:   ...so that will be a question that's raised, but, it's it, uh, we
 2.      really have to be careful because we may all be saying in a few
 3.      minutes or a few hours' time, 'well actually it was a gas explosion'
 4.      and all this political ex- speculation may not be relevant to what has
 5.      happened.
 6. P1:  Yes, I mean I'm just reading as you, as you talk to us Bridget, and
 7.      please stay with us for the moment, um, that the epicentre of the
 8.      explosion at least on some of the newswires seemed to be between
 9.      the Prime Minister's Office and the Oil and Energy Ministry which
10.      were both badly damaged, an' just, an' what, I know you've been
11.      watching these pictures with us Bridget, but, the scale of the blast
12.      does seem to be very large, doesn't it?
13. P2:  It does, but I mean that doesn't mean to say that that means in
14.      itself that it was deliberate. Although, if it was deliberate, uh,
15.      then it has caused a large explosion ...
```

Note that, in the first stages of reporting, the correspondent and reporters talk of an 'explosion' (lines 3, 8) or a 'large explosion' (line 15), but do not ascribe agency or cause. Indeed, they orient to the ambiguity of the event as one that is not yet fully known, as well as the moral need for caution and rush for definition ('we have to be really careful'; 'that doesn't mean to say'). Nevertheless, the sequential environment in which these 'explosions' are talked about involve various forms of collaborative work, accepting and resisting some kind of agency. The participants do their own dialogic retrospective and prospective work, moving from what we know – an explosion – to what we could know in the future. In the next iteration of the story, details begin to change:

EXTRACT 6: BBC ROLLING NEWS (22/07/11)

((Rolling headline across screen: 'Norway Oslo Blast. Reports: blast blew out most windows of PM's office'))

```
 1. P:  Well, I I think it's important to say that still nothing is confirmed,
 2.     um, one expert on this uh has said that the working assumption –
 3.     and I won't say which country this person is in – uh the working
 4.     assumption is that it probably was a bomb but options, you know,
 5.     people are keeping an open mind […] they take away the remains
 6.     from the kind of ground zero where the blast actually came from and
 7.     analyse the explosive to see if its, you know, is it military explosive,
 8.     was it gas, was it, you know, who knows yet, so I think we, we've
 9.     got to be a little bit cautious at this stage. What I would say is this,
10.     though, um, there are, if it turns out, if it turns out this was terrorism,
11.     there are a number of possible, uh, leads, or directions, or causes
12.     that would have come, uh, reasons why this would have happened.
13.     The most obvious is the presence of Norwegian troops in
14.     Afghanistan. They've been there for 10 years. They've had special
15.     forces up in the mountains hunting down Al-Qaeda, uh, they've had
16.     other groups involved in more conventional forms of warfare in
17.     Afghanistan for quite some time […]
```

Extract 6 contains the same kinds of disclaimers and mitigation that we saw in Extract 5 (e.g., 'nothing is confirmed'; 'if it turns out'). At the same time, however, the earlier 'explosion' is beginning to be reconstructed, and recategorised, as a 'bomb'. Technical details and 'expert' sources are discussed using particular inference-rich descriptions, including 'ground zero' (connoting the Al-Qaeda attack on the Twin Towers in 2001), 'blast' and 'military explosive'. Note also how the action of 'bombing' gets tied to the category 'terrorist' (line 10), where the incumbents of that category are, inevitably and without question, Al-Qaeda terrorists. An attempt is made to work back from the possible action to the sort of category, and the sort of incumbent of that category, that would typically and routinely perform that action. The day after Extracts 5 and 6 appeared, and when

institutional sources filled out the vacuum of 'what happened', the retrospective categorisation of the 'explosion' as a 'bomb' and then an 'attack' began to appear in these rolling
news items, in which the actions were increasingly invested with intention (e.g. 'A bomb
has gone off'; 'a huge bomb'; 'a bomb tore through'; 'Norway's day of violence began';
'the first attack occurred'; 'Norway attacks').

As a 'bombing', rather than an 'explosion', the unfolding event now can take the
standardised relational pairing of 'victim–perpetrator'. But what kinds of victims, and
what kinds of perpetrators? Again, in the absence of any institutional certainty, the
perpetrator has to be *prospectively* categorised. We see the work of describing and
categorising hitherto unattributed events, which draw on conventional, historical cultural and categorial resources. Consider Extracts 7–9, this time from newspaper
articles online.

EXTRACT 7: *DAILY MAIL* ('GUN MASSACRE OF THE YOUNG ONES', 23/07/11)

Social tensions within Norway have heightened in recent months
over the country's perceived stance on Islamic issues […] it
has recently increased its military presence in Muslim countries
such as Afghanistan or Libya, a move bound to anger fanatics […]
Last night 'Helpers of the Global Jihad' posted a message on
the internet claiming the bombing was 'only the beginning' of
the retaliation over the cartoons. Other Scandinavian countries
have faced radical Islamic attacks in the past. Violence erupted
in Denmark after a newspaper published a cartoon of the Prophet
wearing a turban in the shape of a bomb in 2005. And last
December an Islamic suicide bomber, who was radicalised in
Britain, set off a bomb in Stockholm.

EXTRACT 8: *DAILY MIRROR* ('SEVERAL REASONS FOR THIS "SOFT TARGET" ATTACK', 23/07/11)

Although it is one of the founders of Nato, it is an international
'sleepy hollow' which sadly may have fallen victim to its relaxed
attitude. There are five possible reasons for this soft-target
attack in the twisted logic of the terrorist.The first is simple – a
revenge attack for the death of Osama bin Laden, given Norway's
Nato role […] There is also an outside chance the bombing was
sponsored by Col Gaddafi. Norway has for many years had fairly
relaxed security measures. But sadly, like much of the post 9-11
West, that is probably not for much longer.

EXTRACT 9: *THE TIMES* ('SIMULTANEOUS ATTACKS BEAR THE HALLMARKS OF AL-QAEDA', 23/07/11)

Oslo has joined a roll call that now includes New York, London,
Mumbai, Bali and Madrid. The goals of yesterday's attack were
indiscriminate death and terror, conveyed in real time to a
global audience. By that measure the attacks achieved their
apparent aim. No group had admitted responsibility last night
for the bombing or the attack on young people camping on an
island. But the multiple nature of the assault, combining an
attack on both the Norwegian State and citizens at a youth camp,
bear the hallmarks of al-Qaeda.

Across these news reports, 'what happened' is gradually consolidating around a clear, but as yet prospectively categorised, standardised relational pairing such that the victim is 'the West', and the perpetrator is 'Islamism'. Norway becomes one of a series of category-pairings in Extract 7, in which it joins other Scandinavian countries as a victim of Islamic perpetrators, and in Extract 9, as joining 'a roll call that now includes New York, London, Mumbai, Bali and Madrid'. Each of these place names themselves work as categories (Stokoe and Attenborough, 2014) – as short-cuts of common knowledge to a story or event that 'Norway' now belongs to. Likewise, in Extract 8, the name 'Osama bin Laden' similarly works as a category, invoked in the construction of motives for the 'attack'. In Extract 9, both the headline and the news report content demonstrate members' orientations to the machinery of categorisation and description, as links are made ('bear the hallmarks'), albeit provisional, between the 'attacks' and 'Al-Qaeda'. Each report also lists historical evidence for Norway's own plausible categorisation as 'victim'.

As the story rolled on, information that was potentially incongruous with the dominant version was initially worked into the accounts unproblematically, again via categories.

EXTRACT 10: *THE SUN* ('NORWAY'S 9/11', 23/07/11)

Witnesses claimed the gun maniac was blond with blue eyes and
spoke Norwegian – raising fears that he was a homegrown al-
Qaeda convert.

EXTRACT 11: *THE SUN* ('RAMPAGE OF THE BLUE-EYED ASSASSIN: AL-QAEDA CONVERT', 23/07/11 – EDITION 2)

Ten were confirmed dead – with more feared to be victims – after
the maniac launched Europe's first Mumbai-style attack on a youth

camp on the tiny Norwegian island of Utøya. The gunman – described
as over 6ft, with blond hair and blue eyes – arrived on the island
by boat posing as a policeman. He spoke fluent Norwegian – raising
fears he was a homegrown Islamic convert.

In these two extracts, we see the pairing of categories that do not conventionally go
together. In other words, we have 'category-puzzles' (Silverman, 2001) in which 'Islam'
and 'Al-Qaeda' are paired with 'blond with blue eyes' and 'blue-eyed'; and 'terrorist'
has been replaced with 'gun maniac' and 'assassin'. The solution to the puzzle in both
reports is the further categories 'home-grown' and 'convert', which enable the 'blond
and blue eyed' perpetrator to remain tied to the category 'Al-Qaeda'.

   The next iteration of the story is the one that started to become 'the facts of the matter'; what 'really happened'. *Retrospectively*, as certainty solidified, the categories
within the standardised relational pairing 'victim–perpetrator' were tweaked and
revised: no longer 'West–Islam', but 'nutter–Norwegians'. We see this clearly by comparing edited selections from *The Sun*'s second and third editions of the same day's
newspaper.

EXTRACT 12: *THE SUN* ('STAND STRONG WITH NORWAY', 23/07/11, EDITION 2)

Carnage in a city centre. A massacre at an island youth rally.
Terrorism, the scourge of the West, brought slaughter yesterday
to the friendly and civilised streets of one of Europe's most
peaceful nations. The Sun and its readers grieve today with the
people of Norway, stunned by the assault on their capital Oslo
and the island of Utøya. How well we remember, from London's
7/7, the shock and misery when an ordinary summer's day turns
into a nightmare of smoke, flames and bodies in the street […]
The lessons for us are clear. Osama Bin Laden may be dead. But
the tentacles of al-Qaeda, and groups linked with it, spread
deep into the heart of Western nations […]

EXTRACT 13: *THE SUN* ('NORWAY'S PAIN', 23/07/11, EDITION 3)

Carnage in a city centre. A massacre at an island youth rally.
Terrorism brought slaughter yesterday to the friendly and
civilised streets of one of Europe's most peaceful nations.
The Sun and its readers grieve today with the people of Norway,
stunned by the assault on their capital Oslo and the island of

Utøya. How well we remember, from London's 7/7, the shock and
misery when an ordinary summer's day turns into a nightmare
of smoke, flames and bodies in the street […] But neither al-
Qaeda nor any other extremist group has exclusive rights to
murder and mayhem. The picture emerging in Norway last night
was of one blond-haired, blue-eyed man being behind the Oslo
bombing AND the island camp massacre. Acts of terror can be
an easy resort for any loner who believes their own personal
grievance against the state is justification for indiscriminate
violence. Take Timothy McVeigh, a US Army veteran whose warped
world view was all the reason he needed to kill 168 innocent
people in the Oklahoma bombing in 1995 […]

The editorial has some similarities, but, of course, is crucially different in the way
events are now categorised. First, consider the other events that 'Norway' is now
duplicatively organised with: it started out in the same family as 9/11 and 7/7 in
Editions 2 and 3, but is now in the new family of crimes of the type committed by
Timothy McVeigh in the USA. Second, the prospective categorisation of the perpetrator as an Islamist, part of a networked Al-Qaeda and targeting 'the West' as a whole,
becomes a 'loner' with 'personal grievances against the state' (Extract 13). In the next
two extracts, the connection between the perpetrator and Islam is broken:

EXTRACT 14: *NEWCASTLE EVENING CHRONICLE* (23/07/11)

NRK and other Norwegian media posted pictures of the blond,
blue-eyed Norwegian. Police said later that the suspect had
right-wing and anti-Muslim views, but the motive for the attacks
was unclear.

EXTRACT 15: *DAILY MAIL* 24/07/11

Media reports in Norway described Breivik as a 'loner', who
lived with his mother in a wealthy suburb of west Oslo, was
well-educated and enjoyed hunting.

Here, the retrospective categorisation work establishes a new victim–perpetrator pairing, with the perpetrator being named as 'Breivik' (Extract 15), which, of course, rapidly
spread across all news sources over 24 July. 'Home-grown convert' was replaced by
'right-wing' and 'anti-Muslim' (Extract 14); and a different narrative began to emerge,
one of the 'loner' killer, with various category-tied predicates including 'lived with his
mother' and 'enjoyed hunting' (Extract 15). As Watson (2009a: 86) notes, 'particulars

may subsequently appear which may occasion a redefinition (again maybe involving nuance and 'fine-tuning' rather than necessarily involving a radical re-casting)'. In our case, a 'radical recasting' was involved in reconstruction of the case, accounts of which consolidated around a sole, white, Norwegian perpetrator who was operating from an anti-Islamic, 'right-wing extremist' ideology. The final extracts are headlines from subsequent days' newspaper headlines:

EXTRACT 16: *SUNDAY MIRROR* (24/07/11)

THE LONE WOLF KILLER

EXTRACT 17: *DAILY MAIL* (26/07/11)

SMIRK OF THE MANIAC

EXTRACT 18: *DAILY MAIL* (26/07/11)

MIGRANT HATING MONSTER

EXTRACT 19: *THE SUN* (26/07/11)

MADMAN RANTS

EXTRACT 20: *DAILY STAR* (27/07/11)

PSYCHO NAZI'S LUXURY JAIL

A week after the initial event, the categories in play were refined further, away from the 'loner' committing a 'Timothy McVeigh' type of crime. Rather, Breivik was now simultaneously categorised in psychopathic terms ('lone wolf killer', 'maniac', 'monster', 'madman', 'psycho'), with a political flavour ('migrant-hating', 'Nazi') and with particular category-tied predicates and activities ('smirk', 'rant').

Overall, our data show the trajectory of rolling news around a particular international news event. Although this is a case study, we hope that we have shown how the practices used by speakers in Extracts 1–4 are resources in this process. We also know, from our wider analysis of rolling news (e.g. Oscar Pistorius, retrospectively categorised following the murder of his girlfriend), that this is a setting in which the *same practices* can be found doing the *same sorts of actions*, in the *same sorts of environments*, counter to the 'needle in the haystack' view of MCA.

Doing Membership Categorisation Analysis

In this chapter, we have attempted to do three things. First, we have illustrated an approach to Membership Categorisation Analysis (MCA) that focuses on sequential and categorial analysis and shows the way categories, and the resourcefulness of their inference-rich quality, can be used prospectively and retrospectively to proffer and solidify on-going accounts, states of affairs, event descriptions, and 'fact'. In addition to the analysis of different kinds of spoken and written interaction, we have also shown how the movement between description and categorisation functions to construct, constrain and produce accounts of 'what is happening' and 'what happened' in news reporting.

Second, we have tried to show Sacks's machinery of membership categorisation in practice. While one reads many descriptions of the terms of MCA, including the notions of 'inference-rich' and so on, these terms can seem complex and can also be used to justify the kinds of 'wild and promiscuous' analysis that Schegloff has criticised MCA for conducting. In contrast, we have shown how the inference-rich nature of categories is built into people's categorial practices. As noted earlier, it is not just that categories are, in theory and before empirical observation, 'inference rich', but that we can see that, and how, people treat categories *as* carrying inferential resources, in the design of their turns in which categorial formulations appear (Stokoe, 2012b). In other words, the inference-rich nature of categories is observable from the endogenous orientations of participants and is a resource for constructing accounts that can be reconstructed, contested, provisional, deniable – on their way to becoming solid, factual and beyond construction.

Third, we have shown how one can build MCA studies of the identification of practices from different sorts of large datasets. As Stokoe (2012b) has argued elsewhere, for MCA to survive as a method, in any way distinct from the more dominant conversation analysis, or as adding something to the analysis of social interaction, studies of practices that can be transferred across settings are required. Not only does such an approach provide an empirical base for other researchers, in the same way that CA has done, but it provides for the possibility of applying research findings to create impact for users and practitioners (Stokoe, 2013). Stokoe (2012b) has described a number of principles and steps for beginning and proceeding with a categorisation study, whether they start with an interest in a particular category in mind (e.g., 'nutter') or categorial phrase (e.g., 'it's human to get angry'; 'speaking as a parent'), or with a more inductive 'noticing' of a set of spoken or written interactional materials. The key is to collect data across different sorts of settings; including both interactional and textual materials. Data collection may be purposive (e.g. gathering together instances of particular categories in use because of an *a priori* interest in that category) or unmotivated (e.g. noticing a category's use and pursuing it within and across multiple discourse sites). Once collected and organised, analysis should look for evidence that, and how, recipients orient to categories, devices or inferences for the interactional consequences of a category's use; for co-occurring component features of categorial formulations; and for the way participants within and between turns build and resist categorisations. In this way, a 'categorial systematics' approach to MCA works with collections of instances of possible categorial phenomena gathered from different discourse contexts, with the aim of uncovering the systematic centrality of categories and categorial practices to action.

Note

1   As such, Garfinkel et al.'s (1981) study of how a particular group of scientists ended up making the optical 'discovery' of a pulsar offers a useful simile with which to understand this process of naming and labelling. For Garfinkel et al., the scientists' pulsar did not emerge as a 'pre-given fact', but rather developed as if a 'potter's object': in the same way that a shapeless piece of clay on a potter's wheel can only 'take shape' as it is worked upon and moulded into shape (as, say, a vase), then for Garfinkel et al.'s scientists working away in their laboratory, the 'first time through' sighting of the pulsar on an oscilloscope could only provide for a crude approximation of what 'the pulsar' was eventually to became. Indeed, as Garfinkel et al. went on to note, the pulsar's existence as 'a pulsar' could not be disentangled from the successive and sequential techniques that progressively made it observable, distinguishable, specifiable, and so on. Here, we want to suggest that in the same way that scientists turn to things like oscilloscopes during moments of investigation and discovery a similar sequential process is involved as people turn to categories during sequentially organised moments of naming and labelling: faced with the task of naming or labelling some hitherto un-named or un-labelled action, behaviour, person and so on, a 'first-time through' categorisation will often be contested, tweaked, rejected, accepted with caveats, and so on, as people interactively try to work out how to name or label some hitherto un-named or un-labelled action, behaviour, person, and so on.

4

Categorisation Work in the Courtroom

The 'Foundational' Character of Membership Categorisation Analysis

Christian Licoppe

Introduction

Conversation Analysis (CA) and Membership Categorisation Analysis (MCA) were simultaneously developed in the work of Harvey Sacks (Sacks, 1992), particularly in respect to his 'interest in the crafting of observation, description and replication' (Lynch, 1993: 232). We will eschew here a discussion of the current debate regarding CA and MCA (Schegloff, 2007a; Stokoe, 2012b; Stokoe and Attenborough, this volume). We will focus here on the idea that both may demonstrably work together in members' practices, for example in 'tying practices' (Watson, 1997a) or in the way conversationalists might 'turn categorical' in question/answer sequences (Stokoe, 2012b): sequence and categorisation are often interwoven within a 'categorical flow' providing for a layered texture of talk-in-interaction in which they are mutually elaborative in the production of social action (Fitzgerald and Housley, 2002). Some kinds of institutional talk have provided fecund sites for studying the use of MCA in conversation, such as police interrogations (Watson, 1983; Stokoe, 2010b), media debates (Cuff, 1993; Housley and Fitzgerald, 2007) or courtroom interaction (Drew and Atkinson, 1979; Matoesian, 2001). In such settings, in which participants debate or investigate varying or contested descriptions of activities, facts and situations, and in which the attributions of blame or responsibility are often salient concerns, categorisation practices are a powerful resource for sense making. Moreover, the use of MCA is usually embedded in extended question-answer (Q/A) sequences, which provide for a particular type of 'categorical flow'.

    The data I will present here comes from a similar setting, that is, the proceedings of a pre-parole judicial commission that hears long-term prison inmates in order to assess their dangerousness. What makes them especially interesting is the place MCA is made to take and what it is made to do in such hearings. I will analyse in some detail one particular extended question-answer (Q/A) sequence within the hearing, to show how the ability to do MCA, that is to commonsensically analyse the situation at hand in terms of relevant membership categories, may emerge as the very focus of the ongoing talk. MCA then appears both as a resource for the intelligibility of the talk-in-interaction and as the object of that talk. Moreover, sequence organisation and MCA appear to be so intricately interwoven that some questions may appear as category-relevant 'riddles' that need to be 'solved' by providing some adequate category in the next slot.

One core feature of MCA is its 'foundational' character. Sacks analysed MCA as a basic and generic sense-making activity and as a set of procedures which make certain features of stories intelligible to any member. While categories may have a decontextualised classificatory relevance, Sacks insisted that categories were constituted for the occasion, to be recognised (and expected to be recognised) by any participant in the course of the talk (Hester and Eglin, 1997a). To be operative, MCA has to function as some kind of *generic* machinery, providing intelligibility 'at a glance', for *any* member, that is, any competent conversationalist in the relevant language. When glossed upon, categorical relevancies appear 'obvious', commonsensical, like cultural clichés, etc., so that MCA has been described as 'culture in action' (Hester and Eglin, 1997a; Housley and Fitzgerald, 2009a): categories are the kind of things about which Harvey Sacks noted that 'members are so committed to their correctness, that if you undercut one, exactly what you've undercut is not clear. And one does not know exactly how we can continue talking' (Sacks, 1992: 25).

However, while members demonstrably display their orientation towards MCA as common sense, it is often somewhat indirectly, '*en passant*', as an integral part of orienting towards categorisation relevancies with respect to the practical business at hand. The data we discuss here displays a more direct, and therefore explicit, orientation towards categorisation work, which becomes the focus of the talk. So much so that the 'foundational character' of MCA is not only an analytic issue; it also becomes consequential within the course of the ongoing interaction. In a sequence oriented towards doing categorisation work, proving unable to do so undermines the possibility of convincingly 'doing being ordinary' (Sacks, 1984b), and makes the concerned party vulnerable to inferences that she is an incompetent 'member', as we will see in more detail below. The data we will discuss here displays a much more direct and explicit orientation towards MCA, so that the foundational character of MCA becomes consequential in the course of the interaction. Categorisation work becomes the focus of the talk, and, in such an environment, if one member can be understood as failing to do MCA competently in a question/answer sequence focused on the provision of categories and the elicitation of what such categories make relevant, that member becomes recognisable by all co-present participants (and not only the questioner) as an incompetent conversationalist, which may warrant further assessments regarding incompetence in other domains of life. Proving unable to do categorisation work when required is oriented-to as undermining the possibility of convincingly 'doing being ordinary' (Sacks, 1984b), and makes the concerned party vulnerable to inferences that she is an incompetent 'member', as we will see in more detail below. The combination of a Q/A sequential organisation and MCA will be retrospectively glossed by participants as a powerful, untaught but expert interactional resource for making medical and social incompetence actually 'perceptible' to any lay participant, a resource uniquely appropriate to the interactional resources and constraints of the judicial setting.

Moreover, as Sacks suggested above, common-sense expectations regarding the routine ability to do MCA in conversation makes MCA into an integral part of the kind of fundamental trust that makes interaction possible. It is the same kind of trust that is threatened and broken in 'breaching experiments', and which accounts for the violent emotional response the latter may elicit (Garfinkel, 1967). Indeed, in the data we analyse here, being in a position to watch that trust broken, in a protracted question/answer sequence focused on the (normally routine) provision of categories, their repeated unavailability occasions visible displays of emotion, with one participant (the inmate's counsel) even 'flooding out' of the interaction (Goffman, 1974) through nervous fits of laughter. A detailed analysis shows how such behaviour is noticed and treated by the participants as responsive to the questions being asked at the time: the latter repetitively request the provision of categories and the resolution of categorical 'riddles' emerging from the interplay of the Q/A sequential organisation and membership categorisation analysis. The observable failure to do MCA may thus provoke the kind of intense emotional feeling that characterises 'breaching experiments', in line with Sacks' notion that with the kind of foundational commitment to correctness which characterises our orientation towards MCA, categorisation trouble may go as far as preventing the very business of talking from going on as usual, in a very fundamental way.

Fieldwork and Data Collection

The judicial proceedings of the *Commission Pluridisciplinaire des Mesures de Sûreté* (COPMES) that are the object of this study are a recently established type of judicial hearing[1] for prisoners having committed serious crimes and having been sentenced to over fifteen years in prison. These hearings are held near the end of the prison term and aim to assess the potential dangerousness of the detainee, that is, the risk of the prisoner repeating the same kind of crime after their release. The committee (the COPMES) is composed of a professional judge, a representative of the prison administration, a psychiatrist, a psychologist, a lawyer from the local *barreau*, a representative of one of the victims' associations, and a representative of the police administration. The inmate's lawyer is invited to attend, but her/his presence is not mandatory, and in practice, in the hearings we attended, lawyers were present in just under half of the cases. The aim of the commission is to provide a collaborative and 'pluridisciplinary' assessment of the potential dangerousness of the prisoners. Its opinion is conveyed to a judge who then makes the final decision. Hearings typically last 20 to 30 minutes, and are followed by a 10 to 15 minute deliberation. The president usually gives the floor to each of the members in succession so that they may ask questions, and the talk that ensues takes the form of extended question/answer sequences. No particular legal text or administrative rule describes the way in which they are supposed to proceed and the management of the hearing is pretty much left to the discretion of the presiding judge.

Six commissions of this type were created in different courts of appeal in France. We worked with one of them, which meets one afternoon a month and hears two to four cases during that time, with inmates appearing from a special room in the prison through a video link. Within the framework of this study, we were allowed to attend and observe the whole proceedings and to record the hearing of the inmates, provided the data would only be used for scientific research and in a way which preserved the anonymity of the participants. This is why we do not provide or have changed places, names, and dates, and have restrained the data we exploit to segments in which the description of the facts of the case do not include recognisable particulars. In this chapter we will provide extracts from a particular case in which MCA played a crucial part which we want to examine. For the Q/A sequences, we use Conversation Analysis transcriptions. For better readability we chose to state the occupation and location of the speakers. Though we will not discuss it here, such a choice, which has some analytic implications (Watson, 1997a), is justified by the fact that participants orient to one another according to their occupation and their mandate within the commission, and also to topics and questions that are considered to be 'owned' (Sharrock, 1974) by a certain occupation and to be relevant to the domain of expertise which is bound to it.

The Emergence of Membership Categorisation Analysis (MCA) as the Object of a Q/A Sequence in a Judicial Setting

The Q/A sequence that interests us here is led by the psychiatrist who has been given the floor by the judge acting as a chair. The psychiatrist begins by asking the inmate to relate what happened with the victim. Then he reformulates the kind of sexual abuse

Figure 4.1 View of the videoconference screens in the courtroom (at the end of the question, Line 8). The left screen is the prison image, with, from left to right, a legal intern, the counsel and her client. The right screen is the control image from the courtroom, with, from left to right, the representative of the victims' associations, the representative of the prefect of police, and the psychiatrist, who has been given the floor and who is currently asking questions.

committed against the victim (we changed all names in this part for reasons of anonymity) and elicits the agreement of the defendant with his description of the latter's past criminal actions. At this point, the psychiatrist initiates a new topic with a question requesting the age of the victim at the time of the events (Extract 1, Line 15 below).

EXTRACT 1: THE EMERGENCE OF CATEGORY-BASED LINE OF QUESTIONING

'Psy' is the psychiatrist, 'I' the inmate, 'C' the inmate's counsel, 'Pen' the representative of the penitentiary administration, 'Pf' the policeman who represents the regional prefect, 'V' the representative of the victims' association. Appended to these identities throughout the transcript is either 'C' or 'P' tags to index that they are either present in the courtroom or in the prison.

```
1     Psy (C)    eu::: vous lui faites une fellation/ c'est ça/
                 er    you perform fellatio on him is that right
2         I(P)   après\
                 after
3     Psy (C)    mh\
4     Psy (C)    vous lui demandez de faire une fellation/*
5                you ask him to perform fellatio
6         I(P)                                              *((nods))
7     Psy (C)    il vous fait une fellation/ (.) et après vous le
                 he performs fellatio on you       and after you
8                sodomisez
                 sodomize him
9         I(P)   oui\
                 yes
10               (1.0)
11      Psy(C)    c'est bien ça ?
                  is that right?
12        I(P)    oui
                  yes
13      Psy(C)    d'accord\
                  okay
14                0.5)
15      Psy(C)    quel ad- quel âge il avait/ Alexandre\
                  how o- how old was he/ Alexandre
16                (0.7)
17                quel âge il a\ enfin (.) quel âge il avait à ce
                  how old is he\  well. how old was he at
18                moment-là
                  the time
19                (1.0)
20        I(P)    euh huit ans/ (..) °ouais°
                  er eight years old/ (..) yeah
21                (0.5)
```

```
22      Psy(C)      *vous trouvez ça normal de faire ça/
23                   do you find it normal to do that/
24                  *((straightens upper body and clasps hands, Fig. 2)
25          I(P)    non\
                     no\
26                  (1.0)
27      Psy(C)      qu'est-ce qui est anormal/ (.) là-dedans\
                     what is abnormal/ (.) in that\
28                  (8.0)
```

(a)   (b)   (C)

Figure 4.2 At the start of the question in Line 22 the psychiatrist has his hands flat on the desk (Figure 4.2a). While uttering 'normal' he straightens up and raises his hands, which he then clasps (Figure 4.2b). He then leans slightly forward with his crossed fingers resting on the desk, while his torso remains straighter than at the start of the question (Figure 4.2c).

The first part of the sequence (Lines 1–13) is focused on a series of polar questions in which the psychiatrist formulates the actions of the inmate with respect to the victim and elicits their ratification by the inmate. With the agreement token at Line 13, the psychiatrist signals the end of that line of questioning, and initiates another question regarding the age of the victim (Line 15), which he self-repairs (Lines 17–18), and which is answered (Line 20). The question takes the form of an information query, projecting a single, discrete item of information as an answer (the age), which is provided in the answer Line 20. All of these questions check information about which the psychiatrist and the inmate are both knowledgeable, so there is no epistemic gradient involved (Heritage, 2012). However, the questions navigate a complex epistemic landscape, particularly regarding the facts of the case, the knowledge of which is available through the written file in the case of the psychiatrist, and through his own experience in the case of the defendant. These questions may be heard as related to B-events (Labov and Fanshel, 1977), as perhaps evidenced in the psychiatrist's repair of his initial question in Line 4 following an ambiguous response of the inmate (Line 3).

The following question ('do you find it normal to do that', Line 22) marks a shift with the previous questions for: (a) it seems to change the topic, by asking for a confirmation not of the facts, but of the inmate's moral assessment of them; (b) it is designed as a polar question with the use of an interrogative morphosyntax (Stivers and Rossano, 2010) which makes relevant a K-/K+ epistemic gradient, since the design of the question asks explicitly for the recipient's current view, regarding which the questioner is not knowledgeable (it is not part of the file); and (c) it is uttered with a repositioning and straightening of the body and the hands, as if the projected answer should be listened to and considered from a greater distance. However, it is also tied to the previous questions through several devices – first, through the use of the indexical pronoun '*ça* (that)', which anaphorically refers to what has been said earlier on; and second, through the question about the normality of 'that', which calls for a common-sense assessment of some actions. It makes relevant a kind of category-based reasoning. By contiguity, the conduct to be assessed is understandable as the actions of the defendant with respect to the victim (the last piece of 'assessable' conduct topicalised in the talk). This transforms what came in between, i.e. the age of the victim, as a potential resource for the assessment. It also frames the preceding questions as embedded in a kind of contrastive structure. Contrasts have been shown to be an important sequential device in adversarial courtroom questioning (Drew, 1990; Matoesian, 2001) operating at the intersection of grammar and sequences (with conjunction devices such as 'but' in initial position). Here, it is the question in Line 22 which makes the previous turns hearable as incorporating a contrast, for it brings into normative tension the past conduct of the recipient and the age of the victim. This shows that 'contrasts' may be produced as the interplay of categorisation and sequence. Contrasts can then be seen as emergent configurations within the 'categorical flow'.

This question strongly projects a negative answer, both because of its design as a polar question, and because of the setting (the recipient is in prison precisely for such actions). Moreover, it is also hearable as involving some blame, since what is referred to through the indexical 'that' at the end of the utterance are actions of the recipient which have already been judged and sanctioned as criminal. However, by providing resources for common-sense reasoning about these facts (as distinct from legal/judicial qualifications of the facts), the question, and to some extent the repositioning of the questioner's body, also project an account or further elaboration as a relevant next, as well as possible expansions: it can be described as a 'query' (Boden, 1994: 122ff.). In that respect, the recipient produces a negative and type-conforming answer (Raymond, 2003), which also appears minimal. The psychiatrist seems to orient to that, for he reformulates/repairs the design of his question, to utter an open 'wh-question' which overtly aims at eliciting the defendant's view (Line 25). The repaired question's design assumes less, in line with the idea that speakers should ask for the smallest increment that they think they need and then escalate towards less assuming or presupposing questions in case their initial informational stance proves inadequate (Levinson, 2012). A consequence of that is that the repaired question is now almost devoid of the accusation which was conveyed by the previous question.

It is common in this setting for the psychiatrist to try to elicit the inmate's current view of his past crimes, to get a sense of how he has now come to terms with them. Answers to these questions usually constitute potent arguments to support later claims in the final deliberation regarding the recipient's potential dangerousness or lack thereof. What is unusual here is that instead of being asked straightforwardly, the question is prefaced by a contrast involving the past actions of the recipient, and the age of the victim. It is followed by a long silence (Line 26) and a partial repeat of the question, followed by a term of address which functions as an intensifier (Line 27, below), and displays the commitment of the psychiatrist towards eliciting an answer to that particular question. At the end of the question he gazes down, and after a two second pause, he gazes up, producing a 'display of recipiency' (Heath, 1986) which eventually elicits an answer from the inmate (Line 31).

EXTRACT 2 (CONTINUED FROM EXTRACT 1)

```
27.   Psy(C)   qu'est-ce qui est anormal/ monsieur
               what is abnormal/ monsieur
28.   Psy(C)   ((gazes down))
29.            (2.0)
30.   Psy(C)   ((gazes up towards screen))
31.     I(P)   ben qu'est-ce que j'ai fait
               bah what I did
32.   Psy(C)   PARDON/
               PARDON/
```

Figure 4.3 The repair of Line 32 is uttered with a much louder voice, and with the psychiatrist bending forward and raising his eyebrows.

```
33.   I(P)     d'avoir fait ce que j'ai fait
               to have done what I did
34.              (0.5)
35.   Psy(C)   oui mais ça on est d'accord/ on savait bien que
               yes but we agree about that/ we knew well that
```

(a)   (b)   (C)

Figure 4.4 (a) The psychiatrist recoils as he produces his agreement + disagreement turn in Line 35; (b) he opens and closes his arms several times on 'on est d'accord'; (c) he joins his hands on 'on savait bien'.

```
36.              que que: (.) *mais qu'est-ce qui est anormal/ euh:
                 that that (.) but what is abnormal/  e:r
37.                           *((joins his hands in front of him))
38.              (5.0)
39.   Psy(C)     d'avoir fait ce que vous avez fait mais avec une
                 to have done what you did but with
40.              personne particulière (..) qu'est-ce qu'elle a
                     a particular person      what is
```

(a)   (b)

Figure 4.5 (a) During the turn unit Lines 39–40 ('mais avec une personne particulière'), the psychiatrist joins his hands so that they form an angle, and brings them close to the desk several times, as if he were pointing to something which was available 'just there'. (b) When he asks the question Lines 40–41 he clasps his hands together.

```
41.   Psy (C)    de particulier cette personne/
                 particular about this person/
42.              (6.0)
```

The answer Line 31, 'bah what I did', is potentially problematic, since it just repeats what the question asked and does not involve what could be perceived as some elaboration on the part of the participant. It may be viewed as a 'transformative answer' which resists the question's agenda (Stivers and Hayashi, 2010) and which might index either the recipient's unwillingness or inability to answer. It is marked as highly troublesome by the psychiatrist, who initiates a repair with an emphatic tone (Line 32), uttered while raising his eyebrows and bending forward as if he were not sure of what he was hearing (Figure 4.3). In spite of all this embodied highlighting of the repair, the recipient produces an almost exact, grammatically corrected repeat of his initial answer (Line 33). He orients towards the repair as signalling only potential hearing problems (which projects repeating), or perhaps grammatical issues (which projects correcting).

This is received by the psychiatrist with an initial token of agreement followed by a negative assessment, which is a way to accomplish a dispreferred, disaffiliative answer (Pomerantz, 1984), here based on an assessment of what is already well known (Lines 35–36). In this setting, the hand gesture in Figure 4.4b is intelligible as the movement of getting something which is there to pass, to move on. Conversely, such an understanding of the hand gesture conveys a sense that some other answer is expected, towards which 'moving on' is relevant, so that it provides a setting in which the repeat of the question 'what is abnormal' may be heard as inviting another answer. A long pause ensues, after which the psychiatrist self-selects again: he produces a repeat of the inmate's answer in initial position, which produces parallelism and ties his turn to that earlier answer, and then utters a contrastive turn construction unit (through the initial 'but'), which makes relevant some undetermined category of which the recipient is an incumbent ('but with a particular person'), before asking specifically for that category (Lines 40–1). This reformulation of the question makes explicit a category-based answer to the initial question of the psychiatrist ('what is abnormal in this'). It embeds a category-based practical reasoning that was until then a potentiality in the question itself. If the right age-related category is found, then the abnormality of the inmate's past actions will appear, for this kind of action is 'abnormal' when it involves an incumbent of that category. This prospectively frames that relevant answers should provide a category for the victim and that the category provided should make the past actions of the inmate appear 'abnormal' in the light of such category-based practical reasoning.

Such category-based practical reasoning is embedded in the sequential organisation of the question/answer sequence through the interplay of the presupposed contrast and the category-targeted final question. Producing an acceptable answer in the next slot amounts to a ratification of the category-based reasoning embedded in the question (which was initially made relevant through a question/answer sequence). Categorical reasoning and sequence organisation are particularly deeply intertwined here (Watson, 1997a). Moreover, when the psychiatrist refers to the category in the contrastive turn construction unit (TCU), he produces a repetitive hand gesture aiming at a spot on the table. The gesture points to something which might be there, and might be perceptively and jointly available to the speaker and the recipient. It iconically constitutes the object of the question that follows as something readily accessible, with respect to which everybody is expected to be 'K+', in line with Sacks's idea of MCA as common-sense practical reasoning or 'culture-in-action' (Hester and Eglin, 1997a). It appears, on the part of the psychiatrist, as a way for him to 'simplify' the work the recipient has to do to answer his questions and displays his orientation towards the recipient's inability to answer the previous questions, rather than his unwillingness to do so. The reliance on MCA as a common-sense resource on the basis of which an answer is expected, and the orientation of the sequence towards the inability of the recipient to answer, are mutually elaborative.

The 'Pursuing' of a Category and the Elicitation of Displays of Emotion

After a significant pause, the inmate eventually answers (Extract 3).

EXTRACT 3 (CONTINUED FROM EXTRACT 2)

```
43.   Pen(C)  ((heavy exhalation))
44.     I(P)  c'est qu'elle habite à côté de chez moi/
              it's that he lives near my place/
45.           (2.0)
46.     C(P)  ((pinches lips, smiles, rises her eyebrows))
47.   Psy(C)  *ah oui/
              ah yes/
48.           * ((turns the head away))
```

Figure 4.6 The psychiatrist turns his head and looks away while uttering his answer, Line 48, and maintains this posture during the following silence, Line 50.

```
49.           (1.5) ((Pf(C) turns towards V(C)and they exchange
                     glances))
50.   Psy(C)  *vous avez eu d'autres relations sexuelles hein/
              you have had other sexual relationships uh/
51.           * ((gazes towards screen))
```

Figure 4.7 The psychiatrist turns towards the screen as he utters his new question, Lines 51–52.

```
52.    Psy(C)    je crois (.) en dehors d'enfants
                 I think       besides children
```

It is type-conforming in the sense of providing a categorisation ('he lives near my place'). It is, however, treated as problematic by the psychiatrist: he replies with a token of agreement, preceded with 'ah' in initial position (Line 47). This 'ah' suggests that the speaker has a different view on the matter, a bit like an initial 'oh' might work in English (Heritage, 2002), while the agreement token may address the fact that the answer is type-conforming. This is highlighted by the psychiatrist's change of body posture. The psychiatrist breaks away from mutual gaze and turns his head away as he answers, and he maintains this position during the following silence, giving the impression that he is considering the matter (Figure 4.6). Other participants also provide signs of treating the answer as particularly noticeable. The defendant's counsel (not shown) raises her eyebrows, while the representative of the prefect turns towards his right (as visible in Figure 4.7) in order to exchange marked glances with his neighbour. Finally, the psychiatrist self-selects to ask a new question about the sexual relationships of the recipient with his adult partner (Lines 50–2). It seems to address a different matter, both lexically (through the reference to '*other*' relationships '*besides* children') and categorically, for the question does not have an obvious immediate and direct bearing on the abnormality of the inmate's past actions. The psychiatrist even provides one of the possible categories which would have resolved the previous matter in a kind of collateral manner ('children'). Sequentially, the psychiatrist's apparent change of tack seems retrospectively to leave the previous matter somewhat 'hanging'. While a category has been provided and 'received', its relevance with respect to the category-based abnormality of the inmate's past actions has not been acknowledged in any way, and the inmate's answer has even been answered in a way that shows that it is deemed problematic by several participants.

After a few questions focused on eliciting the age of his previous girlfriend, the psychiatrist utters a wh-question asking for the difference between the girlfriend and the victim (Extract 4, Lines 1–2 below).

EXTRACT 4: 'FLOODING OUT'

```
1  Psy(C)  c'est quoi la différence entre Marie-Jeanne
              what is the difference between Marie-Jeanne
2          et Alexandre/
           and Alexandre/
3             (3.0)
4  I(P)   j'saurais pas vous dire (.) (inc) quoi
           I wouldn't be able to tell you
5          j'sais pas\
           I don't know
6          (3.0)
7  I(P)   (XX[X)
8  Psy(C)     [pour essayer de trouver quand même des
                 to try to find at least some
```

```
 9              différences/
10              differences
11              (2.0)
12  Psy(C)      déjà Marie-Jeanne Furet elle est quoi comme sexe/
                to begin with what is Marie-Jeanne Furet's gender/
13              (2.0)
14    I(P)      féminin
                female
15              (1.0)
16  Psy(C)      d'accord\        (.) et l- Alexandre/
                okay and th- Alexandre
17              (2.0)
18    I(P)      masculin
                male
19  Psy(C)      °d'accord° (.) ça en fait déjà une différence/
                °okay° (.) it already makes one difference
20                   (2.0)
21  Psy(C)      non ?
                no/
22    I(P)      oui
                yes
23  Psy(C)      vous êtes capable de me trouver une autre
                are you able to find me another
24              différence/
                difference
25   C(P)       ((glances briefly at her client))
26              (7.0)
27    I(P)      a::h d'un côté c'est une femme/ (1.5) c'est une
                a::h on the one side she's a woman   she's a
28              femme (.) un homme c'est un homme
                woman      a man is a man
29   C(P)       ((smiles and starts to laugh))
```

Figure 4.8 The counsel starts to laugh at the answer of her client (Lines 28–9), while the psychiatrist looks away until the start of his question at Line 33.

```
30    Psy(C)    oui d'accord (.) mais une autre différence
                yes okay          but   another *difference
31              *  (2.0)
32    C(P)      *((lowers her head while laughing))
33                                        *((raises her
34              head laughing and hides her mouth with her hand))
```

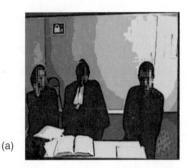 

(a)   (b)

Figure 4.9 (a) The counsel laughs as the psychiatrist agrees, Line 30, and disengages partly by lowering her head and then (b) by raising it again but hiding her mouth with her hand when the psychiatrist utters the second TCU in Line 30.

```
35    Psy(C)    c- c'était/ euh avec Marie-Jeanne c'est normal
36              i-it was    er with Marie-Jeanne it's normal
37              d'avoir des relations sexuelles/
                to have sexual relationships/
38    C(P)      ((has a fit of more intense laughter))
39              (1.0)
40    I(P)      ah oui
                ah yes
41    C(P)      ((turns towards intern who starts laughing))
42    Psy(C)    hein/
                uh
43    I(P)      ((glances briefly towards counsel))
```

  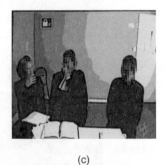

(a)   (b)   (c)

Figure 4.10 (a) Still hiding her mouth, the counsel has a more intense fit of laughter (Line 38). (b) She turns towards the intern, who begins to reciprocate with a large smile (Line 41). (c) The inmate briefly glances at the pair (Line 43).

```
44    Psy(C) je je *fais (.) * l'avocate a l'air de:
              I   I am *making (.)  the counsel looks like\
45                       *((points towards screen))
46                             *((turns head towards president))
```

(a)   (b)

Figure 4.11 (a) the psychiatrist points to the screen while starting his noticing, Line 44, and (b) turns his head towards the president while moving to a third person noticing.

```
47    Pso(C)    oui (.)  (°oui°)
                yes       yes
48    Psy(C)    [de de:
                like like
```

Asking for the difference between the girlfriend and victim makes salient an agenda which might account retrospectively for the previous line of questioning about the age of the girlfriend: it makes the categorisation of the girlfriend, particularly with respect to her age, a relevant issue with respect to the pursuit of an adequate category for the victim, which was left noticeably open before (Extract 2, Lines 1–2). The question presupposes a categorical contrast between her and the victim, embedded in some particular membership categorisation device (MCD). Instead of pursuing an isolated category for the victim, the question appears to be looking for the kind of relevant categorisation device, the existence of which it presupposes. This shift is made possible by the particular organisation of categories and activities here. If the recipient were able to find an age-related category for the girlfriend, then a categorisation of the victim would become salient and available on the basis of the membership categorisation device the question is hinting at.

The psychiatrist is witnessably performing some specific work to redesign his questions and their categorical foundations so as to enable the recipient to provide relevant answers. Following the recipient's declared inability to provide an answer and find a relevant categorical contrast (Lines 4–5) he introduces from his own initiative a particular MCD (i.e. gender) in which the girlfriend and the victim are the incumbents of contrasting categories. The gender MCD is posited as an exemplar of what he is looking for through the initial TCU in Line 8, 'to try to find at least some differences', framing what is to come next as one step in a larger pursuit, and it is followed by a narrow-focused wh-question overtly querying the gender of the girlfriend (Line 12).

It is initiated with the conjunction 'déjà', which marks the provision of the category it aims for as one step in a larger pursuit. The psychiatrist acknowledges the answer with a positive evaluation and follows up with a similar question about the victim's gender (Line 16), getting a type-conforming answer (Line 18), to which he also responds with an evaluation in third position (Line 19). The sequential organisation displays here the ternary pattern of Initiation-Response and Evaluation (IRE) characteristic of pedagogical environments (McHoul, 1978; Mehan, 1979). It reinforces even more the authoritative epistemic status of the questioner while lowering that of the answerer, and it makes more salient the orientation of the questions' recipient design towards facilitating the production of adequate answers by the recipient. The interweaving of sequence organisation and MCA within a particular 'categorical flow' is particularly apparent in the way the category-based reasoning embedded in the psychiatrist's question-based pursuit of some reasons why the past conduct of the inmate was abnormal is made to sound like a category-based 'riddle', with the psychiatrist knowing its solution (a point enacted through the IRE sequence organisation) and trying to get the inmate to solve it through questions that are designed and sequentially positioned as 'hints', such as the one in Lines 8–12.

Finally, the psychiatrist provides a declarative polar question ('are you able to find another difference for me?' (Line 23) by which he makes relevant the elicitation of another difference, that is, another MCD. The question does two different things: (a) it frames the preceding sequence as a template for the kind of categorical work that is expected (another aspect of the pedagogical feel the sequence has now been endowed with); and (b) it makes it even more obvious that the main focus of the question is the question of the recipient's ability to answer, rather than his unwillingness to do so. The answer is type conforming but reformulates the previous gender difference (Lines 26–7). It is made noticeable by the laugh of the counsel (Figure 4.8) and by the fact that the psychiatrist acknowledges it, but instead of positively assessing the answer (which would have been the expected form of agreement in an IRE sequential environment), he provides another question initiated with a 'but' which displays a disaffiliative stance with respect to the preceding answer. The sequence is hearable at this stage as a protracted effort on the part of the psychiatrist to have the recipient achieve common-sense categorisation work related to the victim, in a way in which the answers in themselves matter less than the kind of interactional competencies they might display.

During the pause which ensues the counsel starts to laugh again (Extract 2, Line 30). This is a step up with respect to earlier occasional smiles and a brief laugh (Figure 4.8). The laugh is more continuous than before. Moreover, she breaks eye contact and lowers her head, and then raises her head while covering her mouth and her laugh with her hand. This embodied behaviour displays her orienting towards her laugh as being more intense and requiring her to disengage partly from the public, mutual visual space of the video communication (Lines 32–34; Figure 4.9). The psychiatrist reformulates his question as a yes/no question about whether it was normal for the inmate to have a relationship with his girlfriend, which might be a first step towards the formulation of a membership categorisation device accounting for the normalcy/abnormality of sexual activities with her as opposed to the victim. The format of the question combines with its categorical implications to strongly project a positive answer. After a two-second pause, the psychiatrist produces a negative question tag, 'no?', giving the question a kind of interro-negative twist which makes it even more assertive (Heritage, 2002) and which projects even more strongly a positive answer and displays the commitment of the psychiatrist to elicit an account from the inmate. The latter provides the expected agreement after a one-second pause, preceded by a 'change of state token' (Line 40). However, in between, the counsel has a kind of hiccup, marking a more intense fit of laughter (Figure 4.10(a)). The positioning of this hiccup, just after the psychiatrist's question, provides for a possible sequential reading, that is that her laughter, or more precisely the intensification of her laughter, might be responsive in part to the previous question, and we will see later that the psychiatrist orients towards such an interpretation.

With this intensification of her laughter she turns slightly towards her intern, and seems to exchange a few brief, possibly whispered words with her, while still hiding her mouth. The intern responds by smiling and beginning to laugh with her (Figure 4.10 (a–c)). The psychiatrist provides an isolated 'uh' with a rising end-tone, which is not followed by a next question (Line 42). This suggests he might be orienting towards what is going on with the counsel as somehow blocking his production of another turn, though this is only a gloss. At this juncture the inmate turns for the first time in the sequence towards the counsel (Line 43), displaying an orientation towards what is occurring beside him. This sequence provides a setting for the psychiatrist to start a first-person noticing, by pointing at the screen (Line 44). The noticing is left unfinished, and he repairs this noticing by reformulating at the third person while now looking at the judge, engaging him into the noticed event. His reformulated noticing (that is also left unfinished) has a slightly blaming undertone, for it notices something in a way that both performs what is being noticed as causing a break in the current interaction frame, and as something troublesome enough to be overtly brought to the judge's attention, who is thus made relevant in his role as chair. As shown in the continuation of the extract below, the counsel orients towards the blame implication with an apologetic and silent hand gesture, which marks her as laughing too much to answer (Line 50 and Figure 4.12(a)), an apology which the psychiatrist acknowledges both verbally (Line 52) and with a reciprocal hand gesture (Figure 4.12(b)).

EXTRACT 5 (CONTINUED FROM EXTRACT 4)

```
49      C(P)      [((apologizing hand gesture))
50                    (.)
51      Psy(C)    *non je vous en prie\(.)  *eu:
                  no don't mention it       *e:r
52      Psy(C)    *((acquiescing hand gesture))
53        C(P)                      *((apologizing gesture))
```

(a)   (b)

Figure 4.12 (a) The counsel's apologetic hand gesture (Line 50) and (b) the psychiatrist's reciprocal gesture while he verbally acknowledges the apology (Lines 52–3).

```
54    Psy(C)    c'est c'est [normal d'avoir
                it's  it's  [normal to have
55    Pdt(C)               [(inc) les les   questions/
                                  the the questions
56                         (.)
57    Pdt(C)    *pardon excusez-moi
                 sorry forgive me
58    Psy(C)    *((looks at president))
59     C(P)     ((goes on laughing))
60    Pdt(C)    mais les questions sont sérieuses hein/
                but the questions are serious uh
61              chuis désolé °hein°
                I'm sorry uh
62     C(P)     oui oui non mais (.) chuis désolée aussi/
                yes yes no but      I'm sorry too
63              (.) ya une chose que: je ne: (.) j'ai du
                there's something that I don't  I have
64              mal à contrôler\ ex[cusez-moi
65              difficulties controlling   forgive me
66              (.)
67    Psy(C)    [non mais pas de souci  enfi:n je[::
                no but no problem       well I
68    Pdt       [pas de problème\               [no problem\
69    Psy(C)    mais c'est quand il me semble important
                but it is still it seems important to me
70              quand même de de: poser ce type de question
                still to to ask this type de question
71     C(P)     tout à fait hein/ chuis d'accord avec vous
72              absolutely uh      I agree with you
73              hein/ (.) [bien sûr
74              uh/ (.) of course
75    Psy(C)              [merci beaucoup maître\
76                         thank you very much counsel
77              ((laughs on the court side))
```

The counsel provides another apologetic hand gesture (Line 54) and the psychiatrist begins a justification (Line 55). At that point, and though the matter seems to be moving towards a resolution, the presiding judge, who is legally responsible for what happens in the commission, intervenes with a request for talking (Line 59) and responds to the noticing which was addressed to him by providing another account justifying the seriousness of the ongoing questions. Such an account makes their possibly perceivable levity a possible cause of the counsel's noticeable conduct, and works by reasserting the legitimacy of the questions being asked (Lines 61–2). The counsel responds with a new apology and produces an account of her conduct as due to her inability to control herself (Lines 63–4). She thus recognises the impropriety of her behaviour and frames it as a kind of 'flooding out' of the situation through uncontrollable laughter (Goffman, 1974). The psychiatrist then takes the turn to produce his own justification of his line of questioning ('it seems important to me to ask this type of question', Lines 70–1) to which she agrees somewhat emphatically (Lines 72–4), with an initial 'extreme case formulation' (Pomerantz, 1986) of agreement followed by another turn construction unit marking strong agreement without reservation. Only then does the psychiatrist resume his line of questioning (continued below).

EXTRACT 6 (CONTINUED FROM EXTRACT 5)

```
78      Psy(C)     ((raises his head towards the screen))
79      Psy(C)     je continue alors
80                 I'll go on then
81                 (0.5)
82      Psy(C)     euh:: excusez- moi (.) monsieur\  (.)
                   er      excuse me           sir
83                 *j'essaie de vous (.) de vous faire
                    I'm trying to      to get you to
84       C(P)      *((dries her eyes))
85      Psy(C)     comprendre des différences quand mê:me
                   understand some differences at least
86                 entre: cette personne/ cette dame (.)
                   between this person      this lady
87                 avec qui vous avez eu de:s rapports
                   with whom you've had sexual intercourse
88                 * sexuels/ (0.5) mais qui sont interdits
89                           but which is forbidden
89       C(P)      *((laughs behind her hand))
90      Psy(C)     (.) pourquoi sont-ils interdits/
                       why is it forbidden
91                 (6.0)
92       C(P)      ((looks towards P))
93      Psy(C)     pourquoi/ c'est permis avec eu:: Marie-
                   why is it allowed with er Marie-Jeanne
94                 Jeanne/ pourquoi c'est pas permis (.)
95                 why isn't it allowed
```

```
96                    Avec Alexandre/
                      With Alexandre
97                    (5.0)
98      Psy(C)        vous ne le savez pas\
                      you don't know
99                    (0.5)
100     I(P)          ((nods with a slight smile))
```

The psychiatrist achieves resumption with an explicit performative gloss, which retro-spectively treats what has just occurred as a (finished) interruption ('I'll go on then', Line 81), and he does so with a new question. The latter is prefaced with an overt formulation of what he had been doing with his questions (a gloss which resonates with his prior account on the importance of asking this type of question), stressing his pedagogical strategy ('I am trying to get you to understand'), reformulating his search of an MCD ('some differences at least between this person this lady with whom you've had sexual intercourse …') which would account for the forbidden charac-ter of the recipient's past actions (Lines 83–9). All this is being done while the counsel is visibly trying to regain her composure. Finally, the psychia-trist ends his account with a direct why-question about the forbidden character of the defendant's actions (Line 91). After a pause of several seconds, during which no answer is given, the psychiatrist reformulates the question in a way that highlights the contrast between activities allowed with one person and forbidden with another, and projects the provision of a membership categorisation device as a way to explain that difference (Lines 94–7). The reformulated question achieves the resumption of the line of questioning (or a similar contrastive question) for it would have perfectly fitted the sequence after Line 40, at the moment at which the interruption was made relevant. The account given by the psychiatrist in this resumption is a formulation in the initial ethnomethodological sense (Garfinkel and Sacks, 1970). It glosses what had been going on in the talk as oriented towards doing categorisation work in itself, for pedagogical purposes, and not just the pursuit of particular membership categories or membership categorisation devices. However, the interruption sequence suggests that such categorisation work is not straightforward. After the psychiatrist notices the laughing fit of the counsel, who apologises, it is remarkable that neither he nor the president questions the propriety of her conduct but rather orients to it as if it were a plausible occurrence in such circumstances. Both he and the presiding judge find it relevant at that stage to provide justifications for the questions being asked, and therefore the kind of categorisation work being done, and this with some insist-ence: the presiding judge reminds the counsel that these are 'serious questions' and the psychiatrist finds it necessary to add that it is 'important to ask this type of question'. The design of these accounts makes the counsel's fits of laughter as responsive to and accountable with respect to the kind of questions that were being asked at the time. What warrants such a member's ascription? The fact that, since MCA is considered to be a shared common-sense bundle of conversational practices, available and expected to be available to members at all times, relevant categories are in a sense 'there' to be picked up by any relevant participant, as indicated for instance by the pointing gesture of the psychiatrist in Figure 4.5(a). Such a taken-for-grantedness is crucial to MCA. Evidently 'pursuing' categories that are not provided and doing categorisation work per se therefore appear as a special, marked, kind of behaviour. When some event (here the counsel's conduct and its noticing by the psychiatrist) suggests that there might be some trouble in the way the categorisation work is going, buttressing it with justifications claiming that these are 'serious questions' and that 'it is important to ask this type of question' become relevant next actions.

Moreover, such justifications, being thus positioned just after the treatment of the counsel's nervous fit of laughter as threatening the ongoing participation frame, can also be heard as providing a potential account for her 'flooding out'. How might asking 'this type of question' explain such a visible loss of control, here and then? Such conduct, and this sequence in general, suggests that MCA is not common-sense practical reasoning in just a loose sense but in a way that is foundational to the organisation of the interaction, so that far-ranging inferences may be made of the inability or the unwillingness to accomplish MCA. A sequence in which MCA is pursued almost relentlessly through questions and in which the recipient fails consistently and repeatedly, makes this foundational taken-for-grantedness of MCA for other co-participants problematic. In a way somewhat parallel to Garfinkel's 'breaching experiments' (Garfinkel, 1967; Heritage, 1984), such a moment may be experienced as a 'breaching situation' which disrupts deep-seated and MCA-related expectations about the local moral order of interaction. Therefore, the surge of negative affects and emotions, up to the point of a loss of control (getting into a fit of rage was a feature of members' responses to Garfinkel's initial breaching experiments) and 'flooding out' of the interaction in some way or other (we also observed an inmate getting into a fit of rage in another problematic categorisation sequence not discussed here) become plausible responses. It is such a foundational taken-for-grantedness associated with membership categorisation analysis that is revealed here in the embodied conduct of the co-participants, which, along with the counsel's loss of control, displays their experience of 'lengthy' and protracted categorical pursuit as a moving and painful one. It is the problematic character of the sequence as a breaching of the 'local categorical order' which accounts for such potential 'flooding out' in terms of the kind of categorical pursuit that was the point of the interaction at the time, and to which the members seem to orient when they respond by defending the legitimacy of their questions and such a pursuit.

From the Inability to 'Do MCA' in a Q/A Setting to the Ascription of Mental Retardation

After a brief pause, the psychiatrist re-designs his question so as to explicitly introduce the question of the relevance of age as a categorisation factor, with an interro-negative question which strongly projects assent (Lines 101–102, below).

EXTRACT 7 (CONTINUED FROM EXTRACT 6)

```
101.  Psy(C)  la question de l'âge/ vous ne croyez pas/ que
              the age issue        you don't think it is
102.          important/
              important
103.   I(P)   si
              yes
104.  Psy(C)   alors (.) qu'est-ce qui est important/ (.)
               so        what is important
105.           pourquoi j- je souligne ça/
               why am I highlighting this
106.           (2.5)
107.   I(P)   *si quelqu'un est majeur ou pas
              if someone is of age or not
108.          * ((frowns))
109.  Psy(C)  majeur ça veut dire quoi/
              what does it mean to be of age?
110.          (0.5)
111.   I(P)   ben plus de dix-huit ans/
              well over eighteen
112.          (1.0)
113.  Psy(C)  d'accord/
              okay
114.          (3.0)
115.   I(C)   (inc)
116.  Psy(C)  =hein/ >allez-y allez-y< dites-moi/
              uh      go ahead go ahead tell me
117.          (1.0)
118.   I(P)   (inc) maintenant c'est vingt-et-un ans\
              now it's twenty one
119.          (2.0)
120.          ((inaudible responsive comments in the court))

121.  Psy(C)  non (.) c'est c'est dix-huit ans/ 'fin jusqu'à
              no       it's it's eighteen         that is until
122.           preuve du contraire/
               there is evidence to the contrary
123.          (1.0)
```

After obtaining a type-conforming but minimal assent, the psychiatrist opens up his questioning with a wh-question asking why age is relevant (Lines 104–5). In his reply the recipient at last introduces an age-related categorisation device: being of age/not being of age (Line 107). The questioner responds to this by asking what being of age means (Line 109), getting a correct answer (Line 111). Then the recipient produces an inaudible expansion, on which the psychiatrist prompts him to elaborate (Line 116). The recipient treats that as indicating some trouble with his prior response, and he repairs his definition of being of age to an older, no longer valid one (Line 118), a definition which the psychiatrist states as being wrong (Lines 121–2).

The psychiatrist then moves the categorisation work to a close by asking for the recipient's age and introducing a new topic, that is trying to determine whether the inmate had a legal tutor to take care of his business. This change of topic (towards the issue of incomplete legal responsibility), coming sequentially after a categorisation sequence of which most issues were left open and noticeably unresolved (a wrong definition of being of age, no agreement on an adequate age-related MCD, and therefore no category-based reasoning leading to an account of the abnormal character of the recipient's previous actions) highlights once more the possible incompetency of the recipient, although no inferences from his inability to commonsensically analyse the situation in question in terms of relevant membership categories are overtly made at that stage.

What was the point of such an extensive and, as we have seen, painful categorisation sequence? How is it used? This becomes visible in the final deliberation in which the members of the commission must agree on the future dangerousness of the inmate they have just heard and on the kind of monitoring he should be subjected to (electronic location surveillance, psychotherapy or chemical treatments). Since these were not deliberations leading to a decision with legal effect, I was allowed to attend and to take extensive notes. In the parts which will interest us now I tried to monitor and write down in shorthand the psychiatrist's arguments as accurately as possible, but I missed several short turns, often done in overlap, which accounts for some of the pauses and restarts in the main line of the argument. It is therefore impossible to do a detailed sequential analysis of these sequences on the basis of a partial transcription. We may only note here that, in such an environment, as in the case of jury deliberations in trials, taking turns is tightly articulated with taking sides (Manzo, 1996), and that the kind of overlapping talk produced as the psychiatrist was making his point and which I could not write down were mostly affiliative and expressing assent.

In the following extract, the psychiatrist provides an occasioned gloss on the kind of interactional work which had been done during the hearing itself, and which is uttered to do specific work at that particular moment of the deliberation. After one member started to argue in favour of putting the subject under electronic surveillance after his release, the psychiatrist countered with the following challenge:

EXTRACT 8

Noticeable silences have been marked with (.) but could not be quantified

```
1   Psy(C)  puisque sa capacité de compréhension est si faible
            since his ability to understand is so weak
2           (.) que on peut se demander finalement si ça va servir à
            that one may wonder in the end whether it will be of any use
3           quelque chose/ (.) et moi je ne suis pas certain (.)
                            and me I am not sure
```

```
4        que cela puisse représenter un rempart contre
         that it may constitute a barrier   against
5        une agression sexuelle (.) éventuelle
         a sexual assault          a potential one
```

The gist of the argument relies on the ascription of weak cognitive capacities to the inmate. This is presented as a kind of shared knowledge for the co-participants and it can only refer back to the unsuccessful categorisation sequence we have studied as evidence for such an understanding (it is the only part of the hearing from which such an inference could be made, and, moreover, the reference is made less allusively later on). Such a claim implies that it is possible to infer from what happened, and particularly from a situated failure to do standard MCA, that the person has more generally 'very diminished (cognitive) capacities'. Such reasoning reveals another facet of the foundational character of categorisation work. Being demonstrably displayed as being unable to perform MCA becomes exploitable as a rich source of inferences from which to argue many other forms of incapacity or incompetence (here serious cognitive inabilities: 'his capacity of understanding is so weak', Line 1). Such incompetence-oriented inferences become particularly important in the deliberation phase, for, as evidenced here, they can be used and asserted to support or challenge many claims, in particular those related to the relevance of various types of monitoring and treatment, because all these require some competencies. The psychiatrist goes on to elaborate his point for several turns, arguing first that the inmate is not competent enough to handle the constraints of electronic surveillance, and second that his very deficient cognitive abilities will prevent that form of surveillance from acting as a kind of counterweight to his deviant sexual urges, should the latter manifest themselves again. Then he provides a new gloss of the earlier, 'live' categorisation sequence (Extract 9 below).

EXTRACT 9

```
 1  Psy(C)  Il sait pas ce que c'est qu'un mineur
             he does not know what a minor is
 2             (.)
 3           [((multiple overlaps))
 4  Psy(C)  j'ai passé plusieurs minutes à poser des
             I spent several minutes asking
 5           questions (.) justement pour bien vous montrer ce
             questions      precisely to show you well what
 6           que c'est que le  retard mental
             mental retardation is
 7  Pdt(C)  oui oui
 8  Psy(C)  le retard mental la personne est incapable de
 9           ((multiple overlaps))
10  Psy(C)  ben je sais mais quelques fois parce que (.) même les
             bah I know but sometimes because          even the
11           les internes en psychiatrie les jeunes médecins ne
             psychiatric interns the young doctors don't
```

```
12            savent pas ce que c'est que le retard mental (.) les
              know what mental retardation is
13            gens  ne sont pas capables de faire la distinction
              people are not able to make the distinction
14            entre quelqu'un qui est mineur et quelqu'un qui est
              between someone who is a minor and someone who is
15            majeur
              of age
16            ((brief overlap))
17 C(C)    ni d'ailleurs entre le bien et le mal hein
              nor between right and wrong eh
18 Psy(C)  oui enfin (.) entre le bien et le mal
              yes well      between right and wrong
```

The psychiatrist characterises the inmate as someone who does not know what a minor is (Line 1). This single observation is not, however, the main point. After all, the inmate himself volunteered that category (rather than the MCD child/adult which would have been as admissible in that sequential environment). Moreover, when asked, he initially provided a correct definition of the legal age for majority. He only gave a wrong one when prompted, that is, in a sequential context in which he could hear that prompt as indicating some trouble with his answer. That there is more to hear behind the claim that the inmate does not know what a minor is becomes hearable when the psychiatrist elaborates a little more, and states that he has asked 'all these questions' to show his co-participants 'what mental retardation is'. In light of this reformulation 'not knowing what a minor is' appears to be a gloss for the answers (or the failures to answer) to 'all these questions' and therefore for the kind of MCA work he has been trying to get the inmate to do through his questions. A bit later he redefines mental retardation as the state of not being able to differentiate between a minor and someone who is of age (Lines 13–16), a reformulation which introduces the inability to recognise and use a particular MCD. And this elicits an elaboration from another co-participant, the lawyer who adds 'nor between right and wrong' (Line 27), pointing back to the visible purpose of the categorisation work during the hearing, that is getting the recipient to see the abnormality of his conduct on the basis of MCA-based categorical reasoning. So these different elaborations of what the inmate cannot do are constituted on the occasion of the deliberation as referring to an inability of 'doing MCA'. That the latter is not recognised as such, and that references to the kind of MCA work during the Q/A sequence take an allusive and metonymic form (in which a failed answer to a particular question stands for a series of inadequate answers and what they mean as a whole) highlights the fact that while MCA encompasses a set of common-sense conversational practices or 'culture-in-action' (Hester and Eglin, 1997a), members, even when oriented towards doing MCA in a very direct and hearable sense and as an activity in itself, do not have a specific gloss available to describe such a practice.

I have argued that MCA is a common-sense set of practices in a foundational sense (which accounts for how an enduring inability to do MCA when required to do so could constitute a kind of 'breaching experiment'). We see here that the inability to do MCA on a particular occasion may be used 'ideologically', in the sense that it becomes a basis for the general inference that the person suffers from 'mental retardation', which is a generic or foundational form of incompetence from which many other and more specific forms of incompetence may be derived. Indeed, in the course of the deliberation, on that basis, the inmate will successively be pronounced to be unable to manage electronic surveillance, to be unable to behave normally in the civic domain (hence he should have a tutor on a permanent basis), to be unable to undergo psychotherapy, and to need a special form of support and monitoring just to be able to follow a chemical treatment that he might require. MCA is treated as so foundational to interaction and sociality that being found structurally incompetent with respect to MCA warrants being pronounced incompetent in nearly every domain of social life, though the core inference is couched here in cognitive terms (the inability of doing MCA is equated to 'mental retardation' as a generic cognitive deficiency).

Showing that someone is mentally retarded in this way is a special kind of performance that is described as not being part of standard psychiatric expertise and that is not available to young psychiatrists newly out of medical school. What kind of performance? It is glossed by the psychiatrist to his co-participant in the following way: 'I have spent several minutes asking questions precisely to show you well what mental retardation is' (Lines 4–6). This gloss stresses two features of the kind of questioning done during the hearing which makes it quite different from usual psychiatric interviews: it is time-constrained (the hearing itself rarely lasts more than half an hour as a whole, and for one member to ask ten minutes of questions as above is already rather long and unusual) and it is public, so that questions and answers must be meaningful to lay co-participants, and be usable to support or challenge various claims during the deliberation. It is a retrospective gloss which leans towards redefining both the problem and its solution ex post facto (we saw these were only gradually emerging within the sequence), somewhat like Garfinkel's juries (Garfinkel, 1967). MCA and the sequential organisation of talk appear as crucial strategic resources in such a retrospective reconstruction. Doing MCA is a very powerful resource, because it may be embedded into the particular sequential organisation of questions and answers. In such a move, to paraphrase Rod Watson, the 'categorisation potentiometer' is maximised within the sequential organisation of talk, which harnesses the joint power of both: failures to provide requested categorisations may be recognised as such (a) because what constitutes a relevant (category-wise) answer is available to all competent co-participants on the basis of MCA being a common-sense set of rules and practices; and (b) because the organisation of questions and answers makes the recognisable absence of an adequate answer a noticeable feature and an interactional issue, accountable as an inability or an unwillingness to provide it. In that respect, as shown in our case study, a ten-minute series of questions can demonstrably (in a way that makes sense at least to all competent co-participants) build a plausible case for the inability of the recipient to answer, and from then on, relying on the foundational character of MCA, support far-reaching inferences regarding the latter's generic incompetence with respect to all domains of social life.

Conclusion

The sequence we have analysed here was specific in the sense that categories were not just evoked in the talk; rather, the whole talk gradually evolved into a sequence organised around doing categorisation work and formulated as such. The emergence of categorisation work as the interactional issue at hand was accomplished within the categorical flow of questions and answers. It is through the question/answer sequence that the relevance of doing categorisation flow per se was gradually accomplished. Conversely, doing categorisation work made questions and answers hearable within the category-based kind of practical reasoning: such work made relevant, for instance, questions as hints regarding the larger frame of what could be read as category-based reasoning or 'riddles'. The question/answer sequence and the categorisation work were mutually elaborative and intertwined.

This particular case was one of the few which the participants regularly invoked to justify their practice of hearing inmates rather than just assessing their dangerousness on the basis of the written file, which other similar commissions did elsewhere in France. It was one of the exemplary instances in which they felt something had visibly been accomplished, a particular point regarding the inmate and his potential dangerousness had been intelligibly and even spectacularly made within the hearing in, through and as interaction. The analysis showed how the salience of the accomplishment relied on the foundational character of membership categorisation analysis as a crucial resource. First, MCA was used as a way to display the inability of the recipient to commonsensically analyse the situation in question in terms of relevant membership categories and then as a persuasive ground to support general claims regarding his inability and incompetence in various domains of social life. The generation of a collective consensus over such an assessment on that categorical basis retrospectively enacted and confirmed the foundational character of MCA. Second, the protracted pursuit of categories was displayed as a painful experience by overhearing participants with respect to the ongoing question/answer sequence, also occasioning the counsel's uncontrollable fit of laughter, an interruption and some significant repair of participation frameworks. The counsel's conduct was treated as responsive to the kind of category-based questions that were asked at the time. The inability of doing MCA in the face of the persistent pursuit of category-based reasoning embedded in Q/A sequences was oriented to as something akin to a breaching experiment, as though it violated basic expectations inherent in the organisation of talk, such as that participants should be able to do MCA competently enough for all practical purposes. In line with Sacks's seminal intuitions, Membership Categorisation Analysis appears as foundational to the organisation of interaction as the sequential organisation of talk.

Harnessing the power of sequential organisation and Membership Categorisation Analysis in this way was retrospectively glossed by the psychiatrist as an expert performance on his part. 'Expert' here is not meant in the sense that it invoked expert psychiatric knowledge which might be taught at school (on the contrary it involved shared sequential and categorisation practices in the recognition and use of which everyone is expected by default to be competent), but in the sense that it displayed responsive conduct uniquely fitted to the practical relevancies and concerns at hand in line with Dreyfus's views on expertise (Dreyfus and Dreyfus, 1987). More specifically, it involved being attuned to: (a) the sequential and categorical relevance of successive answers, so that doing categorisation work might gradually emerge as a relevant accomplishment; (b) the temporal constraints of the setting, in which whatever point to be made had to be made through a sequence of questions and answers lasting only a few minutes (as is the case with category-based 'riddles'), much less than the usual psychiatric interview; and (c) the categorical constraints of the setting, in which whatever point was to be made had to be made so that it would be intelligible to lay participants with little or no medical knowledge. This case provides us with an instance regarding MCA of the general point made by Sacks that when one encounters a feature of talk that is commonsensical, one should look for and be able to find a setting in which it is exploited as a resource and put to work for institutional purposes.

Note

1   Their creation was part of a set of reforms introduced in 2007, after a few high-profile cases in which newly freed criminals committed similar crimes again.

5

Challenging Normativity

Re-appraising Category Bound, Tied and Predicated Features

Edward Reynolds and Richard Fitzgerald

Introduction

Research in Membership Categorisation Analysis (MCA) has illustrated a wide and varied use of activities, rights and obligations, variously related to categories and membership devices (Eglin and Hester, 1992; Jayyusi, 1984). As discussed in the Introduction to this volume, while these were initially described by Sacks (1974) as 'category bound activities' and later developed by Watson (1983) as 'category bound predicates', little recent attention has been paid to the subtle differences in the ways category features (rights, knowledge, activities, etc.) are deployed. While the term 'category bound predicate' has proven immensely useful it has also tended to serve as a catch-all term for all relationships between category features and categories, obscuring the action involved in the use of this category resource. In this chapter we touch off from Sacks's initial discussion of predicates and subsequent discussions to explore this relationship further by developing levels of sophistication to understanding the relationship between membership categories and locally invoked associated features. In this instance we examine the way in which participants engaged in a number of public arguments orient to three distinct differences in the types of relationship between categories and category features.[1] In order to explore the use of category features we draw on data taken from public arguments posted on the social media website engaged in what has been described as 'enticing a challengeable' (Reynolds, 2011, 2013). The first of these adopts Sacks's (1995) term 'category tied' to refer to the link between category and category feature which is treated by participants as not taken for granted and needing to be made explicit. The second relationship examines the way in which features are treated by members as naturally related to a category, in a taken-for-granted, but nevertheless explicit way. For this link we use Sacks's (1972a, 1972b) term 'category-bound'. Thirdly we examine where a category feature is directly implied, by the operation of a membership device or category. For this type of relationship we use 'category-predicate' (Eglin and Hester, 1992). These three different relationships between category features and categories/membership devices are explored through an analysis of the operation of the practice of 'enticing a challengeable' (Reynolds, 2013). This term refers to an adversarial method of enacting a strategic manipulation of social knowledge (often using categories and category ties) as a basis for later challenging an opponent's normativity (again, using norms related to a membership device). This chapter uses the description of these three different forms of relationship between category features and categories/devices to develop the argument that further levels of technical sophistication in the labelling of phenomena is now possible in MCA.

Within MCA the term 'category bound predicates' (Watson, 1983) serves as a valuable analytic term to label category-tied actions, knowledge, features or values (e.g. Butler and Fitzgerald, 2010; Fitzgerald and Housley, 2002; Housley and Fitzgerald 2002a; Eglin and Hester, 1992, 1997a; Hester and Francis, 2002; Stokoe, 2003). While initially described by Sacks (1974) as 'category bound activities', the term 'predicate' was incorporated into MCA following a series of papers by Watson (1976, 1978, 1983) which explored and extended Sacks's original use of category-bound activities. As Wowk and Carlin (2004) point out, the term 'category bound predicates' expanded the possible work of category based attribution beyond observed activities to include knowledge, beliefs, entitlements, obligations and typifications of categories, and has proven immensely useful in MCA analysis and fruitful in the cumulative development of MCA. Building on Watson's work, MCA research has sought to examine the way category-bound predicates or category predication can be entwined with a moral ordering whereby behaviour and actions, thoughts and opinions are made normatively sanctionable through category- based attribution (Fitzgerald and Housley, 2002; Housley, 2002; Jayyusi, 1984). More recent work has developed this further through examining the way in which category- bound predicates are tied to individual actions (Fitzgerald, 2012; Fitzgerald et al., 2009; Housley and Fitzgerald, 2009a). These ties are made by invoking social norms with which to make accountable a particular action in relation to a category-based norm. Next, we describe the data used in this chapter and the practice of enticing a challengeable.

The Data and the Practice

Data for this discussion is drawn from videos of arguments which take place in public and have been uploaded to the social media website YouTube,[2] with additional materials from other public sources such as US-based cable news channel Fox News and the UK's public broadcaster the BBC. A collection of 20 instances of a practice entitled 'enticing a challengeable' (Reynolds, 2011, 2013) is used as the basis for the analysis in this chapter. The arguments employed by participants in the data include public political, social, ethical and moral topics and focus on the interlocutor's publicly presented and assumed identity.

The majority of cases were from arguments during protests conducted in public. These had been recorded, either by the protesters themselves, or by individuals heckling the protesters, and then subsequently uploaded to YouTube. In several cases, the camera person is the main antagonist in the argument (as in the heckling videos); in other videos the camera person is peripheral to, or uninvolved in, the argument (usually where the recording is being done by protesters). The videos are posted to YouTube with a brief characterisation of the contents of the video. Most of the recordings also capture other protest activity that does not involve arguments wherein protesters yell or shout protests slogans, chants or statements to camera or passers-by. The other source of data is from broadcast interviews. These are gathered from a variety of formats, multi-party discussion, panel-discussion, radio interviews, phone-ins where arguments between guests or panellists occur (Clayman and Heritage, 2002; Hutchby, 1996).

Each of the instances employ the practice of enticing a challengeable in the midst of conflict talk by invoking norms as a resource for posing problems of orderliness in, and of, their opponent (Housley, 2002; Fitzgerald and Housley, 2002; Housley and Fitzgerald 2009a; Jayyusi, 1991). Challengers use this practice to invoke social order through strategically crafting disorderliness in their opponent, constituting the challenger as the agent of normativity who reveals a normative 'breach' or flaw in their opponent between their category and their action.

The overall practice of enticing a challengeable is identified as following a sequence of distinct phases (Reynolds, 2013). The five phases are the: (a) arguable, (b) preface, (c) pre-challenge, (d) challenge and (e) reaction. The first phase (a – arguable) is a prior point made in the argument. Most frequently, this is a point made by the target, but the sequence may also be used to support a point made by the challenger. This phase is a pre-requisite part of the sequence. Also it is oriented to in the final challenge phase, but it has no routine character, and it may be authored (Goffman, 1979) by either of the parties (e.g. the challenger may argue for their own arguable or argue with the target's). In the preface phase (b), interactional and physical space is made for the challenge and the target is constituted as the target. Challengers may employ work to treat their opponent as the target of the challenge (with talk or gesture) and gain the right to speak for sufficient time to enact the practice. In the third phase, the pre-challenge (c), a key adjacency pair is enacted (the enticing interrogative and enticed-response) using an enticing interrogative with a known answer to bluff the target into providing a pre-figured response. In the challenge turn the response to the pre-challenge is juxtaposed with the arguable in order to propose that there is an implication of the target's current line as evidence that they have failed to adhere to an explicit or assumed mutually ratified norm. The argument is continued in the reaction phase (e) in which the target treats the challenge as any other move in an argument, deflecting, minimising or getting back to the 'bottom line' (Ashmore et al., 1994) of the argument in a myriad of distinct ways. It is through this participant work (particularly phases (c) and (e)) that we explore the way category features are deployed and invoked and how they can be unpacked through the terms category-tied, category-bound or category-predicated actions, in relation to category-based rights, knowledge and norms.

We begin our discussion with an illustrative example of the practice, used to provide a basic overview of the distinct phases of enticing a challengeable. After the initial sketch of the practice and the membership work involved in the basic thrust of the challenge, we present three different relationships between membership phenomena used by parties – category tied, category bound and predicated. We illustrate a category-tied relationship whereby a connection between a category and some related action, attribute or knowledge is treated as locally established and locally contestable. We then highlight category-bound relationships in which the relationship between a category and an activity or attribute is treated by participants as *a priori* and non-contestable. Finally, we present the way in which a predicated relationship between membership devices and norms is implied by participants, rather than an explicit relationship worked up in the course of the talk.

We use these three differing relationships to categories and membership devices to argue that the analysis can usefully differentiate the descriptive language employed based on members' actual conduct.

An Illustrative Example of Normative Challenges as Action

Our first example is from an argument between a protestor maintaining that globalisation (through the G20 summit of leaders) is destroying the environment. He is arguing with a counter-protestor who has taken a 'law and order' stance against the protest thus far. The challenger (C) works to produce a relative ordering of the membership devices for the target (T) through setting up a no-win scenario by proposing that the target is failing to adhere to the norms related to their own membership.

EXTRACT 1: 'ANTI G20 ARGUMENT'

```
URL: http://www.youtube.com/watch?v=9NJKk_IJbUg [01:10-01:22]

 5.T:   a→   so whaddya you want to happen.
 6.C:   a→   I want our world to <su[rvive. > ]
 7.T:                            [you wanna] stop
 8.           [°fishing?°]
 9.C:   b→   [↑you  have] children?
10.T:   b→   I have two grea:t kids.
11.C:        do you have gran[d children
```

```
12. T:         [and they're a lot smarter
13.            than anyone in this park.
14. C:         well that's a [bit subjective]
15. T:                       [including me .]
16. P2:        yeah because they're stupid [that's why.]
17. C:                                      [do you care]=
18.            =about what's gonna [happen   to ]
19. T:                             [NO. They're] educated,
20.            [and they're-]
21. P2:        [>you  just- ] you just called us stupid.<]
22. C:    c→   [do    you    care    a b o u t      t h e i r ]
23.            future?
24. T:    c→   ↑↑of ↑↑course,
25. C:    c→   do you want them to have clean water?
26.            (0.6)
27. C:    c→   clean air?
28. T:    c→   ↑~yeah~.
29. C:    d→   wull, you better oppose the geetwenty,
30.            [because the (maybe) sure as aint gonna have it.]
31. T:    e→   [well I'm sending down to the gulf to get some.]
```

Extract 1 illustrates a challenger constructing this sort of moral ordering with category-tied actions.

The first part of the practice begins in (a) with the question/answer about what the protestor 'wants to happen'. In line 9, in response to his own position, the challenger initiates the preface phase (b) with a pre-question 'you have children?', posing a possible category (parent) incumbency as the basis for what will turn out in the enticing sequence. This turn also works to enact a turn-generated, or turn-formed, categorisation (Hester and Fitzgerald, 1999; Watson, 1997) where the counter-protestor is sequentially categorised as the 'target' of the sequence. The challenger then moves to the pre-challenge phase (c) in lines 22–3, 25 and 27. In this phase the challenger poses three enticing interrogatives, which are also category-tied in so far as caring about your 'kids' is something parents do – a norm that parents should care for their kids. This is evident when the target treats the question as obvious with 'of-course' (line 24), orienting the impossibility of not caring for his 'kids'. That is, the challenger, with the emphatic agreement of the target, has created a relational tie between the category 'parent' and the value 'caring for your kids'. From this the challenger moves to the next phase (d) where, having collaboratively established that the target cares for his kids, and wants them to have clean water and air, the challenger proposes that currently the target is not behaving in line with an implied norm. The protestor's challenge at line 30 treats the target's current line (the arguable) as evidence that he is not adhering to the now mutually ratified norm that parents should care for their kids – the implication being that acting to protect the environment is a required part of category-tied action. In doing this the protestor employs Sacks's 'second viewer's maxim' (Sacks, 1972a) to bring together the sequentially ordered category ties 'caring for your kids' and wanting clean water and clean air to propose a norm that parents should work to prevent damage to the environment.[3]

The second viewer's maxim is described by Sacks (1972b: 339) in relation to the constitutive enactment of norms as implicated in the management of membership devices.

> … on seeing a pair of related actions being done, where those actions are tied to categories; see that the doers of the actions as members of the tied category and treat the relatedness of the actions as a done in conformity with a norm. (Sacks, 1972b: 339)

That is, doing category-tied actions places the doers in that category. In addition, the sequential ordering of category-tied actions (parents caring, wanting clean air) is treated by participants as a 'norm' (parents should care for the environment) (Sacks, 1972b: 338). Most centrally, Sacks observed that '[v]iewers use norms to provide some of the orderliness, and proper orderliness, of the activities they observe' (Sacks, 1972b: 339). That is, norms are used by participants to regulate, control or sanction the actions of others. Thus, in Extract 1 the challenger is sanctioning the target for his apparent disorderliness by using the relationship between the norm and the membership device as a resource for enacting a challenge to the target's normativity.

In proposing that the target is not currently 'being a good parent', by juxtaposing 'caring for his kids' against his arguable activity of counter-protesting, the challenger is attempting to degrade the target's status as a 'good' father. He is implying that he is failing to adhere to the norm that parents should try to stop damage to the environment. The deployment of such norms allows the challenger to degrade the target's normativity by implying that the target is not adhering with the mutually ratified norm established previously.

Three distinct relationships between membership device/category and associated features are apparent in Extract 1 – category-tied, -bound and -predicated links between the categories and features. In lines 22–3 the challenger actively ties being a parent and being concerned about what will happen to their children and is responded to with emphatic agreement with 'of course' – accepting the fact of the relationship, but rejecting the form. Here then the target rejects completely the possibility that he could provide any other answer with his reply 'of course' (Stivers, 2011). This proposes that the category/action should be treated as natural – that it is obvious – and in fact the work done by the challenger in linking the category action was unnecessary. So whereas in the first pairing the challenger worked to tie the category and action, but this was rejected, in the reply the category and action are treated as already bound. The third relationship is evident in the final challenge – the implied relationship between norms about what parents should do and the target's local incumbency as a father. This form of relationship is not treated as explicit, by either party; it is treated as both natural and implied. What is apparent is that here the form of the relationship is as important as the fact of the relationship.

These terms, 'tied', 'bound' and 'predicated', were chosen for their scalar descriptive adequacy in representing the different 'strengths' of relationship between categories and their features. While initially employed by Sacks (1972a, 1972b) and Watson (1983) we take 'tied' to be the weakest, most 'constructed' relationship, 'bound' to be related in a more 'permanent' way and 'predicated' to be an implied relationship. Thus, in the following discussion we examine in more detail these three different relationships between category-tied, category-bound and predicated features. On the basis of this we argue that a greater level of analytic sophistication can be gained through the differentiation of these relationships.

Tying and Binding Category Features to Categories and Membership

In examining the different relationships between category and category feature our analysis below proceeds in three sections. The first two describe two distinct trajectories identified in the practice of enticing a challengeable where the first trajectory highlights a 'let it pass' (Drew, 2005) design in the target's reply to the category-tying work in the pre-challenge phase. In the second trajectory – exhibited above – we examine the contest over whether the pre-challenge turn is a category tie or a category-bound relationship. In the third section we highlight the predicated relationship between membership devices and the norms used in enacting the practice of enticing a challengeable. We begin next with the illustration of uncontested category ties.

An Uncontested Category Tie

Within the data the targets of the challenges are not unwitting dupes. In almost every case they employ some form of resistance.[4] The first straightforward opportunity for such resistance is in the course of the enticed response and this resistance comes in one of two forms – a passive trouble-proposing silence, or rejecting form of relationship of the category tie. The work of the target in the pre-challenge phase exhibits attempts to avoid the pitfalls of flat-out rejection of the pre-challenge while doing their best to maintain their position in the argument and their local social status. The first pattern of resistance is delay coupled with a minimal, yet 'type conforming' (Raymond, 2003), response which belatedly assents to the tie. The second pattern of resistance, a confirming yet non-type conforming response, proposes that the tied relationship should be bound instead.

This rejection is managed with differing orientations to the preference for type conforming responses (Pomerantz, 1984; Raymond, 2003). Raymond (2003) illustrated the
operation of a preference for 'type conforming responses' to yes–no interrogatives. That
is, a preference for conforming to provide a response that falls within the polar yes–no
constraints of the question. He illustrated the way in which participants design their
responses to be sensitive to constraints of providing a fitted response. Answerers may
either conform to the constraints of the polar design, or perform extra interactional
work to provide a non-conforming response. Raymond goes on to demonstrate the way
in which such non-type conforming responses may resist the appropriateness and presuppositions of the interrogative while still providing something which may 'stand in
place' of a response. We argue here that type-conformity is one of the ways participants
have of managing the relationship between categories and activities, features or knowledge and that conforming or not conforming have two distinct treatments in these
questions. Targets of the enticing interrogative thus have two options: (1) conform and
avoid the response being treated as accountable (and thus risk appearing difficult); or
(2) provide a non-conforming response to reject that the relationship is a category tie
and propose it is a category- bound relationship instead – at the risk of appearing indo-
lent. We begin with an illustration of the first of these options.

Extract 2 comes at the beginning of a recording in which a heckler (C, challenger)
has approached a group of protestors including (T, target) located outside of a birth
control clinic.

EXTRACT 2: 'ARGUMENT WITH ANTI-BIRTH CONTROL'

URL: http://youtu.be/tC6GxktGdww [00:20-00:30]

```
 1.C:    is this a religious protest.
 2.T:    this is- this is a: >human rights protest.<=
 3.      we're [we're >standing out here.<]
 4.C:         [well why are you praying over] there then.=
 5.      =look at them.
 6.P1:   people can pray for a cause.
 7.C:    so this is religious right?
 8.      (2.3)
 9.C:    [ is it.]
10.T:    [it's about] human rights.
11.      (0.8)
```

12. C: [uh huh.]

13. T: [just <be]cause> there are people, (0.4) >praying.<

14.   and people are religious, who are involved in it.=

15.   =doesn't (0.5) take away >from the fact that< (0.6)

16.   the issue is about, the <pill killing women.>

17.   (2.0)

18. T: and you can get that message across through

19.   <signs, through t-shirts, education.>

20. C: [uh huh .]

21. T: a→   [>and then] you can pray.<

22.   (0.7)

23. C: c→   does praying work?

24.   (1.2)

25. T: c→   (h)$ye:s$¿

26.   (0.9)

27. C: d→   >then why don't you just stay home and pray.<

28.   (1.0)

29. T: because (0.3) there's (0.3) other ways to do it.

Across lines 1–7 the heckler works to establish that the protest, and the protestors, are 'religious', a point the protestor rejects the relevance of in lines 13–16, while accepting 'religious people' are involved. The heckler is thus proposing a membership device relevant to the activity of 'protesting' currently being engaged in, that it is instead 'religious protesting'. Then at line 23 the heckler works to tie an understanding of the result of 'praying' (that it 'works') to the 'religious' device. The protestor assents to this tie between the device religious and tied-activity praying in line 25. Despite having previously categorised the group as 'religious' the heckler is not taking for granted the link between 'praying' and 'it working' simply based on the device 'religious' (as he well could). Instead, the heckler does additional interactional work to link 'praying working' to the device. That is, he ties 'praying working' to the local assembly of 'religious' people as a basis for challenging the form of their protest.

The next example is from an interview on 'The O'Reilly Factor' on Fox News between Bill O'Reilly, the show's host, and Dr Jeremy Levitt. The point of contention is whether Fox News 'played the race card' in their coverage of demonstrations against US President Obama in 2009. Only the initial part of the sequence is shown for brevity.

EXTRACT 3: 'LAW PROFESSOR'

```
URL: http://youtu.be/m6sOkGZtc6Y [02:05-02:30]

 3. C: b→ but wha I wanna- I wanna get back to you.
 4. T: b→ [okay]
 5. C: c→ [you ] teach law,
 6.        (0.6)
 7. C: c→ the [la:w is based] on logic.
 8. T: c→     [that's right ]
 9.        (0.4)
10. C: e→ I don't see the [logic] in saying that
11. T:                    [yes.]
12. C: e→ attacks on barrack obama, A::LL of them-
13.        I think the kook minority
```

The challenger (C), O'Reilly, categorises the target as someone who 'teaches law' in line 5 and then ties 'being logical' to that category in line 7 (the enticing interrogative). After some delay, and in overlap with O'Reilly, the target provides a confirmation of O'Reilly's asserted tie in line 11, after which O'Reilly proceeds into a challenge which he briefly suspends for some additional business about the 'kook minority'. Again, as in Extract 2 the challenger does explicit work to tie a category feature (the law being based on logic) to a category (law teacher) as the basis for the later challenge.

The targets in these cases employ a 'let it pass' (Drew, 2005) design in the organisation of their responses. That is, after a moment of delay orienting to the possibility of repair they relent, allowing the sequence to progress. The targets' responses, then, conform with the type and the presumptions of the questions they are presented with. Further, they accept that such questions are askable, that the relationships between category features and categories need to be made explicit and cannot be taken for granted (even if they are 'obvious', cf. Reynolds (2011, 2013)). Targets accept the possibility that the two may not be linked by conforming to the binary design proposed by the challenger. Thus, targets both ratify the fact of the relationship between category and feature, and the form of that relationship (as tied).

Extracts 2 and 3 highlight cases in which the descriptive term category-tie is most apt. Participants do interactional work to make a category relevant and also link a feature to that category. Importantly, the category feature is not treated as already having been made relevant due to the fact of any prior categorisation (as was evident in Extract 1). Next we work through two cases in which the nature of the relationship of the category-feature to the category or membership device is contested. That is, the next section illustrates the second trajectory in which the 'weakness' of relationship implied by the need to tie the category to the activity is rejected by the target and a stronger bound relationship is proposed instead.

Contesting Category Relationships

Targets presented with the polar yes–no design of the enticing interrogative are routinely faced with a difficult task. Targets do their best to navigate the competing demands placed on them with these sequence and category resources arrayed against them, while still maintaining an adversarial stance. And yet, these resources find themselves 'crosscutting' (Pomerantz and Heritage, 2012) as the polar design used to propose the category tie is rejected by targets. Targets instead provide a response which aligns with the other preferences deployed in the question (matching the polarity and the candidate response proposed by the challenger) but which proposes that the category feature is bound not tied to the category. In doing so, targets imply a 'natural' relationship between category and the category feature (Hester and Eglin, 1992) rather than a 'worked up' relationship (Edwards, 1998). We argue this relationship may be described as category bound. The next section illustrates the way in which targets adopt this response option.

Extract 4 is from an argument between two Mormons and a 'Son of Israel' (a member of an African-American evangelical movement based on the Old Testament). The Mormons have encountered a Son of Israel (the challenger) in a car park and are soliciting him to read the Book of Mormon, to which the Israelite objects, prompting the following exchange.

EXTRACT 4: 'THE WRONG BOOK'

URL: http://youtu.be/sHEqzEFNVOg [02:17-02:35]

```
1.C:      the scripture says that, if anybody
2.        come into your house, and don't bring the
3.        correct book, you not supposed to bid him
4.        godspeed.
5.C:      so I mean why: would I take the book o' mormon.
6.        we talking about the bi:ble, you pushin on me
7.        the book o' mo:rmon.
```

```
 8. T: a→    cuz it testifies (.) of jesus christ.

 9. C: b/c→  but don't the bi:ble testify o' jesus christ?

10. T: c→    absolutely.

11. C: d→    so then why: do I need the book o' mormons?

12. T:       to help strengthen that faith.

13. C:       oh so go:d's wo:rd is weak and needs to

14.          be strengthened.
```

At lines 5–7 the challenger criticises the Mormon's move to 'push on him the book of Mormons', quoting scripture in lines 1–4 as a basis for his rejection of the move. The challenger's criticism in lines 1–7 positions the challenger as 'faithful'[5] and the targets as 'idolaters' (e.g. one who does not bring the 'correct book') in a bifurcated categorisation constituted by his complaint over their move to give him the Book of Mormon. The target's turn at line 8 proposes that his own 'Mormon' category, and the complained-of 'pushing of the book of Mormon' are tied to a larger Christian membership device via a category-tied feature of the book, namely that it 'testifies of Jesus Christ'. The challengers' enticing interrogative at line 9 is designed with a yes–no format – designing for the possibility of a 'no' response. The design, with the possibility of a (dispreferred) 'no-response', proposes that the relationship between the Bible and Jesus Christ's words is not already established, but in establishing it will tie such response to the current category membership (Christian). The question then, while proposing a yes–no answer, is designed to invoke membership of the category Christian through category-bound knowledge, such that a Christian would have knowledge of the Bible and that this work is to be followed by those in the device Christians. However, the target's response in line 10 rejects the possibility of a no-response, as he instead proposes that such knowledge is naturally bound to the category Christian with 'absolutely'. That is, the target proposes that it should be taken for granted that the Bible 'testifies of Jesus Christ' and that any member of the Christian device knows this.

From this agreement, however, the target is then challenged on the basis that because the Bible is the only testament a Christian should need that the target has failed to properly adhere to this norm of Christianity (evidenced in the scripture quoted prior) by proffering the Book of Mormon. The target has accepted that 'testifying of Jesus' as a category-bound property of 'the Bible' is something that Christians know. He then uses the second viewer's maxim to imply the norm that Christians should only need the Bible and that the target has broken that norm (as a Christian) by advocating for the Book of Mormon. That is, the challenge is questioning the target's normative Christian status.

Extract 5, repeated from Extract 1, presents another such case of responses which reject the need to tie a feature to a category.

EXTRACT 5: 'ANTI G20 ARGUMENT'

URL: `http://www.youtube.com/watch?v=9NJKk_IJbUg` [01:10-01:22]

```
 9. A: b→    ↑you have [children?]
10. C:        I have two grea:t kids.
11. A:        do you have gran[d children
((lines 12-22 omitted))
22. C: c→    [do    you    care    a b o u t      t h e i r ]
23.           future?
24. C: →      ↑↑of ↑↑course,
25. A: →      do you want them to have clean water?
26. T: c→     ↑~yeah~.
27. C: d→     wull, you better oppose the geetwenty,
```

In Extract 5, the protestor asks a pre-question of the target, at line 9, working to position the target as a 'parent', by virtue of his having children. The challenger moves on to tie 'caring about their future' to the already relevant category in lines 22-3, 'working up' a relationship between the two category features. With his use of 'of course' in reply the target treats the enticing interrogative as unaskable (Stivers, 2011) and he proposes instead that the relationship between feature and category is bound – that these two features do not need to be made explicit. In these two examples participants can be seen to clearly differentiate between the work of tying some feature to a category and proposing that it is already bound to that category.

In Extracts 4 and 5 the enticing interrogative works to tie a category feature to the target with the enticing interrogative, which is rejected and treated as bound to an already relevant category instead. In Extract 4, 'being Christian' was the basis for asking about 'the Bible testifying of Jesus'; in Extract 5 'having kids' was the basis of asking about 'caring for his kids'. These activities (e.g. reading books) and traits/ attributes (caring for kids) are tied to the categories by challengers in the design of their turns. In contrast targets treat them as naturally bound to the categories in their response to the turns. Challengers and targets alike differentiate between the strength of category-tied and category-bound relationships between different category features.

As previously discussed in the analysis of Extract 1 above, in Extract 5 the challenger also enacts a norm in order to challenge the target's normativity. The challenger uses the second viewer's maxim to relate the category features 'wanting clean water and air' and 'caring for kids' to the activity 'protecting the environment' to propose that the target should be protesting against the G20 summit of leaders, implying that by not doing so he may not 'care for his kids', and so forth.[6] This behavioural norm, that if you 'care for your kids' you should 'oppose the G20', also has a relationship to the membership devices and categories at hand. We suggest that 'predicate' is the more useful term for this type of relationship because participants treat one as implying the other. In the next section then we explore this use of norms, their relationship to membership devices, and their use as implications, in more detail.

Norms Implied in the Course of Challenges: Predicates

The final relationship we describe in this chapter is 'predicated', a category feature implicationally tied to the membership device or categories employed by participants. In the practice of enticing a challengeable, participants imply the relevance of norms and challengers use them to imply that the target has failed to adhere to said norm. That is, the norms are predicated of the prior category work as the challenge turn is enacted. Unlike the prior relationships (tied, bound) this predication is implied, that is, participants do not *explicitly* link the norm to the category. As highlighted in Extract 1 the juxtaposition work of the final challenge trades on comparing the arguable (a) with the upshot of the pre-challenge phase. This upshot is treated as a norm and the juxtaposition works to propose that the target has failed to properly adhere to this norm. The norm deployed by the operation of the second viewer's maxim works to make the target accountable by juxtaposition with the arguable. It operates as what Housley and Fitzgerald (2009a) describe as a norm-in-action. Housley and Fitzgerald (2009a: 353–4) argue that these moral devices 'provide a praxiological resource for generating difference as an accomplished normative inference and resource which can then be used to make further characterizations of persons, groups or collectivities'. That is, this argues that norms-in-action are predicated of categories and/or membership devices. In this section we detail the way in which this praxiological resource accomplishes the implications generated in the course of enticing a challengeable. In doing so we illustrate the third form of relationship between category and category features discussed – the predicate.

Challengers deploy norms in the final challenge turn as an implied upshot of the prior category work in order to use them as a basis to challenge the normativity of the target. That is to say that the targets are somehow in breach of a norm linked to their membership device. This is evident in the next example (Extract 6) from an argument about a 'stupid sign' (at a protest about same-sex marriage). The challenger is arguing that same-sex marriage is immoral and the target, the cameraperson, has taken a contrary stance.

EXTRACT 6: 'NATIONAL SECURITY'

URL: http://www.youtube.com/watch?v=HLAXe6R6CP8 [01:47-02:25]

```
21. T:        tha:ts the stupidest >thing I've seen.<
22.           (2.0)
23. T:        and you have NOTHing to back that up.
24.           (2.5)
25. C:        bible teaching.
26. T: a→     the bible is a boo:k, written by a ma:n.
27.    a→     there's a lotta books.
28. C: b→     let me ask you a question.=you have a college
29.           education?
30. T: b→     yes I ↑do.
31. C: c→     did you study >books,< or did you read messages
32.    c→     in the sky:?
33. T:        <I read [ ma:::ny    b o o k s. > ]=
34. C:                [then etched in the earth.]
35. T: c→     =>I read [ma::ny books. <]
36. C:                  [you read books.]
37. T:        written  [ b y : : : ] men.
38. C:                 [>do you burn-<]
39. C: d→     YES.=>so you live your life by that right?<
40. T: e→     >No:.<=
41. C: e→     =>↑Yes you do:.<
43.           oh so you live your life by conscience?
44. T:        I↑do.=
```

The challenger works to position V (the target) in the category 'college educated' in lines 28–9 in order to establish whether or not V 'read books' at college in lines 31–2. This category works in the preface phase to prefigure the answer with the reflexive relationship (Hester and Eglin, 1997a) between the category 'college educated' and the category tied to the activity 'studying books'. This orientation to the reflexive relationship between 'studied books' and 'college education' is achieved in lines 31–8 as the target treats 'studying books' as bound to the category 'college educated' instead of tied with his non-type conforming reply 'I read many books'. The challenger then makes an upshot in line 39 in the course of the challenge, based on the membership device 'educated', and the category-tied activity 'studied books', implying[7] that the device 'educated' should govern how you live your life, and that 'reading books' is a pre-requisite feature of that. The implication at line 39 is presented to the target as a challenge to his position, inasmuch as it proposes that 'education' should govern how you live your life. The challenger presents this as a warrant for the challenger's position that 'Bible teaching' is currently governing his own activity, that is, displaying the contested sign. Here then, challenger is employing the second viewer's maxim in the construction of the norm about 'living your life' by specifying a membership device that should govern the way in which that is done (i.e. 'education' via the categories Bible teaching and college). That is, the challenger implies the norm as a resource for the challenge action using the second viewer's maxim. Thus, unlike the category-tied and category-bound features of prior examples, the norm is treated as implied by the membership device.

As in previous examples, in the pre-challenge phase the challenger collects himself in the same device as the target – someone who 'studied books' – working to enact a momentary 'us'. It is this 'us' that the target is resisting with his sarcastic tone. He uses the obviousness of the enticing interrogative as a resource for putting on a patronising tone which works to derogate the challenger – thereby resisting affiliation. The challenger presses the sense of 'us' in the challenge turn as he collects himself and the target in the same 'belief systems' device, but works to hierarchically position himself above the target using the target's normatively challengeable status. As in previous examples the challenger is working to become an agent of normative order by enacting a shared sense of 'us' and then leveraging a normatively challengeable status as a resource for action.

The second viewer's maxim is employed as a resource by challengers to make an inference (about how the target lives his life) and an implication (that in arguing with the challenger the target is not living his life according to his membership obligations). In reaction (line 40 at (e)) the target flatly resists the subsequent characterisation of himself based on this norm, orienting to the possible further trajectory of the challenger's line of questioning. The membership devices are employed as resources to make the implication possible, and the norm deployed by the use of the second viewer's maxim is used as a resource to challenge the target. The challenger treats the norm as predicated of the membership device – and the target flatly rejects that implication (and the associated challenge).

In this section we have highlighted the way in which challenges to norms-in-action 'provide a praxiological resource for generating difference as an accomplished normative inference and resource which can then be used to make further characterizations of persons ...' (Housley and Fitzgerald, 2009a: 354). Challengers invoke these proposed failures to adhere to a norm in order to generate the degrading action of enticing a challengeable, effectively positioning themselves relatively higher in the same moral device in the course of doing so. Challengers imply the norm with the second viewer's maxim, enacting a predicated relationship between the norm and membership device. In the next section we illustrate the way in which targets may work to undercut the relevance of the norm by changing the relevant membership device, illustrating the 'closeness' of the predicated relationship between norm and membership device.

Undercutting Implications by Undercutting Membership Devices

Targets of the practice may resist the challenge to their normativity by working to undercut the relevance of the norm levied against them. In this section we illustrate two ways in which they do so, both orienting to the predicated relationship between norm and membership device. The first method is to reject the membership device, proposing a different one. This illustrates the way in which norms may be implied or inferred by the operation of a given membership device. The second method is to flat out reject the norm (and also reject the membership device), although this has consequences for the target. This latter method illustrates that a norm is relevant, and that both parties do orient to it, although they may choose to contest the norm. We begin with an illustration of a target rejecting the operation of a membership device in the course of trying to evade the challenge.

Extract 7 is from an interview on the BBC's *Hard Talk* between Richard Dawkins (the target) and the interviewer Steven Sackur (the challenger). Dawkins is being questioned about his claim that raising children religious is 'very wicked' (detailed below).

EXTRACT 7A: 'DAWKINS, *HARD TALK*'[8]

URL: http://youtu.be/HSatukeQzFM [00:10–00:56]

```
 7. C:    because you have said that you believe that those
 8.       people with religious beliefs who impose those
 9.       religious beliefs on their children are in effect
10.       responsible for a form of child abuse. You've called
```

```
11. a→    it (.) very wicked.
12. T:    I would like t- to I would like children as far as
13.       possible to be allowed to think for themselves. So for
14.       example to label a small child a catholic child or a
15.       protestant child or a muslim child, that I think is
16.       wicked because the child is too young to know.
17.       And just to give you e- I mean I've used this
18.       illustration often enough before if I said to you
19.       that's a Marxist child or that's a secular humanist
20.       child or that's a keynsian child, you would look at me
21.       as though I was mad. How can the child be a keynsian
22.       child, how can the child be a keynsian child. well
23.       both its parents are keynsians. You see what I mean,
24.       religion has a free ride to label children with the
25.       belief system of its parents.

((00:56-02:14 untranscribed))

26. C:    b→ sti::ll .h as [YOU we::re] >I must say<
27. T:                     [I think-]
28. C:    b→ you were rai:sed (.03) .h as an ↓anglica:[n,]
29. T:                                               [as a-]
30.          >°of course [I was.°<
31. C:    c→              [and you were confi:::rmed,
32. c→    [you went to] chu::[rch,
33. T:    [ ye : : s, ]       [>so what?<]
34. C:    but you're- well- well the poi::nt is, your
35.       pa::rents didn't (.) stop you from thinking
36.       about (.) >other ways of looking
37.       at [the world.< did they?]
```

After categorising the target as 'Anglican' in line 35, Sackur binds the activity 'raised Anglican' to the device 'family' by taking for granted the relationship between the two. In other words Dawkins's 'parents' are 'doing the raising' and are associated with the Dawkins's churchgoing activities. As in Extract 6, they have a moment of agreement and alignment as the target endorses the challenger's statement that he was 'raised an Anglican, was confirmed and went to church'. Then, in lines 34–6, the challenger proposes that despite the target's family labelling him Anglican he was able to choose his own religious values, implying that Dawkin's argument about 'parents being wicked' is contradicted, because he himself was subject to such labelling and turned out 'just fine'. That is, the challenge proposes that Dawkins's own experience does not warrant the blanket attribution to parents who bring their children up as religious are 'wicked' (lines 10–11). The challenge proposes that by Dawkins's own logic he must include his own parents in the device of 'wicked parents' and it implies that making such statements of one's own parents is immoral. In this example there are two forms or relationship between category and device, the taken for granted, but explicit, bound link between 'family' and 'raised Anglican' and the implied predicated relationship between families and the norm to not call one's own 'wicked'.

The continuation of the argument highlights the way in which this resistance to the norm works to resist the action of the sequence.

EXTRACT 7B: 'DAWKINS, *HARD TALK*'

URL: http://youtu.be/HSatukeQzFM [02:10-02:40]

```
38. T:              [no. I been-]
39.       [>by the way, that was nothing]
40. C:    [they- the- you were la:belled]
41. T:    [to do with my parents.<]
42. C:    [you were labelled a christian bo::y¿]
43. T:    the- nothing to do with my pa:rents.
44.       that- that was schoo:l. I mean I- I was sent to
45.       anglican schools. .hhh ahh but sti:ll I mean that-
46.       [thats
47. C:    [so you were LABELLED a- uh- an ANGLican bo::y,=
48. T:    =sure I ↑was.
49. C:    but it didn't stop you:: (0.3) imBIbi:ng lots of
50.       other knowledge about the world.=and seeing the
51.       world in your own particular *↑way*¿
52. T:    well of course not. I as- as- as it happe:ned, and
53.       lots of- >happens often enough,< lots of people
54.       <manage to break free::>
55.       (0.5)
56. T:    from whatever it is that they're >labelled as.<
```

In lines 38–46 Dawkins works to correct Sackur's bound link between 'raising' and 'parents' – that it was his parents who 'raised him Anglican'. Dawkins invokes the device 'school', which he then ties to 'raising' in order to challenge the bound link between 'parents' and the activity 'raising'. By orienting to this category tie Dawkins challenges any possible implications that were and could be drawn about 'being raised religious by parents'. That is, he shifts the implied contradiction and possible inclusion of his own parents in the membership device 'wicked parents' and the moral norms predicated by the device as it is invoked here. Thus, he shifts his own 'raising' to his school, which downgrades culpability of the morally based criticism of his own parents by changing the activity of 'raising children' and by implication the norm of not calling his own parents wicked to not calling your school wicked (a lesser misdeed, or indeed no misdeed at all). In Extract 7b the target differentiates between category-bound activity (raising) and the norms (not calling your parents or school 'wicked') predicated of membership devices.

In the above example (Extract 7) the challenger employs the 'hearer's maxim' (Sacks, 1972b),[9] treating the category 'parents' as bound to the activity 'raising'. The target's resistance works to correct the membership device that collects together the categories 'raised Anglican' and parents along with the category-bound activities 'raising' and 'confirming' from something akin to 'family' to 'school'. By generalising his own 'breaking free' to others by using 'happens often enough', the target is treating the process of breaking free from the 'labels' applied by the membership device school as something which is not uncommon. It is the target's correction of the membership device which establishes grounds for his counter at lines 52–4. The new membership device (people who 'break free' from school) provides for the possibility of new predicates, and relaxes the salience of the previously relevant norm. Thus, by shifting the membership device he is able to undercut the relevance of the norm, thereby resisting the action of the challenge.

The final case presents a stark example of membership devices and norms in conflict as the target flatly rejects any shared membership and uses category-predicated norms to resist the challenger's actions. Extract 8 is a continuation of the argument from Extract 2 some moments later.

EXTRACT 8: 'ANTI BIRTH CONTROL ARGUMENT'

URL: http://www.youtube.com/watch?v=tC6GxktGdww [01:37–01:50]

```
51. T:     [you do at home and pray.]
52. P2:    [just because you   don't ] [ agree      with- ]
53. C:                          [so you're against ]
54.        public displays of re- religiosity?=
55. T:     =oh I just think that this is a religi- now it
56.        becomes a religious issue.
```

```
57.            [y'know.]
58. C:         [no   it ] doesn't.
59. T:         ye:s it [does.   see   look    at    that.  ]
60. C:                 [>just because some people< pray] doesn't
61.            make it all [ re li g io u s. ]
62. T:                      [>they're prayin.<]
63.            yeah well (.) to me it does.
64.            it's very [connected.]
65. C: b→                [>are you< ] anti religion.
66.            (0.5)
67. T: b→      I'm an atheist myself. yes.
68.            °I don't [beli]eve in god.°
69. C:                  [so::]
70.       c→   but- but- don't you respect- don't you tolerate (.)
71.            their religion.=
72. T:         =no I don't tolerate other peoples religion.
73.            =because [it's   unsustai:nable.   ]
74. P2:                 [>you don't tolerate it?]=
75. T:         =no.
76. C:         >>what you ↑mean it's unsustainable.<<
```

In lines 52–64 the argument begins with discussion about the target's opinions on public displays of religion. It culminates in line 65 with the challenger asking the target 'are you anti-religion'. Here, the challenger is aligning with norms of 'freedom of religion and expression', in an attempt to position the target such that a 'yes' answer would paint the target in a bad light. The target instead orients to the dispreferred response in line 67, prefacing his reply ('yes'), with the self-categorising account 'I'm an atheist myself'. That is, he uses the category as explanation for his intolerance of religion, he ties his 'anti-religion' views to his category 'atheist'. The protesters treat his response as accountable, working to solicit confirmation that the target nevertheless still tolerates religion – making explicit their prior implication that he should tolerate their religious display. The challenger asks 'but don't you tolerate it' (line 69); switching to prefer a yes-type answer, she displays a normative assumption that the target does tolerate religion, in spite of his atheism. Instead, the target reiterates that he does not tolerate religion, again confounding the presuppositions in the design of the challenger's reply.

In Extract 8 the target is prospectively oriented to the sorts of inferences and implications available from the category work earlier in the sequence. By calling the protestor's bluff and proposing a new membership device he is working to deny the possible inference that he ought to tolerate what he is treating as what they are doing – religious protest. Having provided the category 'atheist' the protestors can no longer deploy their norm 'that he should tolerate it' uncontested because the target treats the implication as not tied or bound to the category. That is, as an 'atheist' he implies he should be 'anti-religion' and that he need not 'tolerate it'. The target's resistance is premised on claiming membership in a category to which the protestor's norm (people should tolerate religion) is treated as having a different relationship with.

Extract 8, then, highlights participants engaging in a contest of what Jayyusi (1984) termed 'moral ordering'. The target is arguing that the protest is a 'religious issue', and in doing so he partitions the relevance of their protest. His self-categorisation as 'atheist' works to renegotiate the belief 'intolerant of religion' as category-tied and thus warranted by his beliefs. In positioning their protest as 'religious' and positioning himself as 'atheist' and tying 'not tolerating religion' to his category 'atheist', the target is working to place the conflict, and its participants, in the membership device 'belief systems'. In contrast, the protestors take for granted the normative organisation of 'tolerating religion' in the design of their questions and are working to take the device 'religion' out of the argument, proposing that religion is not relevant and that the target should tolerate theirs. Rather than drawing on any particular membership device, the protestors instead propose that norms of religious freedom (not being 'against public displays of religion', line 51) are simply 'normal, mundane, background expectancies' (e.g. Garfinkel, 1967; Jefferson, 2004b; Sacks, 1984b). Thus, here participants are engaged in a contest over whose norms are relevant, the norms that the protestors orient to as held-in-common or the membership-governed norms used by the target to resist the sequence.

The above example also serves to illustrate that norms, and challenges to normativity, are not strictly bound to membership devices. Participants may enact norms as independent, held-in-common features of society that 'anybody' orients to. Participants are enacting multiple social objects in this situation, the activities, values or norms themselves and their differing 'strengths' of link to other category phenomena. Alternatively, participants may enact norms as implied by certain forms of membership, enacted in talk and used to get the business of the moment done (e.g. arguing). This contrast illustrates that participants may on any occasion treat as consequential the *relationship* norms have with other membership features (devices, categories etc.). Thus we see in Extracts 7 and 8 that the targets contest ascribed memberships, norms, or the relationship between them as a resource for their arguing. Parties to talk treat these differing relationships as *distinct*, whether the participants tie some category feature to a category, or whether it is treated as bound to that category or if the participants enact that category feature as predicated by a category. It follows then that it is important and possible to develop a level of sophistication around use of the terms and descriptions used previously in distinguishing between the differing relationships between category and category feature.

Conclusion

In this chapter we have illustrated three distinct forms of relationship between category features and categories – tied, bound and predicated. Drawing on data from public arguments (Reynolds, 2013) we highlighted the way in which challengers may work up an explicit tie between a category and a category feature (as in 'teaching law' being 'based on logic'). We then illustrated the way in which non-type conforming responses were used by targets to propose that while the category feature was correct the challenger had proposed the wrong sort of relationship between category and category feature. We illustrated the way in which these non-type conforming responses proposed a category-bound relationship rather than a category-tied one. Finally, we presented the way in which norms are embedded in an implied relationship, a predicated link, between membership and category feature unlike category-tied or -bound features. Along the way we examined instances of contested membership devices to highlight the very 'close' relationship between norms and membership devices, such that participants may undercut the norm by shifting the relevant membership device. This highlighted the fact that norms may stand apart from membership work or be intimately related to it, thus demonstrating that the relationship between norms and other parts of talk is as relevant and consequential as the norms themselves.

Being able to analytically differentiate between distinct forms of relationship between category features and categories or membership devices not only recognises some of the different ways in which category predicates are used and deployed but also provides researchers with further analytic tools. With the differentiation of category tied and category bound we were able to illustrate distinct phenomena, participants orienting to the *form* of the invoked relationship between category and category feature as well as the *fact* of the relationship; for example, when targets rejected the form proposed by the challengers and proffered their own instead. It was not that the fact of the relationship was contested, it was the 'closeness' of the relationship. Each distinct form of relationship between category and category feature, then, was occasioned by participants for specific purposes and at particular points in the interaction and the interactional flow.

For analysts the required analytic mentality involves continually dissolving any tendency towards a unitary analytic heuristic. Presenting nuances of the distinct relationships between category and category features participants enact offers more complex analytic insights on social action. As the technical sophistication of MCA grows it also moves further away from the tendency towards singular description of relationships between categories and category features, which may overlook the consequential differences between subtle and nuanced relationships which participants may employ.

Notes

1 Jayyusi (1984) uses category features as an overarching term for rights, knowledge, actions, obligations, opinions and activities related (in her terms 'bound') to categories. We acknowledge that just like 'predicate' such generic jargons must be used with care. We use 'feature' in preference to listing the

different things that may be related to categories, noting that future work may determine that such a catch-all gloss is unsuitable.

2   The use of data from YouTube and other such publicly available sites for EM/CA/MCA research is discussed by Reynolds (2013) and Laurier (n.d.). It is done in line with terms of service and copyright provisions.

3   Like membership devices, the specific norm is not explicitly articulated by participants, and does not need to be. It is simply relevant that there is a norm something roughly like what we propose here.

4   For those cases in the data where they evidence no resistance they do so for good interactional reasons.

5   Of course what both parties 'really' believe is irrelevant. It is the display of 'being faithful' via the 'proper' orientation to the Bible as the 'correct book' which is relevant here.

6   Implying is a designedly vague activity. As with the description of unlabelled membership devices it is not our job as analysts to try to label or guess all of the things that might be implied – such a task is endless.

7   This turn in line 39 in fact *infers* and *implies*. The challenger infers 'how (and that) the target lives his life' and implies that the corollary, the challenger living his life 'by a book' (the Bible), is equally acceptable. The 'so' retrospectively proposes an inference.

8   To provide some context without glossing the talk, the first section, lines 9–25, have been presented with a minimal transcription.

9   The hearer's maxim (Sacks, 1972b) is that if a member sees a category-bound activity being done, then, if one can see it being done by a member of a category to which the activity is bound, then: see it that way. It is used by participants as a way to handle the ambiguity of device membership between various categories (Butler and Fitzgerald, 2010; Sacks, 1972b).

6

Omnirelevance in Technologised Interaction

Couples Coping with Video Calling Distortions

Sean Rintel

Introduction

The concept of omnirelevance in Membership Categorisation Analysis refers to participants invoking categories that reflexively treat the understanding of particular interactional moments as controlled by the context of the current activity. This concept is of value to the analysis of computer-mediated communication (CMC), as it relates directly to the field's fundamental interest in exploring how technology effects interaction. When interacting via technology, the affordances of that technology are materially inescapable and thus potentially contextually controlling. However, the control of technology over interaction is not absolute. The affordances of technology are materially inescapable but their relevance as a semiotic resource is a matter for participants. Ian Hutchby (2001a, 2001b, 2003) calls this 'technologised interaction'.

In this chapter I explore examples of how couples cope with audio and video distortions in video calling. The data show that in the face of distortion the couples treat the relationship and technology as omnirelevant (i.e., controlling) devices deployable in a fluid interdependence that differs with respect to how audio distortions and video distortions potentially affect conversational continuity. When coping with audio distortions, relational and technological omnirelevance are used as an organisational feature to *disambiguate* the potential source of trouble in repairs. Coping with video distortions is shown to involve an orientation to *expressive possibilities* of relational and technological omnirelevance.

Omnirelevance, I argue, is a central feature of technologised interaction. While video calling couples are engaged first and foremost to the social activity of doing being couples, their efforts to maintain conversational continuity in the face of distortions orient to doing being a couple in a video call.

Omnirelevance

Omnirelevance is one aspect of Membership Categorisation Analysis's wider attention to the sociological importance of context (Fitzgerald and Housley, 2002). Drawing on examples from automobile and school conversations as well as therapy and military contexts, Sacks first canvassed the possibility of omnirelevant organisational devices in Lecture 5 (1995: 306–19). As discussed in the introductory chapter to this volume, omnirelevance has re-emerged as a topic of interest in Membership Categorisation Analysis research due to its explanatory power for exploring the contextualised underpinnings of *in situ* organisational devices in interaction. Recent omnirelevance research has explored omnirelevant category collections used in children's disputes (Hester and Hester, 2012), playground interaction (Butler, 2008), family interaction (Butler and Fitzgerald, 2010), and relational video calling (Fitzgerald and Rintel, 2013), television interviews (Butler and Fitzgerald, 2011) and radio phone-in programmes (Fitzgerald et al., 2009).

For Sacks (1995: 312), the genesis of the omnirelevance came from bringing together two questions about how interactions could be recognisably organised. First, Sacks noted that participants are able to name the kind and/or context of an interaction, for example as an automobile discussion or therapy session, and thus there must be devices used to enact and recognise an interaction as organisationally 'of a kind' or 'in a context'. Second, taking on a long-standing issue from the philosophy of language (e.g. Austin, 1962; Grice, 1989) he noted that the accuracy of statements alone does not provide for their relevance to an interaction, so again, there must be devices that provide for the relevance of any given turn and that prevent the deployment of just any accurate statement.

Instead of either treating the overall kind or context of interaction as a given (and thus uninteresting to sociology) or seeking maxims by which an analyst could account for relevance (and thus of philosophical or linguistic but not sociological interest), Sacks was looking for evidence of the enactment of society as a public achievement through members' own deployment and analysis of categorical devices as organisationally defining an interaction as of an overall kind or context.

For example, Sacks observed that group therapy sessions could include instances of turns produced by one person that others treated as organisationally relevant to the roles of therapist and patient. For example, around opening periods in a group therapy session a therapist might produce a turn inviting someone at the door to come in and join the group despite that not being responsive to the actual prior turn (Sacks, 1995: 314), or 'patients' might produce an out of place imagined greeting round for a participant marked as notably absent by the therapist (1995: 318). Similarly, he observed that after some time had already passed in a session, the production by the therapist of an apparently topic-opening question, such as 'Well, what's new gentlemen?' (1995:314) could be treated by patients not as a request for more talk but, rather, as indicative of the therapy session being drawn to an end.

As such, Sacks argued, particular sequences within overall activities are sometimes treated by participants as being controlled by a category deployment or an enacted category-bound action so fundamental that 'there is no way of excluding its operation when relevant' (1995: 314). Sacks termed these 'omnirelevant' devices, and noted that omnirelevance may constrain the use of other devices (1995: 316–18). Sacks's (rather complex) example of such constraints concerns cover-identifications used by therapists and teenage patients to interact in public as adult and child in a way that allows for consistency of both sets of identifications. For the purpose of this chapter the more simple point is that omnirelevant devices are resources used by participants to both enable and constrain interactional understandings.[1]

When analysing talk via technology, we must be mindful of Button's (1993b) injunction not to treat technology as omnirelevant in the sense of an external platform that is merely a convenient place in which to gather data or an arena in which to view the playing out of traditional sociological interests. Further, as Greiffenhagen and Watson (2005) warn, as is often a special temptation in mediated interaction research, omnirelevant devices should not be confused with the blunt contextual assumptions of traditional sociology. Categories such as gender or relationship are often treated by researchers as inescapably there *to be found* and amplified in importance rather than found to be relevantly occasioned.

Rather, as for all interactional methods, omnirelevant devices are invoked by participants as needed, both explicitly and tacitly, and while always available they are not always and only the primary device at work (Sacks, 1995: 315). They often appear 'in the cracks, joints, and articulations of touched off-topic devices' (Fitzgerald et al., 2009: 45). Once invoked, the work of an omnirelevant device is to tie the particular interactional moment to the context of the activity by drawing attention to who-we-are-and-what–we-are-doing.

Omnirelevant category devices are related to Goodwin's (2000, 2007) notion of 'participation frameworks', which enable interlocutors to 'build joint action together in ways that take account of both relevant structure in the environment that is the focus of their work and what each other is doing' (Goodwin 2007: 69). However, there is a nuanced distinction. Participation frameworks (and the instrumental, epistemic, cooperative, moral, and affective stances that they are used to convey) are how participants display the context of embodied interaction. While they may be cooperative or contested, Goodwin emphasises that they are essentially unnoticed; unspoken or taken for granted. But this does not quite seem to capture the value of omnirelevant devices, either for participants or researchers. Omnirelevance involves how participants invoke controlling categories to produce meaning – especially, as we shall see, in the case of difficulty with interactional organisation. That is, the distinction is between using a meaning in context (participatory frameworks) versus invoking a context to control meaning (omnirelevance). Omnirelevant devices would seem to be part of the 'language' aspect of Goodwin's (2007: 60) proposed tripartite structure of 'embodied action – language – structure in environment' that constitutes a participation framework, but I will leave that possible integration for the reader's contemplation. For the purpose of this chapter the analytic value comes in the unpacking of the methodical reasoning used by participants to markedly invoke organisational recognisability by using category devices that draw power from an occasioned reflexive oscillation between interaction and context (Fitzgerald and Rintel, 2013).

Technologised Interaction

I turn, then, to introducing the analysis of 'technologised interaction' and how it fits with omnirelevance. An interest in what Hutchby (2001a, 2001b, 2003) treats as technologised interaction is a subset of the wider sociological interest in the interdependence of technology and society (Button, 1993b; Castells, 2001). The classic theoretical debate at the heart of that interest is the direction of the flow of causation. As Hutchby (2001a: 16) explains, technological determinism holds that the inherent characteristics of a technology are thought to have determinate causal effects on social structures (e.g. Bimber, 1990; Ceruzzi, 2005). The opposing position of social constructivism holds that precisely what the characteristics of the technology are, as well as their relationship with social structures, are both seen to be negotiated outcomes of a whole range of social factors and processes (e.g., Bijker and Law, 1992; Grint and Woolgar, 1997; Hutchby, 2001a: 16; MacKenzie and Wajcman, 1999).

Although Ethnomethodology, Conversation Analysis, and Membership Categorisation Analysis (EM/CA/MCA) tend to stay out of the wider debate, the interdependence of technology and society is well known in the fields. The technology of the tape recorder was part of the impetus for Sacks's (1984a) decision to treat naturally occurring interaction as a data source for sociological investigation. Further, both Sacks's earliest lecture (1995: Vols., 1, 3) and Schegloff's (1968) 'Sequencing in conversational openings' specifically rested on the sequential and categorical implications of the telephone as a medium. Both noted that telephone interaction involves the technologically instantiated role categories of caller and recipient and that these categories were oriented to by the participants as having a degree of control over the interaction.

Later researchers following in their footsteps went on to show that there are many practices of telephone interaction that orient to the *technology*. Telephone users have quite sophisticated orientations to the fragility of maintaining mutual engagement with a voice-only connection, as demonstrated by numerous practices for asking others to 'hold on' in circumstances such as transferring calls, switching between two calls, and leaving and returning mid-call (Hopper, 1992). Hutchby and Barnett (2005) and a range of research from Arminen and colleagues (Arminen, 2005, 2007; Arminen and Leinonen, 2006; Arminen and Weilenmann, 2009) has shown that the mobile phone has sparked a range of practices for dealing with location-sensitivity, a mobile intersection of time and space, and being present in the talk while also doing other activities. Unique practices have also been explored in related audio contexts. Sanders (2003), for example, found users of marine radio adapting laughter for situations in which transmission blocked reception and vice versa. Nevile (2004) has explored the careful coordination of pilot and co-pilot with air traffic controllers via radio. Much that is not directly acknowledged by all parties is nevertheless treated as understood through overhearing and there is a crucial skill in understanding who is on and off air at any given time.

As we have moved into the age of Information and Communication Technology (ICT), EM/CA/MCA and allied approaches were initially interested in comparing and contrasting spoken conversation with the typographic quasi-synchronous Computer-Mediated Communication (CMC) systems, exploring issues such as response coherence (Garcia and Jacobs, 1999; Herring, 1999), openings (Rintel and Pittam, 1997; Rintel et al., 2001), and non-responses (Rintel et al., 2003) in Internet Relay Chat (IRC). Critics of this approach have argued that such research treats the specifically scope-limited conversational turn-taking model of Sacks, Schegloff and Jefferson (1974) as a gold standard rather than seeing how members endogenously make sense of, with, and within each given medium on its own terms (see Dourish et al. (1996) and Greiffenhagen and Watson (2005); cf. Reed and Ashmore's (2000) methodological critique that CA mythologises its analytic artefacts as being 'unmediated'). The critique is fairly made, although it leaves open the question of how to treat technology analytically.

MCA's interest in ICT interaction initially started with similar orientations, such as Paul ten Have's (2000) investigation of the use of the specifically categorically oriented 'a/s/l' (standing for 'age/sex/location') as an opening device in IRC interactions. MCA research has concentrated on how communities of practice are enacted in category references (e.g. Stommel and Koole, 2010). Perhaps somewhat ironically, omnirelevance has been a background issue in such work, rarely directly addressed but visible in, for example, Vallis's (1999, 2001a, 2001b) excellent demonstrations of IRC users' devices that orientate to the rights and obligations of 'interacting in a chat room'. The EM 'Studies of Work' programme concentrates less on the mediation of interaction within ICTs and more on the coordination of interaction in technological contexts or with technological artefacts (see overviews in Button, 1993a; Harper, 2010; Heath et al., 2000; Rouncefield et al., 2011; Sharrock and Button, 2011).

While the research above is tied together thematically and through the general methods of the fields, it is highly variable in both the vocabulary and analytic principles by which claims are made about the interdependence of technology and interaction. I follow Hutchby's (2001a, 2001b) approach in using Gibson's (1979) concept of affordances to provide a sufficiently clear but flexible analytic vocabulary.

Gibson's (1979) concept of affordances was first popularised in Human Computer Interaction (HCI) by Donald Norman (1999, 2013) and William Gaver (1992) to explain how designs suggest, or fail to suggest, actions to users (e.g. McGrenere and Ho, 2000). Gibson asserted that actors engage with their environment through making use of the stable actionable material properties of objects. He termed those actionable properties affordances. Affordances that enable action are 'enablements', while affordances that limit action are 'constraints'. Hutchby (2001b: 448) notes that 'for Gibson, 'the *affordance* of something is assumed *not* to change as the need of the observer changes'...' but in Norman's (1999, 2013) extension of the concept, he contends that not all engagement with an object is related to its material properties. Objects also have social affordances (Norman calls them 'perceived affordances') that relate to logical, cultural or conventional enablements or constraints. For example, the field of view of a web camera is limited and participants can often be found urging one another to move around so that one another's face is visible. The technology has no stake in whether a face is in view or not, only people do. The social affordances are thus bound up with the human purposes for using a technology; the material and the social are 'laminated and compounded' upon one another:

> For example, a young child may become interested in a camera found around the house. The camera may be found to have a catch, which affords undoing, and a hinged door, which affords opening. Yet carrying out these actions will lead to problems if the camera contains a roll of film, which is a material affording the development of still photographic images but only if exposed to light under highly restricted conditions. The child may thus learn that there are both social and technological rules delimiting the affordances of the camera's door: namely, that you do not open it while a film is inside unless you want to destroy the film (and incur the wrath of the adult camera-owners). (Hutchby 2001a: 448–9)

In sum, Hutchby argues (2001a: 450), 'When people interact through, around or with technologies, it is necessary for them to find ways of managing the constraints on their possibilities for action that emerge from those artefacts' affordances.' This approach thus accepts a realist but not determinist position because it explores how participants treat materiality as an interactional resource.

As should now be clear, there is a striking relationship between Sacks's observations about the operation of omnirelevant categorisation devices and how the concept of affordances provides a vocabulary for analysing the manner in which people observably orient to ICT features in their interactional practices. Both are ways of pointing to practices of organising behaviour that are always available to frame behaviour but are not necessarily always treated as relevant. Further, I think it is plausible to argue that the reflexive oscillation between interaction and context from which omnirelevance draws its power as an organisational device is the mechanism by which users laminate and compound the material and social possibilities of technology to produce technologised interaction.

Video Calling in Relational Contexts

Video calling has had one of the longest journeys to mainstream use of any post Industrial Revolution communication technology. Much early video calling research was focused on task achievement in institutional settings and conducted experimentally in laboratory settings (see overviews in Finn et al. 1997; Harrison, 2009), largely because of infrastructural requirements. At the turn of the 21st century, domestic video calling has become a near-mainstream reality with the rise in cheap video calling hardware and software for personal computers, improved compression algorithms, and widespread take-up of broadband internet access. However, while it is approaching a level of technological maturity, fitting video calling into domestic life is still normatively unsettled.

Domestic video calling field research has focused initially on two areas. One area of interest is how video calling is the kind of techno-social infrastructural work required to initiate, run and troubleshoot domestic video calls (Ames et al., 2010; Kirk et al., 2010). More interactionally focused research has explored how the sense of intimacy is re-imagined in relational video calling (Neustaedter and Greenberg, 2011) and the management of different expectations about the purpose of video calls and the relative value of visual and audio access in overcoming family separation (Judge et al., 2011; Yarosh and Abowd, 2011; Yarosh et al., 2009), mediated play (Follmer et al. 2010; Yarosh and Kwikkers, 2011), and how always-on video windows between the office and home or between two homes enables and constrains practices for interaction that are quite different to temporally bounded video calls (Judge and Neustaedter, 2010; Neustaedter, 2013).

An oversight in socially focused ICT research, including video calling research, is that researchers concentrate on investigating mediation with respect to the designed *features* of ICTs (e.g. see overviews in Herring, 1996; Jones, 1998; Walther, 2011, 2012). The mediating effects of *distortions* tend to be left either to the engineering-oriented telecommunication paradigm of Quality of Service (QoS) (e.g. Hashimoto and Ishibashi, 2006; Lu et al., 2010; Watson and Sasse, 2000) or the usability paradigm of perceptual thresholds and task effects (Horn et al., 2002; Isaacs and Tang, 2003; Monk and Watts, 1995; Watson and Sasse, 2000). However, there is far less research about how users actually manage such distortions as part of the interaction.

There has been much interest in how media spaces introduce asymmetries into interaction that impact upon getting and keeping an interlocutor's attention (Dourish, 2001; Dourish et al., 1996; Harper, 2010; Harrison, 2009; Heath and Luff, 1991), but these are the result of design constraints of the media spaces rather than distortions. More recent EM/CA research on video calling tends to focus on how video enablements and constraints are entwined with participants' turn-by-turn actions (e.g. Licoppe, Verdier and Dumoulin, 2013; Licoppe et al., 2013; Mondada, 2007b), but again the research focus is on the designed features of the video not distortions. Ruhleder and Jordan's (2001) study is one of the few to have investigated the turn-by-turn results of how network latency distorts the interactional timing associated with preference organisation of turns at talk. However, their study focused on business video call meetings and deliberately set out to investigate distortions that could be shown to effect interaction but were not directly a participant concern due to the subtlety of the distortion.

In terms of the affordances approach, operational problems such as audio/video distortions have rarely been treated as directly considered constraints, perhaps because they result from computational infrastructure issues (e.g. the packet-switched nature of the internet or the complexities of audio/video codecs) rather than user-level design issues, and because they are idiosyncratic mistakes, errors, and in other ways not intended. However, while they are not design features, operational problems are a fundamental material part of the experience of using CTs and, as such, can be considered within the frame of affordances. By employing the technologised interaction approach I am arguing against treating operational problems as mere noise or threshold issues and instead exploring what we might find out about technology, interaction, and society by attending to how operational problems are a participant's concern. Such an argument, of course, depends a great deal on the context in which participants are interacting. In this chapter my illustrations are drawn from the interdependence of technological and relational omnirelevance, especially with respect to couples' talk and teasing (Fitzgerald and Rintel, 2013).

Couples' Talk and Teasing

In contrast to psychologically oriented research into interpersonal communication and relationships (e.g. Knapp and Daly, 2011; cf. Sanders, 1997), EM/CA/MCA research has a long history of arguing that the interpersonal intimacy of being a couple does not consist solely of reciprocal cognitive attitudes nor *a priori*, fixed and stable contexts for action. Sacks noticed early on that intimacy is typically indexed by the absence of ceremonials (1995: Vol. 1, 14–19) and invitations (1995: Vol. 1, 73), but also that on occasion the very absence of ceremonials between married partners might come to be an accountable dilemma which itself indexes intimacy (1995: Vol. 1, 18). Since then many studies have demonstrated that doing being a couple must be accomplished with observable-reportable phenomena between couple members and is as much an interactional achievement as any other social fact (Benwell and Stokoe, 2006; De Stefani, 2013; Edwards, 1995b; Mandelbaum, 1987, 2003; Pomerantz and Mandelbaum, 2004; Staske, 1996, 1998; Stokoe, 2010a; Svennevig, 1999).

Callers and call-recipients have also been shown to orient to the nature of their relationship as enacted via the technology. Two early classic studies on telephone interaction found practices specifically built around the ability to call intimates and family members at a distance. Button (1991c) found practices for telephone closings that propose a 'standing relationship'. Drew and Chilton (2000) found that differences to the canonical telephone opening propose relational maintenance calls as habitualised and 'doing relating'.

Teasing has long been identified as one of the practices used by couples to enact their intimacy (Alberts, 1992; Alberts et al., 1996, 2005; Campbell et al., 2008; Keltner et al., 1998; Pawluk, 1989; Radcliff-Brown, 1940), from younger couples dating (Keltner et al., 1998) to newlyweds (Driver and Gottman, 2004), old married couples (Ingersoll-Dayton et al., 1998) and across cultures (Brown, 1991; Campos et al., 2007; Schiefflin and Ochs, 1986).

Teasing is an ambiguous (Alberts, 1992: 154), paradoxical (Keltner et al., 1998: 1231) blend of 'playfulness with derogation' (Hopper et al., 1981: 28). Campos et al. (2007: 4) define teasing as:

playful provocation that comments on something of relevance to the target (Keltner et al., 2001). The provocation can be verbal ... or nonverbal ... but is commonly a non-literal verbal communication that calls negative attention to another as part of play (Keltner et al., 2001; Wyer and Collins, 1992).

From a social psychological perspective, teasing is interesting because of the relational consequences of its ambiguity: whether teasing will be treated as affiliative or disaffiliative (Alberts et al., 1996; Campos et al., 2007). From an EM/CA/MCA perspective, the interest is more in charting members' methods of recognisably deploying and responding to teases. The method that Drew (1987: 244) finds members using to construct teases is a membership categorisation procedure, 'whereby a kind of innocent activity or category membership which is occasioned, usually in the teased person's prior turn(s), is then transformed in the tease into a deviant activity or category. Something which is normal, unremarkable, etc., is turned into something abnormal.'

This brings us back to couples' talk. Aside from psychological concepts such as affiliation or language in/as context (Alberts, 1992: 168), teases are a valuable part of doing being a couple because they are one of the more special ways of displaying who-we-are-and-what-we-are-doing. In the language of MCA, couple-ness is an omnipresent device for teasing because the attendant category-bound activities, category predicates, duplicative organisations, and positioned categories have special relevance and organisational control with respect to 'we as a couple'.

Methods and Data

The data for this chapter were collected with the goal of exploring whether and how participants oriented to endogenously arising distortions as an interactional issue in long-distance relational maintenance. As noted above, the limitations of consumer-level internet connectivity make video calling a perspicuous setting[2] for exploring the intersection of technological and relational omnirelevance.

Couples in distance relationships were recruited via online and physical flyers in the North-eastern USA and supplied with webcams and the Wave Three Inc. Session video calling software. The couples were asked to try video calling from home to supplement any other regular interaction. They were set a usage goal of video calling for at least 20 minutes per week over a two-month period, but this goal was not strictly enforced. No tasks were required and there were no other controls apart from minimum technology standards. With the couples' consent, an automated remote recording system captured all video calls (see Figure 6.1).

Since the recording system relied on establishing a three-member group call rather than having recording systems at each end of a two-member call, it did not allow for direct or measurable analysis of asymmetrical transmission/reception such as audio/visual latency or clarity in the manner of some prior video-mediated

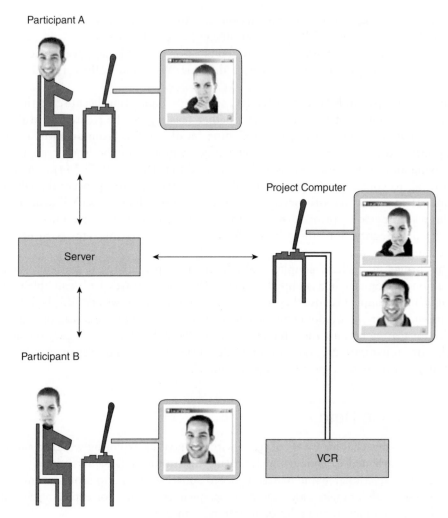

Figure 6.1 Automated remote recording system for video calling data collection.

interaction research (e.g. Harrison, 2009; Ruhleder and Jordan, 2001). However, given the interpersonal context it would have been extremely difficult to recruit participants and record naturalistic intimate relational talk had there been recording devices at either end of the call. Unlike the above-mentioned prior research, the goal of this project was to explore how participants explicitly treated audio/visual distortions as conversationally relevant, so precision timing was not as important as sequential and categorical accountability. Further, the recording system did not capture the entirety of participants' screens, nor their interaction in other media, so it is not claimed that this data represents the entirety of online relational maintenance (e.g. the participants reported talk about distortions on mobile telephones and text-based chat in exit interviews). Again, however, this was a trade-off so that participants did not feel that they were under total surveillance. As such, the system was adequate for the task and this combination of task and technological freedom maximised the ecological validity of the recordings and afforded very naturalistic experiences (see Rintel (2007) for details).

Altogether the six couples each had between five and 11 calls, in which a median of around 8% of their time was spent coping with endogenously arising distortions of varying disruptiveness. One hundred and forty-five total cases of coping with distortions were collected, broadly separable into technology-oriented remedies (57 cases; 39.3%), content-oriented remedies (42 cases; 29.7%) and non-remedial accounts (46 cases; 31%) (Rintel, 2010). This chapter draws on examples from the content-oriented remedies and non-remedial accounts of five of the couples. Some of these examples have appeared in prior analyses (Rintel, 2010, 2013a, 2013b) but not drawn together as in this chapter to demonstrate the analytic value of omnirelevance and its links to technologised interaction.

Distortion and the Omnirelevance of Technology and Relationship

Responses to Distorted Audio

One reason for invoking an omnirelevant device is that it can be used to resolve interactional ambiguities, such as the need for and manner of a repair, because the work of an omnirelevant device is to provide a point of organisational recognisability by reflexively oscillating between interaction and context to produce an observable-reportable account of one's point of view for the other.

Audio distortions can lead to missing or garbled words or phrases, obviously creating the conditions for repair. However, repair is a special issue in video calling because the asymmetrical access to production and reception of audio and video (Heath and Luff, 1991, 1992, 2000; Ruhleder and Jordan, 2001) means that, unlike physically co-present interaction, neither end knows that the other is actually seeing or hearing. In audio distortion cases, then, speakers cannot hear their own distorted sound so self-initiated repair is rare; the onus to initiate repair almost always falls to hearers.

In many cases, repair of audio distortions occurred without ambiguity and even without mention of the technological cause of the distortion. As in co-present interaction, a common repair format involved a hearer initiating repair by indicating a problem and some form of content location, and speakers simply producing the located content (usually a total repetition of the prior turn), as shown in Extracts 1 and 2. In both examples below the repair initiator was treated as unambiguous and the repair was accepted without explanation.

EXTRACT 1: HAL AND EVA 1

```
1.  HAL:  She um broke out the- uh t{SOUND CUTS OUT(0.5)}cake
2.  EVA:  The what?
3.  HAL:  She broke out the cheesecake
4.  EVA:  H↑oh↓ ((laugh)) that's[ nice]
5.  HAL:                          [yeah ]
```
[Case079-p02-c05of05-t11p5307]

EXTRACT 2: CAM AND KIM 1

```
1. CAM:  And I know-] I know that for the entire month
2.       you eat no real food
3. KIM:  .h [no]
4. CAM:     [A-] and don't tell me don't tell
5.       {SOUND CUTS OUT(2.0)}
6.       (1.0)
7. KIM:  What I didn't hear you
8. CAM:  Don't tell me pancakes and toast count as real food
9. KIM:  I didn't say that. What I will say is tha:t
10.      when I don't eat that I don't eat anything
```
[Case139-p05-c11of11-t04p2452]

In both of these cases the only device required for organisational recognisability is the ordinary orientation to conversational repair as part of the turn-taking system itself (Schegloff et al., 1977). No further organisational device that indicates the relational or technological context is made relevant to accomplishing the repair.

However, just as in co-present interaction, open-class repairs (Drew, 1997) may allow for ambiguity – is a repair being initiated because of a hearing problem or some trouble with meaning (something disjunctive, inapposite, possibly indicating a moral problem etc.)? While it is obvious that one or other recipient could point to a technological distortion if it is indeed the cause of trouble, in this data technology was an *omnirelevant* device when it was used to instantiate the technological context as recognisably organisational in the context of an open-class repair of an audio distortion, and thus used to rule out non-technological production or hearing problems, understanding problems, or moral problems. Extract 3 illustrates the simplest sense of the omnirelevant value of the technology for organisational recognisability in repair. After quite a long stretch of talk from Des (lines 1–4), Kay interruptively initiates repair by calling a halt and indicating a problem. With an open-class 'wait what?' (line 5) she does not locate the specifically missed content as Eva's 'The what?' does in Extract 1.

EXTRACT 3: DES AND KAY 1

```
1. DES:    And the wh- most hilarious part was:
2.         Lizzie was on the phone with John when
3.         we discovered this and he's like
4.         {SOUND CUTS OUT(1.0)} -m(h)m s(h)[o-]
5. KAY:                                    [Wa]it what?
6.         (1.5)
7. DES:    What do you mean what
8. KAY:    You cut out I didn't [hear that la-     ]
9. DES:                         [{Oh you mean li-}]
10.        Oh- ah the part that Lizzie was on the phone with?
11. KAY:   Y[eah and then]
12. DES:    [John         ]
13. KAY:   What after that?
14. DES:   And then he was like oh yeah Jan I remember her
15.        so: then I talked to Ann some more
```

[Case019-p01-c03of09-t11p2959]

Since Des does not know his speech has been distorted, he has the job of determining the nature of Kay's need to repair. His solution is to directly ask Kay about the nature of the repair initiation ('what do you mean what', line 7). Kay's response is to report the technological distortion ('You cut out', line 8) and then begin to locate the problematic content. Having heard the nature of the repair as involving a technologically caused hearing problem, Des is able to begin offering a candidate check on the missing content to repair (lines 9–10) in overlap with Kay (line 6). The repair flows without further problem (lines 11–15).

Extract 4 is more complex. Des finishes a story with an upshot (lines 1–2) that Kay does not quite follow (line 3). She does not understand why the protagonist of the story was angry, but repairing this involves some tension between Des and Kay.

EXTRACT 4: DES AND KAY 2

```
1. DES:    He was kinda mad I think it was funny
2.         ((lau[gh))]
3. KAY:        [Why w]as he mad?
4. DES:    Coz she was {SOUND CUTS OUT(1.5)} sausage
5.         and he was like just trying to eat
6.         and she wouldn't leave him alone it was just funny
7. KAY:    Coz what?
8. DES:    ((Deliberate and annoyed intonation)) She was trying
```

```
 9.          to force feed him sausage and he [didn't want] it
10. KAY:                                      [Oh:       ]
11. DES:   Like he just wanted to like chill (.)
12.        and [she was so drunk  ]
13. KAY:       [Sorry . it cut out]
14. DES:   Oh that's okay
```

[Case035-p01-c06of09-t11p0615]

From Kay's perspective, Des's attempted explanation for why the protagonist was mad is distorted early on (line 4) but she lets Des continue with the explanation in an apparent attempt to hear enough to understand. Repair initiation usually follows trouble very rapidly, often at the next possible completion point of the turn (Schegloff et al., 1977). Kay, though, lets Des get through the most obvious completion point ('sausage'), the second possible completion point ('eat'), the third possible completion point ('alone'), and Des's repeated assessment of the anger as 'funny' (lines 4–6). Kay's repair initiator ('Coz what'; line 7) proposes virtually no uptake of Des's long turn. In the context of the unfolding interaction, this repair initiator is almost a repetition of Kay's prior request for clarification (line 3) that occasioned the explanation that is now being treated as troubled. So initiating repair in line 5 amounts to a request for a second repetition. Des produces this second repetition very slowly and deliberately with an annoyed tone (lines 8–9). Kay finally indicates uptake in overlap with the end of Des's repetition (line 10), to which Des orients by returning to his regular intonation as he elaborates the story (lines 11–12) and implicitly proposing an end to the repair.

However, the repair issue is apparently not complete for Kay. Despite indicating uptake of Des's repetition and hearing Des return to storytelling with his regular intonation, Kay retrospectively orients to Des's slower-than-normal talk production method (line 13). She waits for the first possible completion point of Des's next normally produced turn ('Like he just wanted to like chill'; line 11), and then in overlap apologises and reports prior technological trouble ('Sorry . it cut out'; lines 13). The apology casts the repair incident as a whole (that she has made multiple repair requests and that Des has produced long turns, including some produced markedly slower), as potentially blameworthy for the significant effort that it required of Des and because she does not respond to Des's assessment of the humour of the situation. Kay reports the technological trouble with a direct reference to the accountability of the medium as non-human and external to both her and Des's agency/intentions ('it cut out'). The technological distortion, then, is used as an omnirelevant device for reframing the interaction as occurring in that technological context and thus potentially always subject to problems.

As was noted in Rintel (2013b), disambiguation becomes especially relevant when the topic of conversation is *relationally sensitive*. In Extract 5, Des and Kay are making plans for a vacation in another city with a group of friends. Vacations, of course, are relationally important to long-distance couples because they are times to be together and free from other responsibilities. Repair in such a situation is fraught with potential moral consequences, and thus any organisational device is very important.

EXTRACT 5: DES AND KAY 3

```
1.  DES: P→ Um::: someone can probably
2.             sleep on the c{SOUND CUTS OUT(2.5)}s three .h
3.  KAY: I→ Wait what?
4.  DES:Id→ Someone can probably[ sl]eep on- did it cut out?
5.  KAY:                        [oh ]
6.  KAY:      Yeah
7.  DES:      Oh. Someone can probably sleep on the couch
```
[Case052-p01-c09of09-t10p5139]

Des proposes that a third person might stay on the couch in their hotel room (lines 1–2). From Kay's perspective a large proportion of Des's proposal is dropped out (line 2), so Kay initiates repair. As in Example 3, she calls a halt and produces an open-class problem indicator ('wait what'?; line 3), which leaves Des with the responsibility to determine the reason for the repair initiation. Des initially orients to the repair in the simple manner of Extract 1, beginning a repetition of the immediately prior content (line 4).

However, three words into Des's repair, Kay overlaps Des with the change of state marker 'Oh' (line 5). While for Kay this 'Oh' is a retrospective marker of understanding the repaired turn in the midst of its repeated production, for Des this second overlap from Kay is interruptive and potentially indicative that Des's turn-in-progress may not be on the right track. Des cuts off his content repetition to change his repair design. He now specifically requests confirmation of a candidate technological reason for Kay's problem indication ('Someone can probably[sl]eep on- did it cut out?'; line 4). Des is thus attempting disambiguation of whether he can simply repeat the content because the technology distorted it or whether he needs to deal with a meaning issue with the content itself – the relationally sensitive issue of the sleeping arrangements. Kay's confirmation of Des's candidate ('Yeah'; line 6) provides Des with the go-ahead to simply repeat the content (line 7), which he does.

The simplicity of this example belies its importance. Des's immediate jump to a technological candidate is an obvious solution precisely because it is an omnirelevant organisational device that can provide an easy path to resolution. The ease of this path is morally determined by the intertwined omnirelevance of the relationship – this is a relational topic in a longer relationship maintenance activity. These two omnirelevant positions are thus organisational counterpoints – if one is at issue the other is not – but also counterparts – they must both be relevant for one to be foregrounded while the other is backgrounded.

A significantly longer example of such disambiguation can be found in Rintel (2013a: 3346–8), in which Des repeatedly casts Kay's inattention (she is watching a movie while video calling) as technological trouble despite her very obvious inattention. Ironically, ruling out technological unresponsiveness may be relationally awkward in mediated interaction because the asymmetrical constraints of the technology mean that technological unresponsiveness is uncomfortably close – perhaps having almost the same apparent form – to interpersonal unresponsiveness. Treating technology as omnirelevant, then, provides for a level of organisational flexibility for overcoming difficulties.

Responses to Distorted Video

Coping with video or combined audio/video distortions was quite different to coping with audio-only distortions in the data. None of the video or audio/video cases involved *disambiguation* of technological distortion versus a potential relational problem (or, more broadly, any problem of understanding). Rather, what did occur was development of an orientation to technological and relational omnirelevance with respect to the *expressive* needs of the couples' talk. That is, users worked to distinguish frequent low-level operational visual constraints (missing frames, blurriness, etc.) from acute operational problems (long freezes, lack of video), and actively engaged in working out how to treat such distortions as an ongoing part of who-we-are-and-what-we-are-doing-in-this-medium. An acute problem may or may not materially cause interactional perturbation, depending on the relevance of visuals for the activity at hand, but it can be *treated* as relevant – and that, of course, is what it means to be engaged in technologised interaction.

Extracts 6 to 8 show that as the orientation to conversational continuity in the face of visual technological distortion increased, so too did an accompanying mutual expressive orientation to the relationship as enacted through the technology.

EXTRACT 6: HAL AND EVA 2

```
1. EVA:   Joey's pitbull played with Rex the other day (.)
2.        um, cuz he brought him over, and ever since
3.        Rex has been limping.
4.        We think he hurt his l- his uh knee again
5. HAL:   ((\{NO SOUND\}(@Mouths one word@))
6.        \{FREEZES(3.5) UNFREEZES\}
7.        h. So: uh: how was your day?
8. EVA:   ((Small laugh)) D(h)id you hear about my dog?
```

```
 9. HAL:   Yeah you said y- your dog was limping
10. EVA:   Oh yeah okay=I don't-
11.        I couldn't tell if you could hear or not,
12.        coz it keeps going in and out
13. HAL:   {FREEZES(5.0)}
14. EVA:   ((laugh)) And now you're frozen.
15. HAL:   {UNFREEZES}
16. EVA:   There you go you're moving again
17. HAL:   (((@Smiles@)) How was your day?
18. EVA:   It was good u:m (@looks up@) tk what did I do (.)
19.        Oh yeah Lisa's baby I went and saw it, it's so: cute
```

[Case081-p02-c05of05-t11p5418]

In Extract 6 Eva experiences both audio and visual distortions of Hal during a mutual news-of-the-day exchange. The first time Hal's video and audio freezes (line 6), Eva ignores the visual issue and works on ensuring reception and understanding of her news (line 8). The pair make their way through a repair only for Eva to experience Hal as frozen once again (line 13), after which Eva reports him as 'frozen again' (line 14), even as he unfreezes, thus she updates her report on the status of his video as 'now you're moving again' (line 16). Neither Eva nor Hal orient to the visual distortion as relevantly repairable or mutually topicalisable, thus the insertion of these reports without response demonstrates a version of an achieved 'let it pass' omnirelevance in which technological distortion is reportable but not acted upon because it does not trouble conversational continuity.

EXTRACT 7: RAY AND SUN 1

```
 1. RAY:   Actually I wanna watch, uh- {FREEZES(2.0)}
 2.        (2.0)
 3. SUN:   >Okay now you're frozen<
 4. RAY:   {UNFREEZES} ((@Rapidly moves from side to side@))
 5.        Am I out?
 6. RAY:   ((@Rubs lotion [on hands@))]
 7. SUN:                  [Yeah. Unfrozen.]
 8. RAY:   ((@Rubs lotion on hands(6.0) Turns away@))
 9.        {FREEZES(1.0)}
10. SUN:   ((Laugh)) You froze again
11. RAY:   {UNFREEZES} ((@Shakes head from side to side@))
12.        Does it look cool when I freeze
13.        with these stripes on my face.
14. SUN:   Doesn't ma[ke] a difference
```

[Case122-p04-c07of10-t11p0905]

Extract 7 is similar to Extract 6 in that frozen video is reported as not affecting conversational continuity. The pair orient to reporting on whether Ray is 'frozen' or 'out' of being frozen (lines 1–7, 9–14), with limited topicalisation of what Ray's being frozen looks like to Sun (lines 11–13). Having heard the report of being frozen Ray attempts a limited re-framing of the constraint as a resource, shaking his head from side to side and asking Sun 'Does it look cool when I freeze with these stripes on my face'. Although Sun reports that it 'Doesn't ma[ke] a difference' (line 14), in terms of omnirelevance there are some quite important achievements in this example. First, being frozen is initially reportable enough to warrant interruption, despite later being treated as not making a difference (line 3). The ambient sound from Ray's end in this recording indicated that his audio was still functioning correctly (i.e. that this was a production cut-off not a technical reception cut-off) when Ray's visual froze. This coincidence is an apparent perturbation of conversational continuity, which is imminently reportable. However, when Ray resumes speaking and then asks about whether it looks 'cool', Sun reverts immediately to letting it pass. This is crucial, as it indicates the omnirelevance of technology as organisationally recognisable, but that different forms of distortion are to be treated as differently relevant depending on conversational continuity.

EXTRACT 8: ORA AND JED 1

```
 1. ORA:    ((@Arranging her wet hair@))
 2. JED:    Is my video blurry on your screen
 3.         or does it look nice?
 4. ORA:    Um::::::[:]
 5. JED:            [D]oes it look pixelated?
 6. ORA:    Yeah
 7. JED:    Oh okay
 8. ORA:    ((@Looks away towards door@))
 9. JED:    [So does yours]
10. ORA:    [It's fine    ] It doesn't- it doesn't bother me
           it's fine.
11.        As long as I can see your beautiful face @smiles@
12. JED:   The pixelated version of it @raises eyebrow@
13. ORA:   Turn into a dragon again- a dinosaur! ((laug[hs))    ]
14. JED:                                              [((laughs))]
```

[Case142-p06-c04of07-t09p5558]

Ora and Jed take this 'let it pass' agreement that visual distortion is prevalent but not disruptive one step further in Extract 8. Ora is arranging her wet hair in a conversational lull, which Jed takes as an opportunity to topicalise a check similarity of video quality (lines 2–3). Unlike in the previous examples, Jed does not report his view of Ora; rather he asks Ora to report on her view of him. He provides Ora with a choice between two candidates, a view that is negatively valenced via a report of a view state of 'blurry', or the exclusive candidate view that is positively valenced via a report of Ora's evaluative feeling about the video as 'nice'. Ora's first response is a long marker of taking the offered floor but being unsure about the response ('Um::::::[:]'; line 4). Ora's difficulty in responding immediately to this question indicates the potential problems with topicalising non-disruptive technological constraints: Ora may be somewhat absorbed in her own activity of hair brushing, or the candidates may not be mutually exclusive for her, or 'let it pass' may already be operative and thus a change of attention is needed to evaluate the view, or the descriptors may not be as self-evidently representative to her as they are to Jed.

Jed starts a turn in overlap that treats this hesitation as difficulty answering the question by reformulating his check to the simpler proposition of a single negative candidate 'pixelated' that is both more precisely described and can be confirmed or disconfirmed (line 5). Ora's confirmation (line 6) treats Jed's reformulation as answerable and does not mention content perturbation or any form of remedy for the distortion. Jed acknowledges this confirmation (line 7) in the same manner and then reports that the view is mutual (line 9). The floor is thus left open at a point where organisational recognisability of who-we-are-and-what-we-are-doing-in-this-medium is at issue *translucently*. That is, the issue can be let pass or not, but while there has been no perturbation of conversational continuity to overcome, Jed has directed the pair into state of mutual consideration of the technologised view of one another and to a parallel state of mutual consideration of *why* they would want to look at one another. This is a now explicitly relevant and *omnirelevant* orientation to the *interdependence* of the technology and the relationship.

Thus in overlap with Jed's report, Ora orients to this device as organisationally relevant to the next turn. She self-selects and specifically casts the relevance of the pixelation in several ways (lines 10–11): first as not causing trouble ('it's fine'), then as a choice to normalise the distortion by showing that she has accepted its potentially negative valence ('It doesn't- it doesn't bother me it's fine'; line 9). But most importantly, third, Ora follows up her normalisation with relational reasoning, proposing that the warrant for her assessment is that the technological constraints are to be judged against their relational enablements ('As long as I can see your beautiful face'; line 11). Such accounts are crucial to long-distance relational maintenance via video calling because they become part of a couple's collaborative standard for conversational continuity based on expressive practices.

Teases

This brings us, then, to teases. As discussed in the literature review above, teases are common in many forms of intimate relationships, even though – or perhaps because – they involve playing with the ambiguity of affiliation and disaffiliation. It is worth noting that while teases delicately play on the knife-edge of derogation, for these young couples none of the recorded teases misfired or backfired in such a way as to cause a problem. Indeed, even 'po-faced receipts' (Drew, 1987) were not found. Rather, teases were very much part of the expressive fabric of 'doing being couples'.

Some teases in response to video distortions were quite straightforward in their orientation to interweaving the omnirelevance of the relationship and technology.

EXTRACT 9: DES AND KAY 4

```
 1. DES:    ((@Open mouth smile@))
 2. KAY:    ((laugh)) You have no teeth ((laugh))
 3. DES:    ((@Opens mouth with lips over teeth@))
 4. DES:    [((@Closes mouth turns left@))]
 5. KAY:    [Your mouth is like so blurry ]
 6.         it looks like it's sewed shut ((la[ughs))    ]
 7. DES:                                    [Alright ]
 8.         I'll turn up my quality
 9.         it's still choppy I wish it was better
10. KAY:    M:e too but it's not
11. DES:    [Yeah I know   ]
12. KAY:    [. this is why] you can't date people far away
13. KAY:    [((@Open mouth smile and raised eyebrows@))]
14. DES:    [((choked laugh))]
```

[Case021-p01-c03of09-f11p3852-18m57in-02m19s]

In Extract 9, Kay reports that Des's video is distorted in a limited but amusing fashion (he looks as if he 'has no teeth' or his mouth is 'sewed shut', lines 2, 5–6). Des's response is to report that he will undertake a technical solution ('Alright I'll turn up my quality'; lines 7–8). In this software, the technical solution to move the slider that increases video quality make his mouth more clearly visible, but there may be a trade-off in more audio distortion as the system attempts to push more data even though the bandwidth has not increased. The pair have experienced this trade-off before (in this and prior conversations), hence his complaint about the poor audio quality and reported desire for the technology to be 'better' (line 9).

It is at this point that Kay produces both an initial agreement 'M:e too but it's not' (line 10) followed by a teasing upshot '[. this is why] you can't date people far away' (line 12). The tease relies directly on the omnirelevant orientation between the technology and the relationship as an organisational device: that attempting to maintain a distance relationship via video calling is made more difficult when the technology does not live up to the promise of its primary affordance. That being said, the technological distortion is clearly not a barrier to understanding. It is framing what is said but it has not simply caused trouble; rather it has been treated as a resource. The fact of the distortion has been actively converted from a complaint resource into a relational resource for recognising that they are a couple maintaining their relationship via video calling.

While Extract 9 demonstrates quite a straightforward foregrounding of the technologised interaction through an explicit *telling* of the reflexive oscillation between context and content, Extract 10 involves explicitly *enacting* this reflexive oscillation that involves each partner accomplishing quite a feat of intersubjectivity with respect to the organising features of the relationship and technology.

EXTRACT 10: HAL AND EVA 3

```
---EVA and HAL have been experimenting with cartoon video over-
lays---

1.  HAL:    Maybe I'll put a picture of a dinosaur in my wallet
2.          ((@Wink@)) it's prettier
3.          (1.5)
4.  EVA:    Oh: you jer:k
5.  HAL:    ((laughs)) It's great waiting for the delay
6.          coz .h you're like
7.          @Acts out waiting then very animated@
8.          Oh: you jer:k
9.  EVA:    ((laug[hs))          ]+
10. HAL:         [((laughs)) ]
11. EVA:                        +((laughs))  Weirdo
```

[Case056-p02-c01of05-t06p5811]

Eva and Hal have been experimenting with a feature of the supplied webcams that affords them the ability to overlay motion-tracking cartoon characters over their own video. A number of characters are available, including a dinosaur, which Eva has been using. As part of this play, Hal's first tease proposes an alteration of the typical relational practice of putting a picture of a partner or desirable other in a wallet/purse. He proposes that he might put a picture of the cartoon dinosaur overlay into his wallet as opposed to a real photograph of Eva (line 1), and follows this up with a tagged tease that the picture would be prettier (line 2). Eva's response to this tease is to laughingly insult Hal ('Oh: you jerk'; line 4), but this comes after a delay of 1.5 seconds. It is to this delay that Hal addresses a second linked tease, this one addressed directly to the context of the technologised interaction.

Instead of responding directly to Eva's insult, Hal further teases Eva through reporting his amused reaction to the fact that Eva's response was delayed. He jokingly
positively evaluates the fact of Eva's delay after the first tease and then exaggeratedly
re-enacts his view of the response ('It's great waiting for the delay' 'coz .h you're like'
'Oh you jerk'; lines 5–8). The reflexive oscillations between the contents of the first
and second teases and their contextual considerations are quite dizzying.

Both partners need to understand the general constraint of asymmetrical access to
audio and video and thus imagine themselves in one another's position seeing how
the technological constraint of delay stretches out three points of recipiency and
response. The tease target does not know what is coming, the tease target is unlikely
to be able to interdict the tease mid-production, and the tease target's response will
also be delayed, thus increasing the duration of the lived experience of the tease.
Then, the original tease, the distortion, and the teasing report of the distortion all
need to be treated as part of deliberate meaning production, even though the distortion itself was not deliberate and the meanings that are being enacted reflect back
on the situation of doing being a couple via video calling. It would seem crucial that
the engine of this understanding, accomplished in just seconds, is an intertwined
omnirelevant orientation to the technology and relationship-fundamental organisational devices.

Extract 11 shows another version of this kind of elaborate intersubjectivity. Hal's
video has been frozen for some minutes prior to the couple's call-closing sequence.
Clearly, given that this is an intimate couple, closing a call is an activity replete with
the omnirelevance of the relationship as an organisational device. Distortion during a
close, then, is almost inescapably bound up with the relationship. For the purpose of
this chapter the relevant analysis begins with line 9, when Hal is able to see Eva blow
him a kiss as a relationship-relevant parting gesture, but Hal uses the visual distortion
of frozen video to enact a teasing response.

EXTRACT 11: HAL AND EVA 4

```
 1. HAL:    {FROZEN ((@Pulling skin around eyes@))}
 2. EVA:    Alrighty
 3. HAL:    O[kay]
 4. EVA:     [I love] you:
 5. HAL:    I love you t-{SOUND CUTS OUT}
 6. EVA:    {FRAMES MISSING((@Hand flash@))}
 7. EVA:    Did you get that
 8. HAL:    No do it again
 9. EVA:    @Blows a kiss@
10. HAL:    Oo::h
11. EVA:    ((laughs))
12. HAL:    Look I caught it I dunno if you can see that
```

```
13. EVA:   I can't see it (laugh)
14. HAL:   Wow that's too bad
15. EVA:   [I know]
16. HAL:   [In that] case I threw it in the garbage
17. EVA:   Oh: you bastard ((la[ughs)))]
18. HAL:                    [((laughs))]
19. EVA:   Alrighty, I [love you]
20. HAL:               [okay    ]
21. HAL:   I love you too
22. EVA:   Bye sweetie
23. HAL:   Mbye \Logs off\
24. EVA:   \Logs off\
```

[Case076-p02-c04of05-t08p1320-25m03in-00m33s]

In responding to the blown kiss, Hal builds on his initial appreciation (line 10) by describing a physical – but unseeable – performance of catching the kiss, which is a typical second-pair part to the blown kiss. Hal suspects that he is frozen, so he checks Eva's reception ('Look I caught it I dunno if you can see that'; line 12). Eva verifies that she did not see Hal's action (line 13).

With this information, Hal could give up on video and rely on audio, which is demonstrably operative. However, Hal chooses instead to capitalise on the concept of an unseeable performance to tease Eva in a specifically relational manner. He claims that since Eva cannot see his 'catch', in that case he 'threw it in the garbage' (line 16). As noted in Rintel (2013b), this physical performance is unlikely to have actually occurred, but that is irrelevant to the tease itself because of the value that couples ascribe to blowing and catching kisses. In terms of omnirelevance, Hal changes his conversational continuity orientation from distortion as repairable to distortion as an interactional resource for an intimate tease. This form of technologised interaction might be said to almost fully embrace both the enablements and constraints of the video calling into one fluid interdependence that affords mutual orientation to an omnipresent technological and relational sense of who-we-are-and-what-we-are-doing-in-this-medium.

This fluid interdependence within one medium can be taken even further. Example 12, also taken from a call-close, shows Ray teasing Sun through an omnirelevant orientation to technology and the relationship as displayable – and teasable – across multiple media. When Sun's image begins freezing and unfreezing, Ray claims to be able to take a picture of Sun's frozen image and that he will put it up on Facebook (lines 17, 30). While Sun objects violently in between asking him how it can be done (25, 35, 37), the fact of the connection trouble of frozen video in video calling itself is completely subsumed by the possibility of an unflattering picture being publicly available across media other than the one in which the couple are currently enacting their relationship in private.

EXTRACT 12: RAY AND SUN 2

---RAY has been teasing SUN by not telling her the name of someone who called him. SUN is frozen.---

```
 1.RAY:   It's your bedtime
 2.SUN:   No:
 3.RAY:   Alright so uh
 4.SUN:   Wait so tell me who called {UNFREEZES}
 5.        ((@Wipes moisturizer on face@)) {FREEZES}
 6.        (5.0)
 7.RAY:   Gotta go [(((@Raises hand very high and then back
 8.        down))@]
 9.SUN:   [Ra:y! N(h)(h)o! Don't you dare]
10.RAY:   I'm gonna push that button [(((@Hand hovers@))          ]
11.SUN:                              [{UNFREEZES} No {FREEZES} Ray]
12.RAY:   ((@Hand drops below field of view@))
13.       (8.0)
14.RAY:   You're frozen=
15.SUN:   =Don't. No:!=
16.RAY:   =You're frozen with your eyes closed and your mouth open
17.       and your face coming towards the camera. Eeya[hh:!]
18.SUN:                                               [((laughs))]
19.RAY:   Oh I'm going gonna take a picture of this
20.SUN:   {UNFREEZES}
21.RAY:   ((High 'silly' intonation)) Yeah!
22.SUN:   How do you do that?
23.RAY:   Print[scree:n          ]
24.SUN:        [How do you take- ] Wait we can take pictures?
25.RAY:   .hYup!
26.SUN:   {FREEZES} How?
27.RAY:   ((laughs)) Na- [print screen!]
28.SUN:                  [Ra:y!        ] {UNFREEZES}
29.        No:[:  ]
30.RAY:       [Tha]t's the button you press
31.SUN:   Where?
32.RAY:   On your keyboard
33.       (1.5)
34.       I'm putting this up on Fa:ceboo:k
35.       (4.0)
```

```
36. SUN:   This doesn't work you l(h)i(h)ed to me!
37. RAY:   ((laughs)) [This picture is you:! ]
38. SUN:              [{UNFREEZES} ((laughs))]  {FREEZES}
39. SUN:   N(h)o(h)o(h)!
40. RAY:   ((High 'silly' intonation)) Oo:h Sun baby ((laughs))
41. SUN:   ↑No↓! {UNFREEZES} {FREEZES}
42. RAY:   That's what I'm saving it as
43. SUN:   You're a liar
44. RAY:   ((High 'silly' intonation))
45.        You'll see what you get it in your [email]
46. SUN:                                      [{UNFREEZES}]
47. RAY:   ((laughs))
48. SUN:   ((laughs)) When are we gonna take pictures?
49. RAY:   Never I'm doing that this weekend, so I don't need
                                                     your help
```

[Case123-p04-c07of10-t11p1752-49m54in-02m01s]

The tease of interest is 'Oh I'm going gonna take a picture of this' (line 18), initiated as an offshoot Ray to already teasingly threatening to unilaterally end the conversation by hanging up the call (lines 1–14). Both participants, then, are in a state of heightened sense of awareness about the view of the other and, indeed, mutual (if asymmetrical) awareness about how they might be viewed by the other. While the frozen video reported by Ray (lines 13, 15–16) is neither especially strange nor funny in and of itself, it can be treated as *now teasable*. Taking a picture of frozen video becomes an excellent resource for a teasing project because it is both something that Sun cannot herself control or even see, and because taking a screenshot is not an affordance of the video calling application itself but an external function of the keyboard and operating system. So when Sun asks Ray how pictures can be taken (lines 21, 23, 25), Ray's short answer 'Print screen' (lines 22, 26) literally provides her with the correct answer, but in a manner that she cannot make use of without more knowledge. Sun's frustration at both the unflattering frozen video image and inability to know how Ray is taking the picture are fuel for Ray's fire. This, then, is not just interaction about multiple technologies but technologised interaction treated as a relevant organisational feature of relationships that are enacted across a skein of both public and private technological spaces.

Conclusions

This chapter has explored how couples cope with audio and video distortions when video calling to maintain their long-distance relationship. I have argued that while video calling couples are engaged first and foremost to the social activity of doing being couples, their orientation is to conversational continuity. As such, re-establishing conversational continuity in the face of technological distortion involves active appeal to organisational devices that focus on attention to the talk in context: omnirelevant devices. These omnirelevant devices are more than simply opportunistically appealed to in the moment because they are returned to, again and again, in specific moments of interactional difficulty, and are invoked deliberately as controlling the participants shared understandings.

I have shown that couples use a fluidly interdependent sense of both the relationship itself and the technology as omnirelevant devices for such appeals. The devices are central to technologised interaction: the technology is not treated simply as a static and determinative conduit or container and the distortions are not treated simply as threshold issues to repair, undifferentiated negatives, or deviant noise to be remedied. Rather, the technology's enablements and constraints are treated as fundamentally expressive resources that frame but do not determine both the enactment of the relationship and the enactment of coping with distortion. Participants invoke a reflexive oscillation between the local interactional content and the technological and relational context as a controlling organisational practice for understanding the current activity.

I have illustrated that couples treat audio and video distortions differently in terms of the use of omnirelevance as organisational. When couples cope with audio distortions, audio is treated as the primary channel of information and repair. Omnirelevance is the organisational engine for disambiguating a potential source of trouble on the basis that the recognisability of technology is part of the problem and solution. Video is treated as either a subsidiary channel to audio or the channel of performance. When visual action matters, the literally framing field-of-view proposes an omnirelevant performance space and, even when distorted, is open to accounting for in a creative dramatic manner. Thus when coping with video distortions, the orientation is to relational and technological omnirelevance as the engine for expressive possibilities. Couples can opportunistically use audio and video distortions as a relational resource rather than simply treating them as perturbing or outside of relational talk. Distortions of audio and video are anything but epiphenomenal sources of repairable noise in the business of couples maintaining long-distance relationships. They can, and do, become interdependent organisational devices, let pass or made use of, but always contingently crucial to achieving conversational continuity.

Remarkably, some of the most creative methods for achieving conversational continuity involve couples using distortion as the spark of trouble to set up relational teasing. Relational teasing is especially useful in moments of distortion because teasing itself is a practice that relies on omnirelevance. As discussed in the introduction, teases are valuable for doing being a couple because they involve invoking trouble (through taboo, deviance, ambiguity, provocations, etc.) in a manner that reflexively proposes the we-ness of relational intimacy. As Housley and Fitzgerald (2002a) explain, the core principle of omnirelevance is that categories are omnirelevant when they can be seen to operate at both an organisational level and at an immediate level. In the case of video calling, distortions are an immediately inescapable and troubling material fact of mediation. However, as materially inescapable as distortions may be, unless they render interaction completely impossible they draw attention to the activity of talk via technology and thus become very obvious candidates for omnirelevance as a resolution process that involves framing who-we-are-and-what-we-are-doing-in-this-medium.

Couples are not necessarily interested in doing technologised interaction; they are looking to act in social ways. Technology is part of that action, but it is as much a creative moral resource (Jayyusi, 1984) used to account for social actions as it is the container or conduit. The reflexive oscillation between content and context from which omnirelevance draws its organisational power is, I would argue, the mechanism by which users intertwine the material and social possibilities of technology to produce technologised interaction. The concepts of omnirelevance and affordances, wound together such that one provides the method for the other, provides a fruitful approach to exploring the practices through which interaction is technologised and thus the wider sociological interest in the interdependence of technology and society.

Acknowledgements

I would like to thank Richard Fitzgerald, William Housley, Richard Harper, Rod Watson, Christian Greiffenhagen, Christian Licoppe, and Marc Relieu for their comments shaping the draft. Although now defunct, I would also like to thank Wave Three Inc. for use of their Session software for this project.

Notes

1   A note on terminology: in Fitzgerald and Rintel (2013), based on a comment from Rod Gardner, we note that Sacks's use of the term 'omnirelevant', and the later descriptive gloss of controlling, suggests that they are *always* relevant rather than always *possibly* relevant. For that reason we used the term 'omnipresence' in that article to capture the sense that 'such devices are available (present) but not always made relevant within the interaction'. In Rintel (2013a), following Schegloff, Jefferson, and Sacks (1977), I used the term omnipresent in relation to the fundamental orientation to repair that is bound up with turn-taking. These two variations indicate that the term 'omnipresent' is useful but overly broad. 'Omni-available' might be a more accurate term, but rather than introduce a new term I am reverting to the original – omnirelevance – for several reasons. First, it has its historical MCA roots, which makes it easier to trace. Second, while omnipresence connotes availability and downplays that a device is always relevant, omnirelevance still connotes the very important aspects of activity, choice and agency better than 'omnipresence'. Third, the omnirelevance concept also ties to the affordances approach taken to the technology in this analysis.

2   A perspicuous setting is one which 'in its specificity and uniqueness allows us to highlight methodic and systematic features' (Mondada, 2007b: 198). This links to the point that while EM/CA research does have some examples of very large corpus studies (e.g. Stivers, 2005), and Stokoe (2012a) has

advocated for similar practices for MCA research, Fitzgerald (2012: 309) has argued that while such studies have value for showing the regularities of membership categorisation practices, those '... principles regarding data collection and building collections are irrelevant to an ad hoc collection or an ethnomethodologically grounded thick description of a single case in which the layered depth and texture of members' category work is explored'. EM/CA/MCA oriented video calling research has tended to take the rich descriptive route of small data sets (e.g. Heath and Luff, 1992; Licoppe, Verdier and Dumoulin, 2013; Mondada, 2007b; Ruhleder and Jordan, 2001), intended, to borrow a phrase describing Erving Goffman's work, to produce 'a shudder of recognition' (Lemert, 1997).

7

Membership Categorisation and Methodological Reasoning in Research Team Interaction

William Housley and Robin James Smith

Making sense of the social world relies on human interaction and communication. This routine and ubiquitous aspect of human existence relies on a number of resources, methods and techniques, many of which have been identified by ethnomethodology and allied fields of inquiry. A crucial feature for making sense necessarily involves the recognition and use of culture so as to render visible, and reflexively account for, members' actions, descriptions, and so forth, as a routine feature and resource for accomplishing social organisation. Accomplishing social organisation and accounting for it are therefore part of the same practical continuum that constitutes the everyday domain of ethnomethods. The difference between mundane and scientific reasoning remains an active area of inquiry and reflection (Lynch, 1993), as does a concern with the role of expertise in late modern social formations. However, the study of scientific method (including social scientific method) remains an important aspect of any sober form of inquiry that recognises the importance of epistemic reflexivity (Wacquant, 2011) to sociological understanding. A key concern here is the actual and situated characteristics of knowledge production, interpretation and methodological reasoning within contemporary social science and scientific practice more generally. Within this chapter we explore real-time examples gathered from a particular work setting where social scientific matters are being attended to as a routine feature of the day's work. Furthermore, the matters that are being attended to in this case relate to the process of coding data using computer assisted qualitative data software (CAQDAS) within a team-based setting. We note the visibility and centrality of membership categorisation work (Sacks, 1995) to coding practices and methodological reasoning within social scientific research teamwork where large amounts of interview data are being processed.

Methodological Reasoning and the Social Life of Methods?

The ethnomethodological study of social scientific practice has returned to prominence within social science through the emerging concern with the 'social life of methods'

(Law et al., 2011; Savage, 2013). The social life of methods has particular relevance in the context of the rise of networked and digital social research where 'open', 'big' and 'broad' data flows are being harnessed to scope and shape interpretive framings of populations on the move (Burnap et al., 2013; Edwards et al., 2013; Housley et al., 2013; Williams et al., 2013). The 'social life of methods', however, can be found across disciplines and traverses the methodological plenum. The notion of methods as a practical and social organisational matter is famously documented by Aaron Cicourel's classic contribution to social science *Method and Measurement in Sociology* (1964). In this great book Cicourel examines a range of methodological practices that include interviewing, questionnaires, demographics, documents and content analysis, experimental design and variable analysis. As Cicourel (1964: 1) states in the introduction:

> Concern for the foundations of social science research should require the continual examination and re-examination of its first principles. In this book I hope to strengthen sociological research by critically examining the foundations of method and measurement in sociology, particularly at the level of social process.

This drive to examine foundational issues through the lens of social process, and what Max Weber described as social action, is a conceptual root and route for ethnomethodological studies of scientific (including social scientific) practice. Taking a lead from influences such as Alfred Schütz's (1953) writings on common sense and scientific knowledge Cicourel's proto-ethnomethodological work foregrounded an interest in the practical accomplishment of method and measurement both within the social sciences and more generally. Developing at the same time, albeit along a different trajectory and from a different point of origin, was a body of work concerned with the social study of science. Empirical studies and reflections on the ordinary work of science within social constructivist (e.g. Bloor, 1991), Actor-Network Theory (e.g. Latour, 1987), anthropological (e.g. Candea, 2013), Sociology of Scientific Knowledge (SSK) (Collins and Evans, 2008) and ethnomethodological (e.g. Lynch, 1996, 2002) programmes converged around the practical and logical matters of production, interpretation and representation within the accomplishment of scientific knowledge. Furthermore, the attention paid to such practices within the natural sciences, initially asymmetrical with that paid to the claims and methods of social scientists, was paralleled by an interest in the practices of the social sciences and, indeed, with method as practised. Aligned with the general rise in concerns with reflexivity and reflection within social science, the nature and consequence of social scientific method is receiving more attention than ever before. As noted by Mair et al. (2013: 1):

> The social sciences are currently going through a reflexive phase, one marked by the appearance of a wave of studies which approach their disciplines' own methods and research practices as their empirical subject matter. Driven partly by a growing interest in knowledge production and partly by a desire to make the social sciences 'fit-for-purpose' in the digital

era, these studies seek to reinvigorate debates around methods by treating them as embedded social and cultural phenomena with their own distinctive biographical trajectories – or 'social lives'.

Yet despite this 'reflexive turn', it is perhaps surprising that there remain relatively few studies of the actualities and specificities involved in the practical interactional business of realising social science method and measurement (Mair et al., 2013). Existing work in this area has focused on the process of measurement and analysis (Anderson and Sharrock, 1982, 1984; Garfinkel, 1967); the accomplishment and production of data reasoning and logic (Bloombaum, 1967; Greiffenhagen et al., 2011); the sites and spaces of social science research (Gieryn, 2006); the use of analytic software (Konopásek, 2008) and questions of surrounding coding practice, membership categorisation and validity within social science research team interaction (Housley and Smith, 2011).

It is important to note, or at least remind the reader, that neither this work, nor this chapter, entails a criticism of sociological practices per se. As Mike Lynch (1991: 79) notes, ethnomethodological inquiry does not preclude or deny the possibility of measurement, but, rather, insists that the accomplishment of measurement, following the principle of ethnomethodological indifference, is yet another (and alike any other) topic of investigation. In this sense, this chapter seeks to draw from this tradition in order to re-specify social scientific methods not only as 'social' but also as practically situated accomplishments through a particular focus on MCA practices. Membership categorisation is of particular interest due to the way in which such work pervades a range of practices associated with methodological reasoning and the art of collating, inputting and interpreting data. This is inexorably so, due to the way in which social data is inferentially rich as a reflexively constituted socio-cultural product that is rendered interpretable and code worthy (or not) through practical knowledge of the self-same culture that social data is understood to both reside in and emerge from in the first place. Again, the study of membership categorisation practices provides a window into the fine detail of culture-in-action (Hester and Eglin, 1997b) in a variety of settings, including those that deal with social scientific data.

This is particularly recognisable within situations where research is being conducted as a group or team where matters of discussion, interpretation, claims making, disagreement and negotiation within the parameters of a necessary accomplished warrantable consensus for reflexively plausible and accountably feasible team work is both practically necessary and therefore routinely evident. To this extent the social life of methods is routinely built on the situated, practically occasioned and accomplished social life of membership categorisation and related practices.

Coding and Coding Practices

The centrality of 'coding' to social science methods has become increasingly pertinent with the rise of software aids and applications, recording devices, transcription services and the rise and rise of the interview and focus group as a primary source of data production. Coding is also central to the analysis of responses provided in question-naires, surveys and more structured forms of data collection obtained via computational and Web 2.0 means, for example the use of crowdsourcing techniques for feature identification of textual materials for machine learning and automated digital tool refinement, for example sentiment analysis. Coding has become an important practice for sorting and sifting different and similar types of data in a variety of ways and often for different epistemological and practical ends. As we have stated elsewhere (Housley and Smith, 2011: 419):

> Despite variance in the way in which coding is approached, and even greater variance in what it is that might be done with data once coded, coding is conceived of as the management of data via its categorization according to codes which are signatures, or shorthand, for the concepts and concerns which the sociologist brings with them to the procedure. Coding is standardly understood as part of a routine analytical procedure in which the sociologist seeks to link the raw data they have gathered or produced to the theoretical presuppositions of social structure, setting or social context with which they begin in relation to particular research questions, hypotheses or themes ...

In this chapter we explore the role of coding interview data as a collaborative activity amongst an interdisciplinary social science research project team. The importance of team work to the recognisable, accountable and orderly (retrospective) production of decisions has been well documented (Housley, 1999, 2000a, 2000b, 2003) in a range of work settings. The role of team work in the routine business of social scientific meth-odological performance, however, remains under scrutinised. Coding is a core topic for research teams who routinely deal with qualitative materials (although a discussion of cleaning quantitative data is necessary and long overdue) due to the way in which the warrantable application of codes to interview responses and materials highlights practical and professional matters of indexicality and reflexivity as they move between the frame of team interaction and the documentary assemblage of social scientific intel-ligibility and interpretation.

Membership Categorisation Analysis and Coding in Teams

In what follows we further examine social scientific coding practices, paying particular attention to the possibility of the team accomplishing a 'shared perspective' in specific relation to the professional (sociological) documentary method of interpretation in action but also, and more significantly, the conversational technologies and mechanisms (Sacks, 1995) in and through which 'coding perspective' is achieved. What is presented here is a case study of a particular form of life associated with a particular activity and setting; in this case the methodological reasoning practices of a social science research team. We are aware that this form of case analysis is not organised around specific cases of sequential or other forms of organisation in talk (e.g. particular types of repair sequence) although we might begin to identify particular types of categorical work that are regular features of such forms of interaction. However, we argue that highly granular analyses of regular features (both categorical and sequential) within talk can be supplemented and enhanced by local case studies of particular settings and activities that can be replicated over time through a cumulative paradigm of empirical research. Indeed, the particular case of methodological reasoning explored in this chapter draws upon and builds on previous analyses (e.g. Housley and Smith, 2011). With further studies providing a horizontal form of case study proliferation, we envisage an accompanying vertical drilling down into a distinct and singular concern with specific patterns of talk observed and identified by the horizontal corpus of *methodographic* cases as a trajectory and analytic framing for future work and studies in this area.

As such we aim to demonstrate the contribution of MCA to describing the procedures and situated 'rules' of sociological reasoning and analysis made visible in the conversations of the team. The role that membership categorisation plays in work team interaction has been well documented with a specific focus on decision making, claims making, epistemics and the routine local production of role-identity within team meetings (Housley, 2003). The analysis presented in this chapter develops and extends a previous examination of team practices in interdisciplinary social science research team meetings where matters of coding are paramount. In a previous article (Housley and Smith, 2011: 420) we described how:

> ...professional concerns such as 'validity' and 'rigour' are realised, as routine practical matters, in the course of research meetings and how 'criteria of 'validity' and 'rigour' as accomplished in the team interaction are ... found in the practices of social scientific categorization and, further, enabled in the sequential machinery of 'meeting talk'.

As such, the practical work of the team in 'managing the code' was revealed to be a membership categorisation problem, dealt with both sequentially and categorically (Housley, 2000a, 2000b, 2003; Mondada, 2011).

The team observed in this chapter comprised six core researchers drawn from three institutions. The project they are working on here was a large interview-based study of local authority decision-making processes and structures. They were, analytically, also interested in 'teasing out' how interview respondents understood and constructed notions of locality and place and the kinds of knowledge that they drew on to do so. The occasion on which our data were produced is the first of two full-day meetings that the team had scheduled in order to check for consistency, understanding and application of their coding practices. Given the size of their data set, the geographically dispersed nature of the 'home' institutions of the researchers and their interdisciplinary backgrounds, such meetings were seen to be vital in producing 'good (social) science' in terms of rigour and validity.

Previous work has explored membership categorisation work in order to examine the ways in which team members established a shared perspective in relation to what it was that was visible and thus relevant within research team social science data. As we hope to further demonstrate in this chapter, a concern with MCA enables a fine grained analysis and understanding of coding and related practices in research team settings, specifically in relation to demonstrating the relationship between the everyday use of conversational resources and strategies and claims to social scientific analysis. In referring to 'managing the code' we noted practices in and through which the team attempted to provide for and accomplish (appearances of) a shared, and thus seen-to-be-valid-for-practical-purposes, 'coding perspective'. A shared perspective of the codes themselves and their applicability to particular stretches of interview transcript was seen to be essential both in terms of the 'team' element of the coding procedure and for the realisation of the activity as having grounds in a 'scientific' procedure. The code, and its application in the coding of the data, required management in that multiple category–code–data configurations were potentially 'valid' and yet only a select number could be viewed and accounted for by the team as such. Given this context, the practice of agreeing the code found mechanisms and 'technologies' in play that are present in other team settings (see Housley, 2003), such as the limitation of category proliferation and the management of topic by senior members of the team. An important aspect of this practical work is the process of accomplishing and making visible for all practical purposes a 'shared perspective' on coding matters between team members.

This is shaped further by the use of the Computer Aided Qualitative Analysis Software (CAQDAS) package 'Atlas.ti', which enables different participants to code distinct documents and to then combine them in an overarching analysis of an entire 'Hermeneutic Unit' (HU). Whilst enabling remote working and providing a resource for organising a manageable division of labour between team members, the software also, as we shall describe below, introduces further contingencies for both the business of coding and, indeed, the resources in and through which the team can accomplish or account for their jointly produced accountable interactional and analytic work. Importantly, this context, and in particular the team situation in which the coding work is undertaken, renders visible many of the practices of coding which are usually 'black boxed' or, at least, conducted under a 'don't ask, don't tell' policy and, at any rate, not provided along with the finalised findings of a 'qualitative research' project. This is significant in recovering the ways in which categories of data and code are managed in interaction. The following extract (Housley and Smith, 2011: 425) illustrates some of these foundational concerns, which we go on to further develop in describing the significance of category work to the resolution of members' (analytic) reality puzzles (Pollner, 1978).

EXTRACT 1: REACHING AND DISPLAYING SHARED CODING PERSPECTIVE

```
115.FS3: Well basic- (.2) yeah we've put
116.     accountability instead of self positioning
117.FS1: Mm
118.FS3: and the two are about (.7) [where] it's
119.     positioned
120.FS4:                                 [yeah ]
121.FS1: Yeah
122.FS3: so we put it as an external
123.FS1: ok
124.FS3: and he's taking it (.) yeah=
125.FS1: =yeah=
126.FS3: = I get
127.FS1: mm hm
128.FS3: (.3) <°that's fine (.2) I'm willing to°>
129.MS1: I'm happy w[ith      that]
130.FS3:           [°use account]ability°
131.FS1: So (.) we've got self positioning
132.FS4: °yeah°
133.FS1: knowledge providence (.8) and who sets the
134.     agendas:
135.FS3: yep=
```

In the extract above the problem concerns the selection and application of the coding category 'accountability' as opposed to 'self-positioning'. FS3 (lines 115–16) frames the problem as a case of selecting 'accountability' instead of 'self-positioning'. This proposition is followed by a continuer (line 117) that serves to acknowledge the coding discrepancy account as a recipient item, thus inviting further elaboration. FS3's elaboration involves the claim that both 'accountability' and 'self-positioning' are 'about where it's positioned' (lines 118–19). The extent to which this is a satisfactory categorical coding resolution is not a matter for us; indeed our analysis problematises the notion of the 'correct' code. The account, however, provides some form of situated device through which both categories can be made to belong, and can be recognised, as a 'family semblance'. The practical matter of coding discrepancy and the production of a 'coding category device repair account' are recognised by FS4 (line 120) and FS1 (line 121) through identical affirmative tokens. This is followed by FS3 (line 121) who skip connects to a topic discussed earlier in the meeting, where matters relating to the predication of 'accountability' and 'self-positioning' were discussed. On line 127 a display of acceptance in using 'accountability' alongside 'self-positioning' by FS1 is characterised by overlapping affirmation (MS1, line 129) and a co-produced account by FS1 and FS4 (lines 131–3) that reiterates their three coding categories, having accommodated 'accountability' through a conversationally agreed device (lines 118–19), serving as a legitimating resource for all practical purposes at that point in the discussion. To this extent a shared coding perspective is accomplished and produced in a way that does not entirely dismiss 'accountability or 'self-positioning' as commensurable coding categories at this stage of the research team interaction. It may well be that the dual life of these particular categories may need to be revisited at a later stage. We might speculate that this is because the category resemblance of 'self-positioning' and 'accountability' are more recognisable and thus present less of an interactional problem in this particular stage of research team coding talk. Thus the ordinary troubles of interpreting, framing and accounting for 'what it is that is going on here' (Goffman, 1974) – a 'no time out' activity for members – is rendered observable and warrantable within assumed 'sociological reasoning' practices (Greiffenhagen et al., 2011). Central here, and as we develop in this chapter, is the way in which analysis – and perhaps in particular coding in teams – represents a reality puzzle for members. That is to say, at stake here is not simply a 'correct' analysis, but rather a series of interactional exchanges, justifications and claims which must provide for the possibility that what the team are 'seeing' in and through the analysis is a property of the data rather than of their practice. And that is to say that coding is retained as an act of 'discovery' rather than 'construction'. The puzzle, in a manner not readily resolvable, arises in situations when the members of the team cannot see what other members are seeing. Appeals to technical and moral framings of alignment and repair, achieved sequentially and categorically, provide two possible resources with which this puzzle may be resolved within the team interaction.

Alignment and Repair: Technical and Moral Frames

In the following extract we find members of the research team discussing the means by which the software (Atlas.ti) will enable them to review a list of the codes they have used and the frequency of their application in specific documents and the 'Hermeneutic Unit' (the 'master' project data file). The discussion here centres upon the technicalities of doing so – 'using the code manager' – but, by the end of the extract, can also be seen as relating to the adequacy of the affordances of the 'code manager' for the practical matter in hand – that is, producing a 'hierarchy' of code relevance and application. This we suggest, begins to shift the issue from a technical to a moral matter, or, at least, two possible frames for 'what is going on here' (Goffman, 1974) are raised. The significance of this for the team's coding practice – and some interesting problems arising therein – will be returned to later in the chapter.

EXTRACT 2: MANAGING THE CODE

```
11.MS1: =°get on with it° ((whispered)) (3.8) sorry
12.     (.) I'm peering over your shoulder (.8)
```

```
13.FS1: but that it only shows you it does not rank
14.      them in order does it? No:=
15.MS3: =you can if you if you (1.4) if you, er:
16.      (1.1) pull these along so you can see the
17.      name
18.MS1: mm hmm
19.FS1: I don't I I haven't got a mouse so
20.      ((inaudible))
21.MS3: °er:m:°
22.FS1: °ok°
23.MS3: °right (.5) okay°
24.MS1: there is a quick way of doing it as well isn't
25.      there (.) coz you
26.MS3: is yours not coming up (.) oh yes it is
27.FS1: yeah
28.MS1: if you go onto your code manager itself
29.FS1: stakes
30.MS1: it tells you how many times you've used the
31.      code in that document
32.FS1: yeah
33.MS1: and how [many]
34.FS1:         [yeah]
35.MS1: times you've used it in its own hermeneutic
36.      unit=
37.FS1:  =yeah (.) yeah=
38.MS1: =um (.8)
39.FS1:  >that's: (.) sort of dun tell me< (.)
40.      you still kind of get a list (.)so yeah,
41.      I've got stakes as my top code (.2)
```

This extract is concerned with the status of the coding hierarchy (i.e. a list of codes that are being applied to the data). There is some frustration entering in to the exchanges (line 11). MS1, after a significant pause, apologises (although not directly for his softly spoken complaint) before MS3 offers a technical solution – perhaps tied to 'getting on with it'. Indeed, there is a self-repair sequence in the initial exchanges in which a technical solution to the emergent 'problem' is proffered.

The problem is the viewing of the coding list and whether it displays a hierarchy of relevance and application or not. FS1 selects to take MS3's commentary (lines 15–17) literally, and argumentatively, made visible in the complaint that she 'doesn't have a mouse' (line 19) and thus cannot follow the problem formulation as instruction. This is followed by a series of small token exchanges indicating a reluctance of anyone to take the floor, until MS1 offers, again, a technical solution to the issue at hand (line 24), 'a quick way of doing it'. We might note here that what 'it' refers to is an as yet to be settled matter, indicated in blunt terms by FS1's interjection 'stakes' (line 29). This 'un-tied' turn is followed by a series of continuers. Silverman (1998) notes how 'response tokens' such as 'mm hm' are usually employed by a hearer to allow a speaker to continue a particular topic by demonstrating understanding and interest. Where these diverge from the 'no gap, no overlap' sequence of conversation running smoothly, the 'yeah's of FS1 can be heard as continuers which 'hurry along' the turns of others indicating a desire to take 'the floor'. Indeed, the technical framing of the problem through the membership categorisation device – the code manager – is dismissed in the first half of line 39 (the account that the software '>that's (.) sort of dun tell me< (.) you still kind of get a list') before a skip connect (Sacks, 1995; Watson, 1997a) tied to the previous interjection which makes reference to one of the membership categories within the coding list, namely 'stakes'; this then allows for the elaboration of 'stakes' as a category and a 'code' which was used most frequently. Here, then, we begin to see a disjuncture in the possible ways in which coding is to be treated as a practice and how such matters are sequentially and categorially managed and visible in the team's talk. In this case the formulation of a problem concerning an emerging code hierarchy and attempts to align a correction to this problem with technical process through the deployment of a 'master device' (lines 35–6), whose mode of predication is tied to the software through the number of times a code has been used in pre-designated hermeneutic units, is evident.

Putting 'technical matters' aside, as enabled by the sequential work in the previous extract, which never let the technical framing of the issue 'settle', FS1 (successfully) continues to elaborate upon the particular problem with the code and the practice of coding; namely, the business of selecting the 'correct' code as complicated by accomplishing a shared understanding of what it is that a given code is taken to stand for.

EXTRACT 3: CODE SELECTION AND SHARED PERSPECTIVE

```
42.MS1: yep (2.7)
43.FS1: significant actors=
44.MS1: =°yep°=
45.FS1: =and key partnerships underneath and
46.      patch (2.5) hhhhh (15.3)
47.      ((sound of footsteps and 'flopping' into a
48.       chair))
49.MS1: hhhhhhh
50.MS3: which ones haven't you used? (1.5)
51.FS1: at all? (1.1) shared interests and
52.      practices (0.2) knowledge providence
53.      (1.1) shared resources (1.1) shared res:
54.      >thas be: (.) I know I have
55.      actually (.)< I know I've done shared values
56.      but only in a hard copy kind of thing
```

```
57.MS3: thas thas the shared values (.) shared
58.     interests (.) shared resources
59.FS1: shar-(.) actors judgements because I just
60      didn't understand that one
61.MS3: °we used that quite a lot°
62.FS1: (1.2) >cos thas< (1 .4) power relations(.)
63.     bureaucracy(.) actually I didn't
64.     really know what that meant there
```

One immediate and obvious remark to make about this extract is the reversal of the turn taking of FS1 and MS1, with the former now trying to not only 'take the floor', but to secure it for the topic of the application of the code as a (potentially) moral issue rather than a simply technical one. The frustration of MS1 at this topical framing of the conversation is visible in the transcript. Indeed, the long absence of talk (line 46) is evidence of a major disjuncture, and in the noises which fill the gap (the walking around the room and flopping into the chair) we hear MS1 withdrawing from the conversation both in terms of turn taking and spatially, a 'move' closed with an emphatic sigh (line 49).

In an effort to move the meeting on, MS3 offers a repair device (line 50), switching FS1's account of her most frequently used codes with the question 'which ones haven't you used?', which can also be heard as a redirect of FS1's attention to and use of the 'code list' – the significance being that, presumably, it will be a quicker business to list which codes have not been used than the order of the ones which have. The closed question of MS3 is, we might suggest, met with some reluctance, visible in FS1's question 'at all?' (line 51) – an argumentative reading (Silverman, 1998) of MS3's redirection-as-question. Following a significant pause, FS1 proceeds by reading, from the list generated by the 'code manager', the codes that she has not used at this stage of the process of 'coding up' the interview data (lines 50–3). Whilst no account is given for the non-use of the first two codes, the third on the list – shared resources – elicits an account in which FS1 invokes a category 'hard copy' to distinguish between her coding practice using the software and her work in coding in another manner (line 56: 'hard copy' hearable as a paper version of coding, manually produced). MS3 utilises a 'tie-in' mechanism (Sacks, 1995) to review the list provided by FS1 but, recognisably to all, selects to include 'shared resources' in the list. Via the hearer's maxim the category 'shared resources' is now heard as belonging to the device 'not-used' codes (line 58). The effect of this categorical work, employed through a sequential mechanism, downgrades FS1's account of activities taking place outside of the technical framing as not observable (in and through the software) and thus un-reportable for the practical purposes of the business at hand.

FS1 proceeds to list a further 'not-used code' – actors' judgements – this time offering a direct justificatory account: 'because I just didn't understand that one' (lines 59–60). This can be heard as an admission of a simple lack of understanding but, equally, given that the team had spent time developing the 'coding frame' prior to the meeting, is an account that also threatens to return to that process as a topic – and thus render visible the common-sense and implicit grounds through which other members of the team had been understanding and applying 'actors' judgements' in their analytic practice. Indeed, MS3 tries to repair this potential trouble by, quietly, suggesting that 'actors' judgements' was a code that 'we' used 'quite a lot' (line 61); that is, that 'we' had no issue of understanding and applying the code. Note that the account is upgraded by the use of 'we' to indicate a consensus of perspective and, also, that 'a lot' (a predicate of the MCD 'interview data' and the corresponding membership categories of codes identified within the interview data) is mobilised as an indication of validity of both the code and its application and warrantability as 'there' in the data, where frequency provides a resource for accomplishing a hierarchy of relevance. The effect(iveness) of this work from MS3 is visible in the pauses and the aborted turn by FS1 (line 62) before proceeding through an account for the lack of use, against MS3's account of 'frequent' use. FS1, after another significant pause, now elaborates further categories drawn from the description of the code itself[1] – power relations, bureaucracy – as an account of her non-use of the code: 'didn't really know what that meant there' (lines 63–4). This has some affinity with the method of 'topical complexity' utilised by politicians in political news interviews where promiscuous category generation provides a means for 'fudging the issue' in broadcast news exchanges (Housley, 2002; Housley and Fitzgerald, 2003). In this case, the code in question is being fudged through the suggestion that it is a promiscuous category and open to multiple readings. This is significant in the course of the meeting as it switches focus from the application of the code to interview data to the code itself. This is a matter that must be dealt with by the team as it represents 'analytic trouble'.

EXTRACT 4: SEQUENTIAL ALIGNMENT AND REPAIR THROUGH TECHNICAL FRAMING

```
65.FS1:  yeah (.) or I mean that there I haven't
66.      used this actors' judgement code (.) at all:
67.      (1.5) um: (.) because I didn't really
68.      understand what bureaucracy uniting >wz
69.      what the explanation is< is power relations
70.      bureaucracy uniting action n I was thinking
71.      quite often bureaucracy um .hh(.)
72.      ham(.)strings action so I just sort of
73.      thought there was [a dif]ficulty I
74.      jus I just didn't understand what it
75.      meant so I haven't coded for it but
76.      assuming that it's power relations and
77.      bureaucracy generally what what people
78.      think about tha::=
79.FS3:                   [Yeah]
80.MS1:  =that's how [I've] used it.
81.FS1:              [then] (.) right (.) >okay<
```

```
82.      so I could probably go back through mine=
83.MS1: =OK=
84.FS1: =and a lot of the stuff I've put under
85.      knowledge relations: (.)
86.MS1: yeah=
87.FS1: =I would probably code:
88.MS1: Yeah. What you'll (.) what we found (.)
89.      you're right(.) yeah you code that (.)
90.      and you you'll you ge- you cou- you could
91.      dump code it alternatively you could (.)
92.      on your viewer
93.FS1: mm
94.MS1: you could click on um ((crashing sound of
95.      chair in background))
96.FS1: Where it's already highlighted (.) you've
97.      double coded again
```

In this extract FS1 continues to elaborate on the promiscuous status of the 'actors' judgment' code (lines 65–7) and provides further identification of analytic trouble through the identification of contradictory modes of predication associated with the membership category 'actors' judgment code', which is part of the list of codes that has been initially applied to the interview data corpus. This *analytic trouble* talk is met with an interjection by MS1 (line 80). This interjection is latched on to the account (lines 69–77) where FS1 provides a reading of how certain activities and forms of predication might be understood to relate to the code in question, albeit in a 'general' manner. The further interjection by MS1 (line 88) appeals to the fact that this is how they have used and applied the code; an invitation to build on the previous account proffered as an adequate and shared reading and therefore a suitable point from which to initiate repair in order to reaffirm shared analytic perspective and reinstate the code as analytically and interpretively stable.

In the following extract we find the team attempting to resolve a further, related, issue arising from the process. That is, attempting to retain codes-as-membership categorisation devices whilst allowing for their promiscuity and potential 'misuse'.

EXTRACT 5: MORAL ACCOUNTING, 'MISUNDERSTANDING' AND BLAME

```
 98.MS1: You just go back through (.) but again (.)
 99.      on when we're viewing it as a group or going
100.      through th the the the er the: analysis we
101.      could select to make a code of um three part
102.      C (.) self positioning and action for
103.      example(.2)
```

```
104.FS3: mm
105.MS1: and (.) f:ive part D which is actors
106.       judgements and bureaucracy
107.FS3: mm
108.MS1: and very much >kind of thing< people say to
109.       you we are doing this because we've been told
110.       we have to do it
112.FS3: mm
113.MS1: which again (.) also refers to bureaucracy
114.FS3: yeah
115.MS1: and then you you you join those codes up
116.       on the analysis (.6) um (.) as
117.       I said (.) I do find (.7) I'm very wary of
118.       getting rid of any codes at the
119.       moment because (.4)
120.FS3: mm
121.MS1: if people have used it and others haven't it
122.       could play havoc with the HU (.)
123.       an:d if its simply a matter of just
124.       making another code (.) which merges those
125.       two °things°
126.FS3: mm
127.MS1: much the same way like this morning in
128.       the: (.2) statistics (1.2) er bit
129.       whereby she was making new output you know
130.       the kind of ((inaudible))
131.FS1: yeah (.) yeah (.) yeah
132.MS1: you can pretty much do that with Atlas
133.FS1: yeah yeah
134.MS1: so you combine all of your quotes
135.       highlighted on on one part and all
136.       of them highlighted somewhere else, it
137.       doesn't matter where in where
138.       in this document they are .h and we:ll make
139.       a new code (.) but if we get rid of them it
140.       means people are going to have to go back
141.       through the transcripts again (.8)
142.FS3: mm
143.MS1: an (.) so practically (.) as a practical
144.       issue(.3)
145.FS1: mm
146.MS1: it's better not to get rid of the codes=
147.FS1: = I think were going to have to go back
```

```
148.        through the transcripts again
149.        >because as we< become more familiar with
150.        it (.) >and after this process the codes
151.        are going to make more sense< (.) or ones
152.        that we didn't really kind of get we might
153.        get (.) so I think there's going to
154.        have to be an iterative process at some
155.        stage anyway (.) .h re:coding
156.MS1:   Okay
157.FS1:   I mean not not sending all that out again
158.        (.) but jus us individually or
159.        individually (.) I'm going to have to go back
160.        and kind of code for actors judgements now
161.        >coz I you know<. did you did you write that
162.        explanation Kerry? of power, of power
163.        relation bureaucracy uniting
164.        action(.) because the reason I <didn't code
165.        anything at all:> into that is because
166.        I was thinking >actually quite a lot of the
167.        time people are talking about< bureaucracy
168.        (.) inhibiting action or constrai:ning
169.        action (.) so I was thinking
```

In the extract above, MS1 is attempting to offer a repair account for the continued issue of managing 'failed' (redundant) or 'misapplied' (over-used) codes (lines 98–103). Here he suggests that the codes are treated as categories, not category devices. That is to say, that for the practical purposes of progressing the analysis and avoiding exposing their previous decisions and categories as flawed or irrelevant the codes can be treated as unproblematic at this point before recognising their duplicative organisation and reorganising and renaming them, made explicit in suggesting that 'it's simply a matter of just making another code which merges those two things' (lines 123–5). As we noted before, the technicalities of the software itself also play a significant part in the reasoning here and, in fact, might be heard as taking precedence in avoiding any 'havoc with the HU' (line 122). Here we see that the production of a 'new code' – which, in Sacks' (1995) terms, becomes a categorisation device under which the other categories might be duplicatively organised in the analysis of the team – is intended to avoid the practical trouble of people having to 'go back through the transcripts again' (lines 147–8). Here, then, any potential trouble with the code frame itself is resolved through a technical framing and categorisation of the problem and its repair. In this technical framing, any misunderstanding or misapplication of the code might be accounted for and resolved at a later stage in the analysis. Furthermore, through the use of the category 'people' (line 121) MS1 ties the problematic consequence of the action as affecting the group equally – as members – and the elicitation, or further proliferation of categories in and through which blame might be apportioned, is avoided. The categorisation of the consequence as a practical one ('people are going to have to go back through the scripts again'), however, affords an opportunity for FS1 to recast the issue not simply as one of resolvable technical practicalities but as a potentially moral one which threatens to expose and unsettle the 'reality' of the code and its application to the data as a matter of qualitative social scientific measurement, rather than active construction or even 'application by fiat' (to borrow a term from Cicourel (1964)). The concern of FS1 is to highlight how the practice of coding is an iterative one and, perhaps more problematically in terms of the team's documentary method of interpretation, how their understanding, and thus use, of the codes will change over time (lines 147–55). Whilst this is not a revelation to the team in the sense that they weren't aware of this, it is an account of the organisation of their practice (and of course, in this case, their reputedly and necessarily-produced-and-seen-to-be-thus *scientific* practice) that must be reconciled within the shared definition of the situation of 'what is going on here'. This account of the iterative, *ad hoc* even, nature of their understanding of the code serves to predicate a further account in which FS1 initiates a self-repair by downgrading her account from 'us' to 'me' (lines 158–9). This, however, elicits some further categorical work in which this situation now becomes categorised outside of the technical framing and repair offered by MS1 in the preceding turns. The topic now shifts from what can be done about misunderstandings and misapplications through affordances of the software to a question of the individual's understanding based on the written descriptions of the code. Here, FS1 (line 162) seeks to apportion blame for her misunderstanding to 'Kerry' (FS2). Whilst this may seem to be a matter of 'passing the buck' and FS1 seeking to apportion blame for her apparent misuse of the 'actors' judgement' code, we want to demonstrate, in the final two sections of this chapter, how, fundamentally and essentially, the business of 'correct' coding is tied not to social scientific principles but to the 'machinery' of membership categorisation and team interaction.

The Coder's Maxim? Accomplishing 'Codes-as-Devices' as a Requirement of Coding Practice

The initial turns of the following extract are a continuation of the repair and alignment work discussed earlier in this chapter. Here we find an appeal to, and mobilisation of, frequency as a frame in and through which alignment work might be carried out. Quantitative discrepancies (and, as we saw in the previous extracts the reasons for such discrepancies) are subject to attempts at repair via the introduction of a frequency device. This, however, raises further issues which must be practically managed through the course of the team's discussions and, as we discuss below, produce a practical (and, in this case, analytical) reality puzzle (Eglin, 1979; Pollner, 1978) to be solved by the team.

Here the team is making evaluations of the 'top five codes' based on the frequency with which particular codes are being utilised. A further problem emerges in this work, over and above a measure of frequency taken as fact, in relation to the problem of 'over coding' and 'under coding'. These terms are salient within the team's work here, as they are membership categories of the device 'correct coding', indicating both the possibility of using a given code in a manner that might be found to be 'excessive' or 'inappropriate' and the possibility of 'missing' opportunities to apply the code to given strips of data. Again, we note here that in and through the team's categorical work the understanding that the data exist *a priori* to the team's work with it is sustained (that is to say, the possibility of seeing the 'facts' of the matter as discoverable properties, awaiting the 'correct' analysis and measurement through coding, is retained, obscuring the ways in which such 'facts' might be found to be accomplished in and through the practice of coding itself). Here the team uses the quantitative analysis of their practice provided by the software to raise and resolve these matters.

EXTRACT 6: 'DOUBLE CODING' AND ESTABLISHING CODES-AS-DEVICES

```
180.FS1: [Actors judgements] (.) yeah a lot of them
181.      do double up
182.MS3: [We need to know ] where we're over coding
183.      and under coding where some people might
184.      have (.7) you know coded it forty six times
185.      [and (.) other people might have coded it]
186.      twenty
187.FS2: [°well     yeah     my     number     is°]
188.      twenty four is almost half what yours is
189.MS2: Yeah
190.FS3: How many have you done though compared to
191.FS2: Four
192.MS2: I've done
193.FS2: so only one less.
194.MS2: One less (.) I've done just five.
195.FS3: It's not a big difference is it?
196.MS2: °No°
197.FS3: Double coding is not a problem (.) in itself
198.      (.) it's just if we continue using the same
199.      codes twice for the same thing
200.MS2: yeah
201.FS3: then obviously one of them's redundant
202.FS1: yeah
203.FS3: but if we are often using an (.)
204.      ((shuffling papers)) one particular code with
205.      another pair with another with another one
206.      that's not a problem (.) thats really
207.      interesting (.)
208.FS1: yeah
```

The issue at stake in the above extract is a very large difference in the frequency between the use of a particular code between MS2 and FS2. The initial repair account for this discrepancy is offered by FS3 (line 190) in asking how many interviews each had coded (allowing for the possibility that the discrepancy in frequency of use might be understood through a discrepancy in the number of documents that the code had been applied to). When this is unsuccessful (MS2 has coded five interviews to FS2's four), FS3 takes the floor (line 197) to provide an extended account of the frequency issues by mobilising (and in doing so addressing an underlying concern) the category of 'double coding'. This category, heard within the device 'coding practices' (along with 'under' and 'over coding'), requires further explication and elicits accounts of two scenarios.

Lines 197–9 contain a further account of the phenomenon of 'double coding': a matter that concerns the team for some time following its explicit introduction as a topic here. Double coding – an outcome of coding work whereby two codes can warrantably be applied to, or, perhaps better, taken to stand for, the same object – is accounted for as indicating, on the one hand, a problem with the coding frame, and, on the other, an 'interesting' device which allows for a further analytic reading to be accomplished by the team. This work is presented through a preference organisation accomplished through the predicates of 'redundant' and 'not a problem', which is later upgraded (Housley, 2000a) to 'really interesting'. A question to be considered at this point concerns what practical work might codes be unproblematically – that is to say, seen, within an aligned analytic perspective and within parameters of professional (sociological) reasoning – applied to a given object?

The Problem of 'Double Coding' and the Coder's Maxim

In each instance a code begins as a member's category. This is a basic and important recognition and one that should be retained. Codes do not exist *a priori* to their use in the process of research analysis. Codes are only constituted as such in and through the work of the team. They begin as 'worked up' members' categories used to denote a particular item, or 'theme', of interest that might be reasonably expected, and thus 'discovered', in the data. We might note, although we do not elaborate further here, that these expectations are, of course, inextricably tied to the elicitation device or 'interview schedule' in the first instance and are a signature thereof. These initial categories-as-codes, worked up from these expectations, what-it-is-we-know-about-our-study, must stand a practical correspondence test against the interview materials themselves and are modified, rejected or joined and replaced by new categories; a process that was the stuff of our previous analysis (Housley and Smith, 2011). We might look at the ways in which teams select, apply, modify and reject certain categories-as-codes in dealing with the interview materials as a practical matter. And we recognise that there is much to the practice of coding, for example the actual manipulation of the mouse to highlight certain stretches of data that a transcript does not capture. Yet, even using video data to capture that physical process, we might still be left with the question of *how* it is that such selections are made. That is, in and through what category and reasoning work, rendered visible here in our case of a team setting, do some coding events come to be accomplished as 'really interesting' and others as 'redundant'. Here, in this penultimate section, we examine a form of categorical correspondence test that appears to be operation. We aim to demonstrate the ways in which this test is accomplished in, and enabled by, members' category work through what we might call 'the coder's maxim'. Here, then, we seek to uncover something of the categorial nature in which 'the point of view of a body of accepted rules of procedure of thinking called the method of science' (Schütz, 1953) is accomplished. In exploring the fine granularity of this particular instance of the documentary method of interpretation (Garfinkel, 1967; Mannheim, 1936), we seek to demonstrate not only the ways in which members, in this instance, find the applicability of certain 'codes' to certain 'data', but, moreover, how the 'technologies of conversation' in and through this work are enabled.

Coding work is, of course, in the first instance and final analysis, a matter of membership categorisation. To return to our initial discussion of the contribution of MCA to describing matters of sociological reasoning and analysis we might look at how definitions of members' devices might equally be heard as applicable to a professional 'code'. It is worth returning to that definition here. A membership categorisation device (MCD) is:

> [a]ny collection of membership categories, containing at least a category, which may be applied to some population containing at least a member, so as to provide, by the use of some rules of application, for the pairing of at least a population member and a categorisation device member. A device is then a collection plus rules of application. (Sacks, 1972a: 332)

So we might recognise that codes are membership categories that are subject to rules of application that include the economy and consistency rule where:

> A single category from any membership categorization device can be referentially adequate. (Sacks 1972a: 246)

> If some population of persons is being categorized, and if some category from a device's collection has been used to categorize a first member of the population, then that category or other categories of the same population, then that category or other categories of the same collection may be used to categorize further members of the population. (Sacks1972a: 225, 238–9, 246)

> If two or more categories are used to categorise two or more members to some population and those categories can be heard as categories from the same collection, then: hear them that way. (Sacks, 1972a: 221)

Of course, in terms of the reconsidered model of Membership Categorisation Analysis the population field and the membership set may also consist of non-personal objects, things and artefacts (Housley and Fitzgerald, 2003) as well as persons. Another aspect of this is the way in which predicates are tied to devices and membership categories as duplicatively organised entities. Codes as membership categories are tied to the membership categorisation device 'the interview data corpus', but can also act as devices in their own right, particularly where their status as a viable code is being negotiated and interpreted through research team discussions and being tied to relevant parts, or objects, in the interview data through manual or electronic annotation. Coding therefore sets up unique opportunities for duplicative organisation and category positioning within a hierarchy of relevance, especially where there may be disagreement about the practical applicability, relevance and disciplinary coherence of certain codes as opposed to others in relation to particular parts or 'objects' contained within the interview data in question.

To return to the previous extract (Extract 6) FS3 states, 'Double coding is not a problem in itself; it's just if we continue using the same codes twice for the same thing then obviously one of them's redundant ...' (lines 197–201). In one sense this conforms to and reflects the economy rule in action as it applies to matters of research team coding talk. However, FS3 (line 203–7) continues by stating, 'but if we are often using one particular code with another pair, with another one that's not a problem, that's really interesting'. In this sense there is an attempt to introduce frequency as a principle for managing duplicative organisation of dual codes for data extracts or 'objects' within the contextual frame of CAQDAS software. This becomes a reasoning procedure for navigating dual codes that may be about disciplinary differences that are expressed through different disciplinary vocabularies of motive (e.g. spatial categories as opposed to class, race and gender) that can be applied to different text extracts and objects within the teams' data corpus as viable coding categories. Alternatively, it may well be read as a more situated concern with everyday interpretive flexibility and matters of consistency within team-based research.

EXTRACT 7: REPORTING AND REFLECTING ON MATTERS OF CONSISTENCY

```
247.MS2: >so I think this issue thi: this i: s< again
248.     er er this consistency between us all
249.     theres also consistency within myself as well
250.     because I know sometimes I've coded one thing and I
251.     won't have coded it the same I'm sure if I'd done
252.     it at a different time of day I kind of that's
253.     what I'm worried about as well is whether I've been
254.     consistent (1.2) I think this comes down to this
255.     thing we were talking about earlier about sometimes
256.     you've got so many codes
257.FS3: mm, ok yeah
258.MS2: you're focussing on a few of them and sometimes you
```

```
259.        forget or (.) >speaking for myself< (.) I forget and
260.        overlook something.
261.FS3:    We musn't forget though (.) we are at the (.8) initial
262.        stages of
263.MS2:    yeah yeah yeah
264.FS3:    it's only when you've read, and re-read, and re-read
265.        and re-read then you can sure that you yourself are
266.        being consistent
```

Matters of consistency and coding of 'social data' remain matters for team member categorisation and analysis. This is because interview talk as sociological data is built upon mundane cultural reasoning whereby the accountability of categories, predicates and action are practical members' concerns. The issue of double coding as a particular practically generated form of duplicative organisation of categories and devices is accounted for in two distinct ways in this instance. Firstly, through a quantified reasoning device – that of 'frequency' of double coding and, as indicated in the above extract, through a reflexive acknowledgement of the 'interpretive flexibility' device that members may or may not be an incumbent of. The matter of consistency is an important norm for research practitioners when dealing with category code proliferation (as indicated, particular devices-as-accounts are mobilised to manage the analytic and mundane breach presented by double coding). The practice of reading and re-reading is presented as a predicate that can be standardly and relationally mapped to codes and code frames in order to realise the normative research principle of 'consistency', a key feature of related matters such as validity and reliability. To this extent we may also understand the issue of consistency and double coding as a 'reality puzzle' when viewed through the lens of mundane reason (Pollner, 1974a, 1974b, 1975, 1978, 1979, 1987). According to Pollner (1987: xi):

> Mundane reason is viewed as an idiom or 'language game' ... constituted through deep assumptions regarding persons and reality. In a fashion akin to the anthropologist, we examine how the 'tribe' of mundane reasoners use their beliefs about reality to make inferences, raise and resolve puzzles and exercise tact and ingenuity.

Whilst the study of MCA looks forwards, it is also necessary to look across the ethnomethodological programme, both past and present, in order to refresh, renew and formulate our studies in ways that remain concerned with the social life of categorisation practices by members as an aspect of situated action within and through a variety of settings, domains and practices. Pollner's concern with mundane reason and Sacks's concern with members' categorisation practices provide powerful resources for interrogating methodological reasoning practices in the human and social sciences. To this extent we recognise the importance of membership categorisation to reasoning procedures and reality disputes (Housley and Smith, 2011) – a key feature of team-based research and ethnomethodologically informed methodography.

Conclusion: Membership Categorisation, Mundane and Methodological Reasoning

This chapter draws upon and develops a concern with membership categorisation within team-based settings where claims, counter-claims and practical decision making are evident. Furthermore, we develop our interest with current debates regarding the social life of methods, albeit as situated features and accomplishments of routine work practices in this instance. Furthermore, we have identified the importance of categorical work, situated within the sequential environment of talk, to an understanding of the social organisation of methodological reasoning as a practical matter. Finally, we note that whilst analyses of membership categorisation work are, correctly in our view, engaged with the sequential concerns of conversation analysis, this chapter also affirms the importance of allied domain practices. For example, there seems ample opportunity for a rigorous understanding of MCA to inform the identification of routine procedures associated with mundane reason and its role within methodological argumentation. In turn, the study of membership categorisation work in relation to methodological reasoning and practice within the social sciences identifies relevant epistopics (Lynch, 1993) within routine social scientific practice that are central organising themes for reflexive social inquiry into and reflection upon our own practices of knowledge production wherever we may find them.

Membership categorisation work is not simply the flip side of the analysis of the sequential organisation of talk-in-interaction, although it can fruitfully inform and enhance studies of sequential organisation particularly in relation to epistemics (Heritage, 2012). Furthermore, MCA is not the technical junior or 'milk float' to the 'juggernaut' of CA (Stokoe, 2012a), though it is worth noting that such temple carts reputedly crushed devotees under their wheels whilst milk floats, on the other hand, are known to be quiet, energy efficient and deliver a healthy staple to the doorstep. Membership categorisation refers to a set of crucially important routine practices carried out by people who are part of a society, culture, form of life and therefore necessarily and inevitably engaged in its mundane reflexive and accountable accomplishment; it is therefore key to understanding the classic sociological question of how social organisation is possible (Button, 1991b); Housley and Fitzgerald, 2008). The analyses of membership categorisation practices as case studies within a cumulative paradigm of research are well established and opportunities are now being presented for studies of MCA to inform computational analysis and digital tool development for the interrogation of big text data sets (Burnap et al., 2013; Procter et al., 2013; Williams et al., 2013). This is not without problems or issues; however it does demonstrate the salience of human practices to machine learning and design and the importance of membership categorisation practices to this task.[2] The role of ethnomethods, including membership categorisation, in feature identification is an important application of ethnomethodological work to a particular set of technical and methodological problems associated with the emerging field of digital social science. However, whilst this type of analytic influence affirms the practical and applied benefits of studying members' in vivo practices, it also, at the same time, requires sustained epistemic reflexivity in relation to the constant moves and the attendant problems of transposition between the study of informal shared everyday practices and the construction of formal inquiry. To this end we are happy to hitch a ride on the milk float delivering the necessary staples where we can, and at a pace commensurate with epistemic reflexivity, reflection and an ongoing concern with the everyday routine grounds of social action and the situated accomplishment of social organisation.

Notes

1   It is standard practice to produce 'code descriptions' alongside the labels themselves to explicate what the code stands for. Clearly in the context of a distributed team analysis, these descriptions pose potential organisational troubles for the team, and some nice examples for our analysis.
2   Indeed, we note the programmatic issues with turning the findings of MCA and associated work into further research and/or analysis strategies (see Button, 1990; Housley et al., forthcoming).

Transcription Key

This book uses Jefferson's (2004b) transcription conventions (see also Hutchby and Wooffitt, 1998; Markee and Kasper, 2004; Psathas, 1995; ten Have, 1999), in accordance with the following key.

Simultaneous Utterances

huh [oh] I see   Left square brackets mark the start of overlapping talk.
    [what]   Right square brackets mark the end of an overlap.

Contiguous Utterances

=   Equal signs indicate that the turn continues at the next identical symbol on the next line or that talk is latched (no interval between the end of prior turn and the start of next turn).

Intervals Within and Between Utterances

(0.4)   Numerals in parentheses mark silence, in tenths of a second.
(.)   A period in parentheses indicates a micropause less than 0.1 second long.

Characteristics of Speech Delivery

hhh hee hah   Laughter or breathiness.
hh   Indicates audible exhalation.
.hh   Indicates audible inhalation.
<u>dog</u>   Underlining indicates marked stress.
HUH   Capitals indicate increased loudness.
°thanks°   Degree signs indicate decreased volume.
$yeah yeah$ Dollar signs indicate the talk was in a smile voice.
news   Asterisks indicate the talk was in creaky voice.
föh   The German umlaut indicates pronunciation of the vowel as in German.
><   Inward-facing indents embed talk which is faster than the surrounding speech.
<>   Outward-facing indents embed talk that is slower than the surrounding speech.

| go:::d | One or more colons indicate extension of the preceding sound or syllable. Each colon represents extension by one beat. |
| no bu- | A single hyphen indicates an abrupt cut-off, with level pitch. |

Intonation Contours

yes?	A question mark indicates rising intonation at turn completion.
yes.	A period after a word indicates falling intonation at turn completion.
so,	A comma indicates low-rising intonation at turn completion, suggesting continuation.
so;	A semi-colon indicates a slight falling intonation at turn completion.
↑	A mid turn sharp rise in intonation.
↓	A mid turn sharp fall in intonation.

Commentary in the Transcript

((hand clap))	Double parentheses indicate transcriber's comments, including description of non-verbal behaviour.
the (park)	Single parentheses indicate an uncertain transcription.
*	An asterisk locates the onset of an embodied action.
@smiles@	Describes some facial action.

Other Transcription Symbols

| • | Vertical ellipse indicates that intervening turns at talk have been omitted. |
| → | An arrow in the transcript margin draws attention to a particular phenomenon the analyst wishes to discuss. |

References

Alberts, J. K. (1992). An inferential/strategic explanation for the social organisation of teases. *Journal of Language and Social Psychology*, 11(3), 153–77.

Alberts, J. K., Kellar-Guenther, Y., & Corman, S. R. (1996). That's not funny: Understanding recipients' responses to teasing. *Western Journal of Communication*, 60(4), 337–57.

Alberts, J. K., Yoshimura, C. G., Rabby, M., & Loschiavo, R. (2005). Mapping the topography of couples' daily conversation. *Journal of Social and Personal Relationships*, 22(3), 299–322.

Ames, M. G., J. Go, et al. (2010). Making love in the network closet: the benefits and work of family videochat. *Proceedings of the 2010 ACM conference on Computer supported cooperative work*, ACM.

Anderson, R. J., & Sharrock, W. W. (1982). Sociological work: Some procedures sociologists use for organising phenomena. *Social Analysis*, 11, 79–93.

Anderson, R. J., & Sharrock, W. W. (1984). Analytic work: Aspects of the organisation of conversational data. *Journal for the Theory of Social Behaviour*, 14(1), 103–24.

Anderson, R. J., Sharrock, W. W., & Hughes, J. A. (1991). The division of labour. In B. Conein, M. De Fornel & L. Quéré (Eds.), *Les formes de la conversation* (pp. 237–52). Paris: CNET.

Antaki, C., Biazzi, M., Nissen, A., & Wagner, J. (2008). Accounting for moral judgements in academic talk: The case of a conversation analysis data session. *Text and Talk*, 28(1), 1–30.

Arminen, I. (2005). Social functions of location in mobile telephony. *Personal and Ubiquitous Computing*, 10(5), 319–23.

Arminen, I. (2007). Mobile time-space – arena for new kinds of social actions. *Mobile Communication Research Annual*, 1, 89–108.

Arminen, I., & Leinonen, M. (2006). Mobile phone call openings: Tailoring answers to personalized summonses. *Discourse Studies*, 8, 339–68.

Arminen, I., & Weilenmann, A. (2009). Mobile presence and intimacy – reshaping of social actions in mobile contextual configuration. *Journal of Pragmatics*, 41, 1905–23.

Ashmore, M. T., Edwards, D., & Potter, J. (1994). The bottom line: The rhetoric of reality demonstrations. *Configurations*, 2(1), 1–14.

Atkinson, P., & Housley, W. (2003). *Interactionism*. London: Sage.

Austin, J. L. (1962). *How to do Things with Words: The William James Lectures delivered at Harvard University in 1955*. Oxford: Clarendon Press.

Baker, C. D. (2000). Locating culture in action: Membership categorization in texts and talk. In A. Lee & C. Poynton (Eds.), *Culture and Text: Discourse and Methodology in Social Research and Cultural Studies* (pp. 99–113). London: Routledge.

Benwell, B. M., & Stokoe, E. (2006). *Discourse and Identity*. Edinburgh: Edinburgh University Press.

Bijker, W., & Law, J. (Eds.) (1992) *Shaping Technology/Building Society: Studies in Sociotechnical Change*. Cambridge, MA: MIT Press.

Bimber, B. (1990). Karl Marx and the three faces of technological determinism. *Social Studies of Science*, 20: 333–51.

Bittner, E. (1974). The concept of organization. In R. Turner (Ed.), *Ethnomethodology* (pp. 69–82). Harmondsworth: Penguin Publishers.

Bloombaum, M. (1967). The logic-in-use of sociologists at work. *The Pacific Sociological Review*, 10(2), 54–60.

Bloor, D. (1991). *Knowledge and Social Imagery* (2nd ed.). Chicago: University of Chicago Press. [First published 1976.]

Boden, D. (1994). *The Business of Talk: Organizations in Action*. Cambridge: Polity Press.

Brown, E. E. (1991). *Human Universals*. New York: McGraw-Hill.

Burnap, P., Rana, O. F., Avis, N., Williams, M., Housley, W., Edwards, A., Morgan, J., & Sloan, L. (2013). Detecting tension in online communities with computational Twitter analysis. *Technological Forecasting and Social Change*. http://dx.doi.org/10.1016/j.techfore.2013.04.013.

Butler, C. (2008). *Talk and Social Interaction in the Playground*. Aldershot: Ashgate Publishing.

Butler, C. W., & Fitzgerald, R. (2010). Membership-in-action: Operative identities in a family meal. *Journal of Pragmatics*, 42(9), 2462–74.

Butler, C. W., & Fitzgerald, R. (2011). 'My f*** ing personality': Swearing as slips and gaffes in live television broadcasts. *Text and Talk: An Interdisciplinary Journal of Language, Discourse and Communication Studies*, 31(5), 525–51.

Button, G. (1990). Going up a blind alley: Conflating conversation analysis and computational modelling. In P. Luff, N. Gilbert & D. Frohlich (Eds.), *Computers and Conversation* (pp. 67–90). London: Academic Press.

Button, G. (1991a). Introduction: Ethnomethodology and the foundational respecification of the human sciences. In G. Button (Ed.), *Ethnomethodology and the Human Sciences* (pp. 1–9). Cambridge: Cambridge University Press.

Button, G. (Ed.). (1991b). *Ethnomethodology and the Human Sciences*. Cambridge: Cambridge University Press.

Button, G. (1991c). Conversation-in-a-series. In: D. Boden & D. H. Zimmerman, (Eds.) *Talk and social structure: studies in ethnomethodology and conversation analysis*. Cambridge: Polity Press. pp. 251–77.

Button, G. (Ed.). (1993a). *Technology in Working Order: Studies of Work, Interaction and Technology*. London: Routledge.

Button, G. (1993b). The curious case of the vanishing technology. In G. Button (Ed.), *Technology in Working Order: Studies of Work, Interaction and Technology* (pp. 10–28). London: Routledge.

Campbell, L., Martin, R. A., & Ward, J. R. (2008). An observational study of humor use while resolving conflict in dating couples. *Personal Relationships*, 15, 41–55.

Campos, B., Keltner, D., Beck, J. M., Gonzaga, G. C., & John, O. P. (2007). Culture and teasing: The relational benefits of reduced desire for positive self-differentiation. *Personality and Social Psychology Bulletin*, 33(1), 3–16.

Candea, M. (2013). Habituating meerkats and redescribing animal behaviour science. *Theory, Culture and Society*, 30(7–8), 105–28.

Castells, M. (2000). *The Rise of the Network Society: The Information Age: Economy, Society and Culture Vol. I* (2nd ed.). Cambridge, MA: Blackwell.

Ceruzzi, P. E. (2005). Moore's Law and technological determinism: Reflections on the history of technology. *Technology and Culture*, 46(3), 584–93.

Cicourel, A. V. (1964). *Method and Measurement in Sociology*. New York: Glencoe, The Free Press.

Cicourel, A. V. (1970). The acquisition of social structure: Toward a developmental sociology of language and meaning. In J. D. Douglas (Ed.), *Understanding everyday life: Toward the reconstruction of sociological knowledge* (pp. 136–168). London: Routledge and Kegan Paul.

Cicourel, A. V. (1974). *Cognitive sociology: Language and meaning in social interaction*. New York: Penguin.

Clayman, S., & Heritage, J. (2002). *The News Interview: Journalists and Public Figures on the Air*. Cambridge: Cambridge University Press.

Clifton, J. (2009). A membership categorization analysis of the Waco siege: Perpetrator–victim identity as a moral discrepancy device for doing subversion. *Sociological Research Online*, 14(5), 8, http://www.socresonline.org.uk/14/5/8.html.

Collins, H., & Evans, R. (2008). *Rethinking Expertise*. Chicago, IL: University of Chicago Press.

Conein, B., Felix, C., Relieu, M., & Watson, R. (2013, August). *Holding Doors Open for Others as Coordinated Action: Some Instances Analyzed*. Paper presented to the Conference in Ethnomethodology and Conversation Analysis, Ontario, Canada.

Coulter, J. (1983). Contingent and a priori structures in sequential analysis. *Human Studies*, 6(1), 361–76.

Coulter, J. (2001). The social construction of what? *Science Technology and Human Values*, 26, 82–6.

Crews, F. C. (1987). *Skeptical Engagements*. New York: Oxford University Press.

Cuff, E. C. (1993). *Problems of Versions in Everyday Situations*. Washington, DC: International Institute for Ethnomethodology and Conversation Analysis and University Press of America.

De Stefani, E. (2013). The collaborative organisation of next actions in a semiotically rich environment: Shopping as a couple. In P. Haddington, L. Mondada & M. Nevile (Eds.), *Interaction and Mobility: Language and the Body in Motion* (pp. 123–51). Berlin: Walter de Gruyter.

Deppermann, A. (2011). Notionalization: The transformations of descriptions into categorizations. *Human Studies*, 34, 155–81.

Dourish, P. (2001). *Where the Action is: The Foundations of Embodied Interaction*. Cambridge: MIT Press.

Dourish, P., Adler, A., Bellotti, V., & Henderson, A. (1996). Your place or mine? Learning from long-term use of audio/video communication. *Computer-Supported Cooperative Work*, 5(1), 33–62.

Drew, P. (1978). Accusations: The occasioned use of members' knowledge of 'religious geography' in describing events. *Sociology*, 12(1), 1–22.

Drew, P. (1987). Po-faced receipts of teases. *Linguistics*, 25, 219–53.

Drew, P. (1990). Strategies in the contest between lawyer and witness in cross-examination. In J. Levi & A. Graffam Walker (Eds.), *Language in the Judicial Process* (pp. 39–64). New York: Plenum Press.

Drew, P. (1997). 'Open' class repair initiators in response to sequential sources of troubles in conversation. *Journal of Pragmatics*, 28, 69–102.

Drew, P. (2005). Is confusion a state of mind? In H. Molder & J. Potter (Eds.), *Conversation and Cognition* (pp. 161–83). Cambridge: Cambridge University Press.

Drew, P., & Atkinson, J. M. (1979). *Order in Court: The Organization of Verbal Interactions in Judicial Settings*. London: Macmillan.

Drew, P., & Chilton, K. (2000). Calling just to keep in touch: Regular and habitualized telephone calls as an environment for small talk. In J. Coupland (Ed.), *Small Talk* (pp. 137–62). Harlow: Pearson Education.

Dreyfus, H. L., & Dreyfus, S. E. (1987). From Socrates to expert systems: The limits of calculative rationality. In P. Rabinow & W. Sullivan (Eds.), *Social Science: A Second Look* (pp. 327–50). Berkeley: California University Press.

Driver, J. L., & Gottman, J. M. (2004). Daily Marital Interactions and Positive Affect During Marital Conflict Among Newlywed Couples. *Family Process*, 43, 301–314.

Dupret, B. (2011a). *Practices of Truth: An Ethnomethodological Inquiry into Arab Contexts*. Amsterdam and Philadelphia: John Benjamins Publishing Company.

Dupret, B. (2011b) *Adjudication in Action: An Ethnomethodology of Law, Morality and Justice*. Farnham, UK: Ashgate Publishing Ltd.

Duranti, A., & Goodwin, C. (Eds.). (1992). *Rethinking Context: Language as an Interactive Phenomenon.* Cambridge: Cambridge University Press.

Edwards, A., Housley, W. Williams, M., Sloan, L. & Williams, M. (2013). Digital social research, social media and the sociological imagination: surrogacy, argumentation and re-orientation. *International Journal of Social Research Methodology, 16*(3), 245–260.

Edwards, D. (1991). Categories are for talking: On the cognitive and discursive bases of categorization. *Theory & Psychology, 1*(4), 515–42.

Edwards, D. (1995a). Sacks and psychology. *Theory & Psychology, 5*(4), 579–96.

Edwards, D. (1995b). Two to tango: Script formulations, dispositions, and rhetorical symmetry in relationship troubles talk. *Research on Language and Social Interaction, 28,* 319–50.

Edwards, D. (1998) The relevant thing about her: Social identity categories in use. In C. Antaki & S. Widdicombe (Eds.), *Identities in Talk* (pp. 15–33). London: Sage.

Eglin, P. (1979). Resolving reality disjunctures on Telegraph Avenue: A study of practical reasoning. *Canadian Journal of Sociology/Cahiers canadiens de sociologie, 4*(4), 359–77.

Eglin, P., & Hester, S. (1992). Category, predicate and task: The pragmatics of practical action. A discussion of Lena Jayyusi (1984) *Categorization and the Moral Order*: International Library of Phenomenologyand Moral Sciences London: Routledge and Kegan Paul. *Semiotica, 88*(3/4), 243–68.

Eglin, P., & Hester, S. (1999). 'You're all a bunch of feminists': Categorization and the politics of terror in the Montreal Massacre. *Human Studies, 22,* 253–72.

Eglin, P., & Hester, S. (2003). *The Montreal Massacre: A Story of Membership Categorization Analysis.* Waterloo, Ontario: Wilfrid Laurier University Press.

Erikson, E. H. (1993). *Childhood and Society.* New York: W.W. Norton & Company.

Finn, K., Sellen, A., & Wilbur, S. (Eds.). (1997). *Video-Mediated Communication.* Hillsdale, NJ: Lawrence Erlbaum.

Firth, A. (2009). Ethnomethodology. In S. d'Hondt, J.-O. Ostman and J. Verschueren (Eds.), *The Pragmatics of Interaction* (pp. 66–76). Amsterdam and Philadelphia: John Benjamins Publishing Co.

Fitzgerald, R. (2012). Membership categorization analysis: Wild and promiscuous or simply the joy of Sacks. *Discourse Studies, 14*(3), 305–11.

Fitzgerald, R., & Housley, W. (2002). Identity, categorization and sequential organization: The sequential and categorial flow of identity in a radio phone-in. *Discourse & Society, 13*(5), 579–602.

Fitzgerald, R., & Rintel, S. (2013). From lifeguard to bitch: How a story character becomes a promiscuous category in a couple's video call. *Australian Journal of Communication. 40*(2), 101–18.

Fitzgerald, R., Housley, W., & Butler, C. (2009). Omnirelevance and interactional context. *Australian Journal of Communication, 36*(3), 45–64.

Follmer, S., Raffle, H., Go, J., Ballagas, R., & Ishii, H. (2010). Video play: Playful interactions in video conferencing for long-distance families with young children. In *Proceedings of the 9th International Conference on Interaction Design and Children,* 49–58. doi:10.1145/1810543.1810550.

Frake, C. O. (1962). The ethnographic study of cognitive systems. In W. Sturtevant (Ed.), *Anthropology of Human Behaviour.* Washington DC: Anthropological Society Publications.

Frake, C. O. (1964). How to ask for a drink in Subanun, *American Anthropologist, 66*(6) (part 2), 127–32.

Garcia, A. C., & Jacobs, J. B. (1999). The eyes of the beholder: Understanding the turn-taking system in quasi-synchronous computer-mediated communication. *Research on Language and Social Interaction, 32*(4), 337–67.

Garfinkel, H. (1959). Aspects of the problem of commonsense knowledge of social structures. *Transactions of the Fourth World Congress of Sociology, 4*, 51–65.

Garfinkel, H. (1964). Studies of the routine grounds of everyday activities. *Social Problems*, 225–50.

Garfinkel, H. (1967) *Studies in Ethnomethodology*. Englewood Cliffs, NJ: Prentice-Hall.

Garfinkel, H. (2002). *Ethnomethodology's Program: Working Out Durkheim's Aphorism*. Boston, MA: Rowman and Littlefield.

Garfinkel, H., & Sacks, H. (1970). On formal structures of practical actions. In J. C. McKinney & E. A. Tiryakian (Eds.), *Theoretical Sociology: Perspectives and Developments* (pp. 338–66). New York: Appleton-Century-Crofts.

Garfinkel, H., Lynch, M., & Livingston, E. (1981). I. 1 The Work of a Discovering Science Construed with Materials from the Optically Discovered Pulsar. *Philosophy of the social sciences, 11*(2), 131–158.

Gaver, W. W. (1992). The affordances of media spaces for collaboration. In *Proceedings of the 1992 ACM Conference on Computer-Supported Cooperative Work*, 17–24. doi: 10.1145/143457.371596.

Gellner, E. (1975). Ethnomethodology: The re-enchantment industry or the Californian way of subjectivity. *Philosophy of the Social Sciences, 5*(4), 431–50.

Gibson, J. J. (1979). *The Ecological Approach to Visual Perception*. Boston, MA: Houghton Mifflin.

Goodwin, C. (2000). Action and Embodiment within Situated Human Interaction, *Journal of Pragmatics 32*: 1489–1522.

Goodwin, C. (2007) 'Participation, stance and affect in the organization of activities', *Discourse and Society 18*(1): 53–73.

Gieryn, T. (2006). City as truth-spot: Laboratories and field-sites in urban studies. *Social Studies of Science, 36*(1), 5–38.

Goffman, E. (1961). *Asylums*. New York: Doubleday Anchor.

Goffman, E. (1974). *Frame Analysis: An Essay on the Organization of Experience*. New York: Harper & Row.

Goffman, E. (1979) Footing. *Semiotica, 25*(1/2), 1–30.

Greiffenhagen, C., & Watson, R. (2005). Teoria e Método na CMC [Theory and method in computer-mediated communication]. In A. Braga (Ed.), *CMC, Identidades e Género: Teoria e Método* (pp. 89–114). Covilhã: Universidade da Beira Interior.

Greiffenhagen, C., Mair, M., & Sharrock W. W. (2011). From methodology to methodography: A study of qualitative and quantitative reasoning in practice. *Methodological Innovations Online, 6*(3), 93–107.

Grice, H. P. (1989). *Studies in the Way of Words*. Cambridge, MA: Harvard University Press.

Grint, K., & Woolgar, S. (1997). *The Machine at Work*. Cambridge: Polity.

Gurwitsch, A. (1964). *The Field of Consciousness*. Pittsburgh, PA: Duquesne University Press.

Hansen, A. D. (2005). A practical task: Ethnicity as a resource in social interaction. *Research on Language and Social Interaction, 38*(1), 63–104.

Harper, R. (2010). *Texture: Human Expression in the Age of Communications Overload*, Cambridge, MA: MIT Press.

Harrison, S. (Ed). (2009) *Media Space: 20+ Years of Mediated Life*. London: Springer-Verlag.

Hashimoto, Y., & Ishibashi, Y. (2006) Influences of network latency on interactivity in networked rock-paper-scissors. In *Proceedings of the 2006 NETGAMES Conference* (pp. 23–9).

Haslam, S. A., Ellemers, N., Reicher, S. D., Reynolds, K. J., & Schmitt, M. T. (2010). The social identity perspective today: An overview of its defining ideas. In T. Postmes & N. R. Branscombe (Eds.), *Rediscovering Social Identity* (pp. 341–56). New York: Psychology Press.

Hauser, E. (2011). Generalization: A practice of situated categorization in talk. *Human Studies*, *34*, 183–98.

Heath, C. (1986). *Body Movement and Speech in Medical Interviews*. Cambridge: Cambridge University Press.

Heath, C., & Luff, P. (1991) Disembodied conduct: Communication through video in a multi-media office environment. In *Proceedings of the SIGCHI Conference on Human Factors in Computing Systems: Reaching through Technology* (pp. 99–103).

Heath, C., & Luff, P. (1992). Media space and communicative asymmetries. Preliminary observations of video mediated interactions. *Human Computer Interaction*, *7*, 315–46.

Heath, C., & Luff, P. (2000) *Technology in Action*. Cambridge, UK: Cambridge University Press.

Heath, C., Knoblauch, H., & Luff, P. (2000). Technology and social interaction: The emergence of workplace studies. *British Journal of Sociology*, *51*, 299–320.

Heritage, J. (1978) Aspects of the flexibilities of natural language use: a reply to Phillips. *Sociology*, Special issue on Language and Practical Reasoning, *12*(1), 79–104.

Heritage, J. (1984). *Garfinkel and Ethnomethodology*. Cambridge: Polity Press.

Heritage, J. (2002). The limits of questioning: Negative interrogatives and hostile questions content. *Journal of Pragmatics*, *34*, 1427–46.

Heritage, J. (2005). Conversation analysis and institutional talk. In K. L. Fitch & R. E. Sanders (Eds.), *Handbook of Language and Social Interaction*. Mahwah, NJ: Lawrence Erlbaum.

Heritage, J. (2012). Epistemics in action: Action formation and territories of knowledge. *Research in Language and Social Interaction*, *45*(1), 1–29.

Heritage, J. (2013). Action formation and its epistemic (and other) backgrounds. *Discourse Studies*, *15*(10), 551–78.

Herring, S. C. (ed.) (1996). *Computer-Mediated Communication: Linguistic, Social and Cross-Cultural Perspectives*. Pragmatics and Beyond Series. Amsterdam: John Benjamins.

Herring, S. (1999). Interactional coherence in CMC. *Journal of Computer Mediated Communication* 4(4).

Hester, S. (1994). Les catégories en contexte. In B. Fradin, L. Quéré, J. & Widmer, (Eds.) *L'enquête sur les catégories*. Paris: École des Hautes Études en Sciences Sociales [Raisons pratiques: Épistémologie, sociologie, théorie sociale/5] (pp. 219–42).

Hester, S., & Eglin, P. (1992). *A Sociology of Crime*. Abingdon and New York: Psychology Press.

Hester, S., & Eglin, P. (1997a). Membership Categorization Analysis: An introduction. In S. Hester & P. Eglin (Eds.). *Culture in Action: Studies in Membership Categorization Analysis* (pp. 1–23). Washington, DC: International Institute for Ethnomethodology and Conversation Analysis & University Press of America.

Hester, S., & Eglin, P. (Eds.) (1997b). *Culture in Action: Studies in Membership Categorization Analysis*. Boston, MA: International Institute for Ethnomethodology and University Press of America.

Hester, S., & Fitzgerald, R. (1999). Category, predicate and contrast: Some organisational features in a radio talk show. In P. Jalbert (Ed.). *Media Studies: Ethnomethodological Approaches*. Lanham, MD: University Press of America.

Hester, S., & Francis, D. (2002). Category play in a school staff-room. *Ethnographic Studies*, *5*, 42–55.

Hester, S., & Francis, D. (2003). Analysing visually available mundane order: A walk to the supermarket. *Visual Studies*, *18*(1), 36–46.

Hester, S., & Hester, S. (2012). Category relations, omnirelevance, and children's disputes. *Sociological Studies of Children and Youth*, *15*, 1–25.

Hill, Richard. J. & Crittenden, Kathleen S. (Eds.) (1968). *Proceedings of the Purdue Symposium on ethnomethodology*. Lafayette, Indiana: Purdue Research Foundation

Hopper, R. (1992). *Telephone Conversation*. Bloomington, IN: Indiana University Press.

Hopper, R., Knapp, M. L., & Scott, L. (1981). Couples' personal idioms: Exploring intimate talk. *Journal of Communication*, 31: 23–33.

Horn, D. B., Olson, J. S., & Karasik, L. (2002). *The Effects of Spatial and Temporal Video Distortion on Lie Detection Performance*. Short Paper presented at CHI 2002, the Association for Computing Machinery conference on Human Factors in Computer Systems, Minneapolis. http://www-personal.umich.edu/~danhorn/reprints/horn_2002_lie_detection_chi_2002.pdf.

Housley, W. (1999). Role as an interactional device and resource in multidisciplinary team meetings. *Sociological Research Online*, 4(3).

Housley, W. (2000a). Category work and knowledgeability within multidisciplinary team meetings. *TEXT*, 20(1), 83–108.

Housley, W. (2000b). Story, narrative and team work. *The Sociological Review*, 48(3), 425–43

Housley, W. (2002). Moral discrepancy and fudging the issue in a radio news interview. *Sociology*, 36(1), 5–21.

Housley, W. (2003). *Interaction in Multidisciplinary Teams*. Aldershot: Ashgate.

Housley, W., & Fitzgerald, R. (2002a). The reconsidered model of membership categorization. *Qualitative Research*, 2(1): 59–83.

Housley. W., & Fitzgerald, R. (2002b). National identity, categorisation and debate. In S. Hester & W. Housley (Eds.), *Language, Interaction and National Identity*. Aldershot: Ashgate.

Housley, W., & Fitzgerald, R. (2003). Moral discrepancy and political discourse: Accountability and the allocation of blame in a political news interview. *Sociological Research Online*, 8(2).

Housley, W., & Fitzgerald, R. (2008). Motives accounts and social organisation. *Qualitative Research*, Response paper and reply, 8(2), 237–56.

Housley, W., & Fitzgerald, R. (2009a). Membership category analysis, culture and norms in action. *Discourse and Society*, 20(3), 345–62.

Housley, W., & Fitzgerald, R. (2009b). Motives and social organization: Sociological amnesia, psychological description and the analysis of accounts. *Qualitative Research*, 8(2): 237–56.

Housley, W., & Smith, R. J. (2011).Telling the CAQDAS code: Membership categorization and the accomplishment of 'coding rules' in research team talk. *Discourse Studies*, 13(4), 417–434.

Housley, W., Williams, M. L., Williams, M., & Edwards, E. (2013). Special issue: Introduction. *International Journal of Social Research Methodology*, 16(3), 173–5.

Hutchby, I. (1996). *Confrontation Talk: Argument, Asymmetries and Power on Talk Radio*. Hillsdale, NJ: Erlbaum.

Hutchby, I. (2001a). *Conversation and Technology: From the Telephone to the Internet*. Cambridge, UK: Polity Press.

Hutchby, I. (2001b). Technologies, texts and affordances. *Sociology*, 35(2): 441–56.

Hutchby, I. (2003). Affordances and the analysis of technologically mediated interaction: A response to Brian Rappert. *Sociology*, 37, 581–9.

Hutchby, I., & Barnett, S. (2005). Aspects of the sequential organisation of mobile phone conversation. *Discourse Studies*, 7(2), 147–71.

Hutchby, I., & Wooffitt, R. (1998). *Conversation Analysis*. Cambridge, UK: Polity Press.

Ingersoll-Dayton, B., Campbell, R., & Mattson, J. (1998). Forms of communication: A cross-cultural comparison of older married couples in the USA and Japan. *Journal of Cross-Cultural Gerontology*, 1, 63–80.

Isaacs, E., & Tang, J. C. (1993). What video can and can't do for collaboration: A case study. In *Proceedings of the ACM Multimedia '93 Conference* (pp. 199–206).

Jaworski, A., Fitzgerald, R., & Constantinou, O. (2005). Busy saying nothing new: Live silence in TV reporting of 9/11. *Multilingua*, 24, 121–44.

Jayyusi, L. (1984). *Categorization and the Moral Order*. Boston: Routledge & Kegan Paul.

Jayyusi, L. (1991). Values and moral judgement: Communicative praxis as moral order. In G. Button (Ed.), *Ethnomethodology and the Human Sciences* (pp. 227–51). Cambridge: Cambridge University Press.

Jefferson, G. (2004a). 'At first I thought': A normalizing device for extraordinary events. In G. Lerner (Ed.), *Conversation Analysis: Studies from the First Generation* (pp. 131–67). Amsterdam and Philadelphia: John Benjamins.

Jefferson, G. (2004b). Glossary of transcript symbols with an introduction. In G. Lerner (Ed.), *Conversation Analysis: Studies from the First Generation* (pp. 13–31). Amsterdam and Philadelphia: John Benjamins.

Jones, S. G. (Ed.) (1998). *New Media Cultures: Cybersociety 2.0: Revisiting Computer-mediated Communication and Community.* Thousand Oaks, CA: Sage.

Judge, T. K., & Neustaedter, C. (2010). Sharing conversation and sharing life: Video conferencing in the home. In *Proceedings of the 28th International Conference on Human Factors in Computing Systems* (pp. 655–8).

Judge, T. K., Neustaedter, C., Harrison, S., & Blose, A. (2011). Family portals: Connecting families through a multifamily media space. In *2011 Annual Conference on Human Factors in Computing Systems* (pp. 1205–14).

Keltner, D., Capps, L., Kring, A. M., Young, R. C., & Heerey, E. A. (2001). Just teasing: A conceptual analysis and empirical review. *Psychological Bulletin, 127,* 229–48.

Keltner, D., Young, R. C., Heerey, E. A., Oemig, C., & Monarch, N. D. (1998). Teasing in hierarchical and intimate relations. *Journal of Personality and Social Psychology, 75,* 1231–47.

Kirk, D. S., Sellen, A., & Cao, X. (2010). Home video communication: Mediating closeness. In *Proceedings of the 2010 ACM Conference on Computer Supported Cooperative Work* (CSCW 10) (pp. 135–44).

Knapp M. L., & Daly, J. A. (Eds.). (2011). *The Handbook of Interpersonal Communication* (4th ed.) (pp. 443–79). Thousand Oaks, CA: Sage.

Knorr-Cetina, K., & Cicourel, A. V. (Eds.). (1981). *Advances in Social Theory and Methodology: Toward an Integration of Micro- and Macro-sociologies.* London: Routledge.

Konopásek, Z. (2008). Making thinking visible with Atlas.Ti: Computer assisted qualitative analysis as textual practices. *Forum: Qualitative Social Research, 9*(2), Article 12

Labov, W., & Fanshel, D. (1977). *Therapeutic Discourse.* New York: Academic Press.

Lakoff, G. (1987). *Women, Fire, and Dangerous Things: What Categories Tell Us about the Mind.* Chicago: Chicago University Press.

Latour, B. (1987). *Science in Action: How to Follow Scientists and Engineers Through Society.* Cambridge, MA: Harvard University Press.

Latour (1999). On recalling ANT. *The Sociological Review, 47*(S1), 15–25.

Laurier, E. (n.d.). *Youtube: Using Third Party Video as Research Data.* Available at: www.ericlaurier.co.uk/resources/Writings/Laurier_2013_Youtube_3rd_party.pdf

Law, J. (1994) *Organizing modernity.* Oxford: Blackwell.

Law, J. (2009). Actor network theory and material semiotics. *The New Blackwell Companion to Social Theory,* 141–158.

Law, J., Rupert, E., & Savage, M. (2011). The Double Social Life of Methods, *CRESC Working Paper Series,* Paper 95.

Lee, J. R. E. (1984). Innocent victims and evil-doers. *Women's Studies International Forum,* Special Issue on Men and Sex, L. Stanley & S. Wise (Eds.), *7*(1), 69–73.

Lemert, C. (1997). Goffman. In C. Lemert & A. Branaman (Eds.). *The Goffman Reader* (pp. ix–xliii). Malden, MA: Blackwell.

Leudar, I., & Nekvapil, J. (2000). Presentations of Romanies in the Czech media: on category work in television debates. *Discourse & Society, 11*(4), 487–513.

Leudar, I., Marsland, V., & Nekvapil, J. (2004). On membership categorization: 'Us', 'them' and 'doing violence' in political discourse. *Discourse & Society*, *15*(2–3), 243–66.

Levinson, S. (2012). Interrogative intimations: On a possible social economics of interrogatives. In J. D. Ruiter (Ed.), *Questions. Formal, Functional and Interactional Perspectives* (pp. 11–32). Cambridge: Cambridge University Press.

Licoppe, C., & Dumoulin, L. (2010). The 'curious case' of an unspoken opening speech act: A video-ethnography of the use of video communication in courtroom activities. *Research on Language and Social Interaction*, *43*(3), 211–31.

Licoppe, C., & Morel, J. (2012). Video-in-interaction: 'Talking heads' and the multimodal organization of mobile and skype video calls. *Research on Language and Social Interaction*, *45*(4), 399–429.

Licoppe, C., & Morel, J. (2013). Interactionally generated encounters and the accomplishment of mutual proximity in mobile phone conversations. In P. Haddington, L. Mondada & M. Nevile (Eds.), *Interaction and Mobility: Language and the Body in Motion* (pp. 277–299). Berlin: De Gruyter.

Licoppe, C., Verdier, M., & Dumoulin, L. (2013). Courtroom interaction as a multimedia event: The work of producing relevant videoconference frames in French pre-trial hearings. *The Electronic Journal of Communication /La Revue Electronic de Communication (EJC/REC)*, Special Issue on Videoconferencing in Practice: 21st Century Challenges, *23*(1&2), http://www.cios.org/www/ejc/v23n12toc.htm.

Liebes, T. (1998). Television's disaster marathons: A danger for democratic processes? In T. Liebes & J. James Curran (Eds.), *Media, Ritual and Identity* (pp. 71–84). London: Routledge.

Lu, Y., Y. Zhao, et al. (2010). Measurement study of multi-party video conferencing. *NETWORKING 2010*, *6091*, 96–108.

Lynch, M. (1991). Method and measurement. In G. Button (Ed.), *Ethnomethodology and the Human Sciences* (pp. 77–108). Cambridge: Cambridge University Press.

Lynch, M. (1993). *Scientific Practice and Ordinary Action. Ethnomethodology and Social Studies of Science*. Cambridge: Cambridge University Press.

Lynch, M. (2002). Protocols, practices, and the reproduction of technique in molecular biology. *British Journal of Sociology*, *53*(2), 203–20.

MacKenzie, D., & Wajcman, J. (1999). *The Social Shaping of Technology* (2nd ed.). Buckingham, UK: Open University Press.

Mair, M., Greiffenhagen, C., & Sharrock, W. W. (2013). Social studies of social science: A working bibliography. *National Centre for Research Methods Working Paper Series, Working Paper 08/13*.

Mandelbaum, J. (1987). Couples sharing stories. *Communication Quarterly*, *35*, 144–70.

Mandelbaum, J. (2003). Interactive methods for constructing relationships. In P. Glenn, C. LeBaron & J. Mandelbaum (Eds.), *Studies in Language and Social Interaction: In Honor of Robert Hopper*. Mahwah, NJ: Lawrence Erlbaum. pp. 207–20.

Mannheim, K. (1936). *Ideology and Utopia*. London: Routledge.

Manzo, J. (1996). Taking turns and taking sides: Opening scenes from two jury deliberations. *Social Psychology Quarterly*, *59*(2), 107–25.

Markee, N., & Kasper, G. (2004). Classroom talks: An introduction. *Modern Language Journal*, *88*(4), 491–500.

Matoesian, G. (2001). *Law and the Language of Identity*. Oxford: Oxford University Press.

Maynard, D., & Wilson, T. P. (1980). On the reification of social structure. In S. McNall & G. Howe (Eds.), *Current Perspectives in Sociological Theory: A Research Annual* (pp. 287–322). Greenwich, CT: JAI Press.

McGrenere, J., & Ho, W. (2000). Affordances: clarifying and evolving a concept. In *Proceedings of Graphics Interface, Montreal, Quebec, Canada* (pp. 179–86).

McHoul, A. (1978). The organization of turns at formal talk in the classroom. *Language in Society, 7*, 183–213.

McHoul, A. W., & Watson, D. R. (1984). Two axes for the analysis of 'commonsense' and 'formal' geographical knowledge in classroom talk. *British Journal of Sociology of Education, 5*(3), 281–302.

McNally, M., & Watson, R. (2013). *Understanding and Constituting Housing Markets in a Public Policy Context.* Paper presented at the European Network for Housing Research Conference Overcoming the Crisis: Integrating the Urban Environment, Universitat Rovira y Virgil, Tarragona, Spain (June).

Meehan, A. J. (2006). Using talk to study the policing of gangs and its recordwork. In P. Drew, G. Raymond & D. Weinberg (Eds.), *Talk and Interaction in Social Research Methods* (pp. 190–210). London: Sage Publications.

Mehan, H. (1979). 'What time is it Denise?' Asking known information questions in classroom discourse. *Language in Society, 28*(4), 285–94.

Mondada, L. (2003). Working with video: How surgeons produce video records of their actions. *Visual Studies, 18*(1), 58–73.

Mondada, L. (2007a). Multimodal resources for turn-taking: Pointing and the emergence of possible next speakers. *Discourse Studies, 9*(2): 195–226.

Mondada, L. (2007b). Operating together through videoconference: Members' procedures for accomplishing a common space of action. In S. Hester & D. Francis (Eds.), *Orders of Ordinary Action* (pp. 51–67). Aldershot, UK: Ashgate.

Mondada, L. (2011). The interactional production of multiple spatialities within a participatory democracy meeting. *Social Semiotics, 21*(2), 283–308.

Monk, A. F., & Watts, L. (1995) A poor quality video link affects speech but not gaze. In *Proceedings of the 1995 ACM Conference on Human Factors in Computing Systems* (pp. 274–75).

Nacos, B. L. (2003). Terrorism as breaking news: Attack on America. *Political Science Quarterly, 118*(1), 23–52.

Nekvapil, J., & Leudar, I. (2002). On dialogical networks: Arguments about the migration law in Czech mass media in 1993. In S. Hester & W. Housley (Eds.), *Language Interaction and National Identity* (pp. 60–101). Aldershot, UK: Ashgate.

Neustaedter, C., (2013). My life with always-on video. *The Electronic Journal of Communication /La Revue Electronic de Communication (EJC/REC)*, Special Issue on Videoconferencing in Practice: 21st Century Challenges, *23*(1&2), http://www.cios.org/www/ejc/v23n12toc.htm.

Neustaedter, C., & Greenberg, S. (2011). *Intimacy in Long-distance Relationships Over Video Calling Research Report 2011-1014-26.* Department of Computer Science, University of Calgary.

Nevile, M. (2004). *Beyond the Black Box: Talk-in-Interaction in the Airline Cockpit.* Aldershot, UK: Ashgate.

Norman, D. A. (1999). Affordances, conventions, and design. *Interactions, 6*(3), 38–41.

Norman, D. A. (2013). *The Design of Everyday Things* (Revised and Expanded Edition). Cambridge, MA: MIT Press.

Pawluk, C. J. (1989). Social construction of teasing. *Journal for the Theory of Social Behaviour, 19*, 145–67.

Pike, K. L. (1964) Towards a theory of the structure of human behaviour. In D. Hymes (Ed.), *Language in Culture and Society* (pp. 54–62). New York: Harper and Row.

Plunkett, R. (2009). Fashioning the feasible: Categorization and social change. *Australian Journal of Communication, 36*(3), 23–44.

Pollner, M. (1974a). Mundane reasoning. *Philosophy of the Social Sciences, 5*, 35–54.

Pollner, M. (1974b). Sociological and commonsense models of the labelling process. In R. Turner (Ed.), *Ethnomethodology*. London: Penguin.

Pollner, M. (1975). The very coinage of your brain: The anatomy of reality disjunctures. *Philosophy of the Social Sciences*, 5, 411–30.

Pollner, M. (1978). Constitutive and mundane versions of labelling theory. *Human Sciences*, 3, 285–304.

Pollner, M. (1979). Self explicating settings: Making and managing meaning in traffic court. In G. Psathas (Ed.), *Everyday Language: Studies in Ethnomethodology*. New York: Irvington Press.

Pollner, M. (1987). *Mundane Reason: Reality in Everyday and Sociological Discourse*. Cambridge: Cambridge University Press.

Pomerantz, A. (1984). Agreeing and disagreeing with assessments: Some features of preferred/dispreferred turn shapes. In J. M. Atkinson & J. Heritage (Eds.), *Structures of Social Action* (pp. 57–101). Cambridge: Cambridge University Press.

Pomerantz, A. (1986). Extreme case formulations: A way of legitimizing claims. *Human Studies*, 9, 219–29.

Pomerantz, A., & Heritage, J. (2012). Preference. In J. Sidnell & T. Stivers (Eds.), *The Handbook of Conversation Analysis* (pp. 210–28). Chichester: Wiley-Blackwell.

Pomerantz, A., & Mandelbaum, J. (2004). A conversation analytic approach to relationships: Their relevance for interactional conduct. In K. Fitch & R. E. Sanders (Eds.), *Handbook of Language and Social Interaction* (pp.149–71). Mahwah, NJ: Lawrence Erlbaum.

Pomerantz, A., & Mandelbaum, J. (2005). Conversation analytic approaches to the relevance and uses of relationship categories in interaction. In K. L. Fitch & R. E. Sanders (Eds.), *Handbook of Language and Social Interaction*. Mahwah, NJ: Lawrence Erlbaum Associates.

Potter, J. (1996). *Representing Reality: Discourse, Rhetoric and Social Construction*. London: Sage.

Procter, R., Housley, W., Williams, M., Edwards, A., Burnap, P., Morgan, J., & Rana, O. (2013). Enabling social media research through citizen social science. In *ECSCW 2013 Adjunct Proceedings*.

Psathas, G. (1995). *Conversation Analysis: The Study of Talk-in-Interaction*. Thousand Oaks, CA: Sage Publications.

Radcliff-Brown, A. (1940). On joking relationships. *Africa: Journal of the International African Institute*, 13(3), 195–210.

Raymond, G. (2003). Grammar and social organization: Yes/no interrogatives and the structure of responding. *American Sociological Review*, 68, 939–67.

Raymond, G., & Heritage, J. (2006). The epistemics of social relationships: Owning grandchildren. *Language in Society*, 35(5), 677–705.

Reed, D., & Ashmore, M. (2000). The naturally-occurring chat machine. *M/C: A Journal of Media and Culture*, 3(4), http://journal.media-culture.org.au/0008/machine.php.

Reynolds, E. (2011). Enticing a challengeable in arguments: Sequence, epistemics and preference organisation. *Pragmatics*, 21(3), 411–30.

Reynolds, E. (2013). *Enticing a Challengeable: Instituting Social Order as a Practice of Public Conflict*. Unpublished PhD, The University of Queensland.

Reynolds, L. T., & Reynolds, J. M. (Eds.) (1970). *The Sociology of Sociology: Analysis and Criticism of the Thought, Research and Ethical Folkways of Sociology and Its Practitioners*. New York: David McKay Company.

Rintel, S. (2007). Maximizing environmental validity: Remote recording of desktop videoconferencing. In *Proceedings of the 12th International Conference on Human-Computer Interaction: Interaction Design and Usability* (pp. 911–20).

Rintel, S. (2010). Conversational management of network trouble distortions in personal videoconferencing. In *Proceedings of the 22nd Conference of the Computer-Human Interaction. Special Interest Group of Australia on Computer-Human Interaction* (pp. 304–11).

Rintel, S. (2013a). Tech-tied or tongue-tied? Technological versus social trouble in relational video calling. In *Proceedings of the Forty Sixth Hawaii International Conference on System Sciences* (pp. 3343–52).

Rintel, S., (2013b). Video calling in long-distance relationships: The opportunistic use of audio/ video distortions as a relational resource. *The Electronic Journal of Communication /La Revue Electronic de Communication (EJC/REC)* Special Issue on Videoconferencing in Practice: 21st Century Challenges, *23*(1&2), http://www.cios.org/www/ejc/v23n12toc.htm.

Rintel, S. & Pittam, J. (1997). Strangers in a strange land: Interaction management on Internet Relay Chat. *Human Communication Research, 23*, 507–34.

Rintel, S., Mulholland, J., & Pittam, J. (2001) First things first: Internet Relay Chat openings. *Journal of Computer-Mediated Communication, 6*(3), http://onlinelibrary.wiley.com/ doi/10.1111/j.1083-6101.2001.tb00125.x/full.

Rintel, S., Pittam, J., & Mulholland, J. (2003) Time will tell: Ambiguous non-responses on Internet Relay Chat. *The Electronic Journal of Communication, 13*(1), http://www.cios.org/ EJCPUBLIC/013/1/01312.HTML.

Rouncefield, M., Slack, R., & Hartswood, M. (2011). Technology. In M. Rouncefield & P. Tolmie (Eds.), *Ethnomethodology at Work* (pp. 191–210). Farnham, UK: Ashgate.

Ruhleder, K., & Jordan, B. (2001). Co-constructing non-mutual realities: Delay-generated trouble in distributed interaction. *Computer Supported Cooperative Work, 10*(1): 113–38.

Sacks, H. (1963). Sociological description. *Berkeley Journal of Sociology, 8*, 1–16. Reprinted in J. Coulter (Ed.) (1980). *Ethnomethodological Sociology*. London: Edward Elgar Publishers.

Sacks, H. (1966). *The Search For Help: No-One To Turn To*. Unpublished PhD dissertation in Sociology, University of California, Berkeley.

Sacks, H. (1972a). An initial investigation of the usability of conversational data for doing sociology. In D. Sudnow (Ed.), *Studies in Social Interaction* (pp. 31–74). New York: Free Press

Sacks, H. (1972b). On the analysability of stories by children. In J. J. Gumperz & D. Hymes (Eds.), *Directions in Sociolinguistics: The Ethnography of Communication* (pp. 325–45). New York: Rinehart and Winston.

Sacks, H. (1974). On the analysability of stories by children. In R. Turner (Ed.), *Ethnomethodology* (pp. 216–32). Harmondsworth: Penguin.

Sacks, H. (1979). Hotrodder: A revolutionary category. In G. Psathas (Ed.), *Everyday Language: Studies in Ethnomethodology* (pp. 7–14). New York: Irvington Publishers Inc.

Sacks, H. (1984a). Notes on methodology. In J. M. Atkinson and J. Heritage (Eds.), *Structures of Social Action: Studies in Conversation Analysis* (pp. 21–7). Cambridge: Cambridge University Press.

Sacks, H. (1984b). On doing 'being ordinary'. In J. M. Atkinson & J. Heritage (Eds.), *Structures of Social Action: Studies in Conversation Analysis* (pp. 413–29). Cambridge: Cambridge University Press.

Sacks, H. (1992). *Lectures on Conversation* (Vols. I and II, edited by G. Jefferson). Oxford: Blackwell. (Hardback)

Sacks, H. (1995). *Lectures on Conversation* (Vols. I and II, edited by G. Jefferson). Oxford: Blackwell. (Paperback)

Sacks, H., & Garfinkel, H. (1970). On formal structures of practical action. In J. C. McKinney & E. A. Tiryakian (Eds.), *Theoretical Sociology* (pp. 338–66). New York: Appleton-Century-Crofts.

Sacks, H., Schegloff, E., & Jefferson, G. (1974). A simplest systematics for the organization of turn-taking for conversation. *Language, 50,* 696–735.

Sanders, R. E. (1997). Find your partner and do-si-do: The formation of personal relationships between social beings. *Journal of Social and Personal Relationships, 14,* 387–415.

Sanders, R. E. (2003). Conversational socializing on marine VHF radio: Adapting laughter and other practices to the technology in use. In P. Glenn, C.D. LeBaron & J. Mandelbaum (Eds.), *Studies in Language and Social Interaction: In Honor of Robert Hopper* (pp. 309–26). Mahwah, NJ: Lawrence Erlbaum.

Savage, M. (2013). The social life of methods: A critical introduction. *Theory, Culture & Society, 30*(4), 3–21.

Schegloff, E. A. (1968). Sequencing in conversational openings. *American Anthropologist, 70*(6, 1075–95.

Schegloff, E. A. (1972). Notes on a conversational practice: Formulating place. In D. Sudnow (Ed.), *Studies in Social Interaction* (pp. 75–119). New York: The Free Press of Glencoe.

Schegloff, E. A. (1992). Introduction to Sacks' Lectures on Conversation. In H. Sacks, *Lectures on Conversation* (Vols. I and II, edited by G. Jefferson). Oxford: Blackwell.

Schegloff, E.A. (1995). Introduction to Sacks' Lectures on Conversation. In H. Sacks, *Lectures on Conversation* (Vols. I and II, edited by G. Jefferson). Oxford: Blackwell.

Schegloff, E. A. (2007a). A Tutorial on Membership Categorization. *Journal of Pragmatics, 39*(3), 462–82.

Schegloff, E. A. (2007b). *Sequence Organization in Interaction: A Primer in Conversation Analysis, Vol. 1.* Cambridge: Cambridge University Press.

Schegloff, E. A. (2007c). Categories in action: Person-references and membership categorization. *Discourse Studies, 9,* 433–61.

Schegloff, E. A., Jefferson, G., & Sacks, H. (1977). The preference for self-correction in the organization of repair in conversation. *Language, 53,* 361–82.

Schegloff, E. A., & Sacks, H. (1973). Opening up closings. *Semiotica, 8*(4), 289–327.

Schegloff, E., & Sacks, H. (1974). Opening up closings. In R. Turner (Ed.), *Ethnomethodology: Selected Readings* (pp. 216–323). Harmondsworth: Penguin.

Schiefflin, B.B., & Ochs, E. (Eds.) (1986). *Language Socialization Across Cultures.* New York: Cambridge University Press.

Schütz, A. (1953). Commonsense and scientific interpretation of human action. *Philosophy and Phenomenological Research, 14*(1), 1–38.

Schütz, A. (1962). *Collected Papers,* 3 Vols. The Hague: Martinus Nijhoff Publishers.

Schtüz, A. (1964). Collected papers, vol. II. *Studies in social theory.* The Hague: Martinus Nijhoff

Schütz, A. (1966). Collected Papers III. *Studies in Phenomenological Philosophy,* ed. I. Schutz, The Hague: Martinus Nijhoff.

Schütz, A. (1973). *The Structures of the Life-world, Vol. 1.* Evanston, IL: Northwestern University Press.

Sharrock, W. (1974). On Owning Knowledge. In R. Turner (Ed.), *Ethnomethodology: Selected Readings* (pp. 45–53). Harmondsworth: Penguin Education.

Sharrock, W., & Button, G. (2011). Conclusion: Ethnomethodology and constructionist studies of technology. In M. Rouncefield & P. Tolmie (Eds.), *Ethnomethodology at Work* (pp. 211–229). Farnham, UK: Ashgate.

Silverman, D., & Gubrium, J. F. (1994). Competing strategies for analyzing the contexts of social interaction. *Sociological Inquiry, 64*(2), 179–198.

Silverman D. (1998). *Harvey Sacks: Social Science and Conversation Analysis.* Cambridge: Polity.

Silverman, D. (2001). *Interpreting Qualitative Data: Methods for Analysing Talk, Text and Interaction*. London: Sage.

Slack, R. S. (2000). Reflexivity or Sociological Practice? *Sociological Research Online*, 5(1).

Smith, D. E. (1974). The Social Construction of Documentary Reality[1]. *Sociological Inquiry*, 44(4), 257–268.

Speer, S.A., & Stokoe, E. (Eds.) (2011). *Conversation and Gender*. Cambridge: Cambridge University Press.

Stam, K. R., Stanton, J. M., & Guzman, I. R. (2004). Employee resistance to digital information and information technology change in a social service agency: A membership category approach. *Journal of Digital Information*, 5(4), http://journals.tdl.org/jodi/index.php/jodi/article/view/150/148.

Staske, S. (1996). Talking feelings: The collaborative construction of emotion in talk between close relational partners. *Symbolic Interaction*, 19, 111–35.

Staske, S. (1998). The normalization of problematic emotion in conversations between close relational partners: Interpersonal emotion work. *Symbolic Interaction*, 21, 59–86.

Stivers, T. (2005). Non-antibiotic treatment recommendations: Delivery formats and implications for parent resistance. *Social Science and Medicine*, 60(5), 949–64.

Stivers, T. (2011). Morality and question design: 'Of course' as contesting a presupposition of askability. In T. Stivers, L. Mondada & J. Steensig (Eds.), *The Morality of Knowledge in Conversation*. Cambridge: Cambridge University Press.

Stivers, T., & Hayashi, M. (2010). Transformative answers: One way to resist a question's constraints. *Language in Society*, 39, 1–25.

Stivers, T., & Rossano, F. (2010). Mobilizing response. *Research on Language and Social Interaction*, 43(1), 3–31.

Stokoe, E. (2003). Mothers, single women and sluts: Gender, morality and membership categorization in neighbour disputes, *Feminism & Psychology*, 13(3), 317–44.

Stokoe, E. (2009). Doing actions with identity categories: Complaints and denials in neighbour disputes. *Text and Talk*, 29(1), 75–97.

Stokoe, E. (2010a). 'Have you been married, or ...?': Eliciting and accounting for relationship histories in speed-dating interaction. *Research on Language and Social Interaction*, 43(3), 260–82.

Stokoe, E. (2010b). 'I'm not gonna hit a lady': Conversation analysis, membership categorization, and men's denial of violence against women. *Discourse Studies*, 21(1), 59–82.

Stokoe, E. (2012a). Moving forward with membership categorization analysis: Methods for systematic analysis. *Discourse Studies*, 14(3), 277–303.

Stokoe, E. (2012b). 'You know how men are': Description, categorization and the anatomy of a categorial practice. *Gender and Language*, 6(1), 231–53.

Stokoe, E. (2013). Applying findings and creating impact from conversation analytic studies of gender and communication. *Economic and Industrial Democracy*, 34(3), 537–52.

Stokoe, E., & Attenborough, F. T. (2014). Gender and categorial systematics. In S. Ehrlich, M. Meyerhoff & J. Holmes (Eds.). *Handbook of Language,Gender and Sexuality*. Hoboken, NJ: John Wiley and Sons, Inc.

Stokoe, E., & Edwards, D. (2015). Mundane morality: Gender categories and complaints in familial neighbour disputes. *Journal of Applied Linguistics and Professional Practice*.

Stommel, W., & Koole, T. (2010). The online support group as a community: A micro-analysis of the interaction with a new member. *Discourse Studies*, 12, 357–78.

Sudnow, D. (1965). Normal crimes: Sociological features of the penal code in a public defender office. *Social Problems*, 12, 255–76

Svennevig, J. (1999). *Getting Acquainted in Conversation. A Study of Initial Interactions* (Pragmatics & Beyond New Series). Amsterdam: John Benjamins.

Tajfel, H., & Turner, J. C. (1986). The social identity theory of intergroup behaviour. In S. Worchel & W. G. Austin (Eds.), *Psychology of Intergroup Relations* (pp. 7–24). Chicago, IL: Nelson-Hall.

ten Have, P. (1999). *Doing Conversation Analysis: A Practical Guide*. London: Sage Publications.

ten Have, P. (2000). Computer-mediated chat: Ways of finding chat partners. *M/C: a Journal of Media and Culture* 3(4).

Turner, R. (Ed.). (1974). *Ethnomethodology: Selected Readings*. Harmondsworth: Penguin Education.

Turner, J., Hogg, M., Oakes, P., Reicher, J., Stephen, D., & Wetherell, M. S. (1987) *Rediscovering the Social Group: A Self-categorization Theory*. Cambridge, MA: Basil Blackwell.

Turner, J., & Reynolds, K. J. (2010). The story of social identity. In T. Postmes & N. R. Branscombe (Eds), *Rediscovering Social Identity: Key Readings* (pp.13–32). New York: Psychology Press.

Vallis, R. (1999). Members' methods for entering and leaving #IRCbar: A conversation analytic study of internet relay chat. In K. Chalmers, S. Bogitini & P. Renshaw (Eds.), *Educational Research in New Times* (pp. 117–27). Flaxton: Post Pressed.

Vallis, R. (2001a). Applying membership categorization analysis to chat-room talk. In A. McHoul & M. Rapley (Eds.), *How to Analyse Talk in Institutional Settings: A Casebook of Methods* (pp. 86–99). London: Continuum.

Vallis, R. (2001b). *Sense and Sensibility in Chat Rooms*. Unpublished PhD, The University of Queensland.

Van Dijk, T. (1987). *Communicating Racism: Ethnic Prejudice in Thought and Talk*. London: Sage.

Verdier, M. (2010). *Le Temps de la Conversation: Anthropologie Linguistique des Chats dans les Cybercafés de Tanarive (Madagascar)*. PhD thesis, Paris, C.E.L.I.T.H., Ecole des Hautes Etudes en Sciences Sociales.

Wacquant, L. (2011). From Public Criminology to the Reflexive Sociology of Criminological Production and Consumption: A Review of *Public Criminology?* by Ian Loader and Richard Sparks. London: Routledge, 2010. *British Journal of Criminology*, 51(2), 438–48.

Walther, J. B. (2011). Theories of computer-mediated communication and interpersonal relations. In M. L. Knapp & J. A. Daly (Eds.), *The Handbook of Interpersonal Communication* (4th ed.) (pp. 443–79). Thousand Oaks, CA: Sage.

Walther, J. B. (2012). Affordances, effects, and technology errors. In C. T. Salmon (Ed.), *Communication Yearbook, 36* (pp. 190–3). New York: Routledge.

Watson, A., & Sasse, M. A. (2000). The good, the bad, and the muffled: The impact of different degradations on internet speech. In *Proceedings of the Eighth ACM International Conference on Multimedia* (pp. 269–76).

Watson, R. (1976). Some conceptual issues in the social identification of victims and offenders. In E.C. Viano (Ed.), *Victims and society*, Washington D.C: Visage Press. 60–71.

Watson, R. (1977). *Making Racial and Religious References in Conversation*. Paper presented at 3rd International Conference on Ethnomethodology and Conversation Analysis, Boston University.

Watson, R. (1978). Categorization, authorization and blame-negotiation in conversation. *Sociology*, 12(1), 105–13.

Watson, R. (1983). 'The presentation of victim and motive in discourse: The case of police interrogations and interviews. *Criminology: An International Journal*, 8(1–2), 31–52.

Watson, R. (1994). 'Harvey Sacks's sociology of mind in action', *Theory, Culture & Society, 11*, 169–86.

Watson, R. (1997a). Some general reflections on categorization and sequence in the analysis of conversation. In S. Hester & P. Eglin (Eds.), *Culture in Action: Studies in Membership Categorization Analysis* (pp. 49–75). Washington, DC: University Press of America.

Watson, R. (1997b) The presentation of 'victim' and 'motive' in discourse: The case of police interrogations and interviews. In M. Travers and J. F. Manzo (Eds.), *Law in Action: Ethnomethodological and Conversation Analytic Approaches to Law* (pp. 77–98). Aldershot, UK and Brookfield VT, USA: Ashgate Publishing Ltd.

Watson, R. (2008). La socioloqie comparative, ordinaire et analytique: quelques remarques critiques sur la comparaison dans l'Analyse de Conversation. *Cahiers de praxématique*, (50).

Watson, R. (2009a). *Analyzing Practical and Professional Texts: A Naturalist Approach.* Farnham, UK: Ashgate Publishing.

Watson, R. (2009b). *Harvey Sacks.* In S. d'Hondt, J.-O. Ostman & J. Verschueren (Eds.), *The Pragmatics of Interaction* (pp. 206–14). Amsterdam and Philadelphia: John Benjamins Publishing Co.

Whitehead, K. (2009). Categorizing the categorizer: The management of racial common sense in interaction. *Social Psychology Quarterly*, 72(4), 325–42

Whitehead, K. (2013). Managing self/other relations in complaint sequences: The use of self-deprecating and affiliative racial categorizations. *Research on Language and Social Interaction*, 46 (2), 186–203.

Widmer, J. (2010). *Discours et Cognition Sociale: Une Approche Sociologique* (pp. 69–72). Paris: Editions des Archives Contemporaines.

Wieder, D. L. (1974). *Language and Social Reality: The Case of Telling the Convicts Code.* The Hague: Mouton Publishers.

Wilkinson, S. (2011). Constructing ethnicity statistics in talk-in-interaction: Producing the White European. *Discourse & Society*, 22(3), 343–61.

Williams, M. L., Edwards, A., Housley, W., Burnap, P., Rana, O., Avis, N., Morgan, J., & Sloan, L. (2013). Policing cyber-neighbourhoods: Tension monitoring and social media networks. *Policing and Society*, 23(4), 461–81.

Wootton, A. (1975). *Dilemmas of Discourse: Controversies about the Sociological Interpretation of Language.* London: George Allen.

Wowk, M. T. (1984). Blame allocation, sex and gender in a murder interrogation. *Women's Studies International Forum*, 7, 75–82.

Wowk, M. T., & Carlin, A. (2004). Depicting a Liminal Position in Ethnomethodology, Conversation Analysis and Membership Categorization Analysis: The Work of Rod Watson. *Human Studies*, 27: 69–89.

Wyer, R. S., & Collins, J. E. (1992). A theory of humor elicitation. *Psychological Review*, 99, 663–88.

Yarosh, S., & Abowd, G. D. (2011). Mediated parent–child contact in work-separated families. In *Proceedings of the 2011 Annual Conference on Human Factors in Computing Systems* (pp. 1185–94).

Yarosh, S., Chew, Y. C., & Abowd, G. D. (2009). Supporting parent–child communication in divorced families. *International Journal of Human Computer Studies*, 67(2), 192–203.

Yarosh, S., & Kwikkers, M. (2011). Supporting pretend and narrative play over videochat. In *Proceedings of the 10th International Conference on Interaction Design and Children* (pp. 217–20). New York: ACM.

Zimmerman, D. H., & Pollner, M. (1970). The everyday world as a phenomenon. In J. D. Douglas (Ed.), *Understanding Everyday Life: Toward a Reconstruction of Sociological Knowledge* (pp. 80–103). Chicago: Aldine.

Index